ISBN: 9781407673943

Published by:
HardPress Publishing
8345 NW 66TH ST #2561
MIAMI FL 33166-2626

Email: info@hardpress.net
Web: http://www.hardpress.net

DIARIES OF THE EMPEROR
FREDERICK

DIARIES OF THE EMPEROR FREDERICK

DURING

THE CAMPAIGNS OF 1866 AND 1870-71

AS WELL AS

HIS JOURNEYS TO THE EAST AND TO SPAIN

EDITED BY

MARGARETHE VON POSCHINGER

TRANSLATED INTO ENGLISH

BY FRANCES A. WELBY

LONDON: CHAPMAN & HALL, LD.
1902

PREFACE

It has been repeatedly suggested to the under-signed publisher by his friends and patrons that he should re-edit the Diaries of the august Monarch, as published in "Kaiser Friedrich: a New and Authorized Presentment," by Margarethe von Poschinger (3 vols., 1899–1900), thus making them accessible to a wider circle of the German nation. In view of the inestimable value which these notes possess, with regard to our knowledge of the thoughts and feelings of their distinguished Author, and as a contribution to the History of his Time, the firm has felt itself justified in acceding to the request.

No one could paint a clear picture of the character of this Prince with greater sympathy, or make it appear more worthy of respect, than it is, as it stands out from his own Diaries. The very spirit of his noble soul breathes to us from his writings.

A further reason for the appearance of this book is the wish to celebrate the approach of the seventieth birthday of our well-beloved Sovereign by some adequate publication throughout the Fatherland.

RICHARD SCHRÖDER.

(Late Ed. Däring's Heirs.)

Berlin,
October, 1901.

TRANSLATOR'S NOTE

I HAVE to express my warmest thanks to Fräulein Idè Clausius for assisting me in the translation of these Diaries.

For the campaigns of 1866 and 1870–71, I have also availed myself of the authorized translations of the German Reports, prepared at the Topographical and Statistical Department of the War Office.

FRANCES A. WELBY.

LONDON,
    October, 1901.

CONTENTS

INTRODUCTION

FROM a very early period, the Emperor Frederick formed the admirable habit, to which he remained faithful all his life, of jotting down in Diaries the fugitive images of the moment, its events and experiences, perceptions and sensations, so as to preserve them from oblivion. If, on the one hand, it seemed to him a worthy task thus to keep the book of his life, and to be the chronicler of his own history, on the other it was no less the intimate joy of literary work and creation that led him to prosecute the development of the habit.

The first of the Kaiser's notes in Diary form date from his eleventh year, followed by others in the next three years. The youthful author in these describes, boy-fashion, and with extreme brevity, Court functions, a Cadets' manœuvre, and, among other things, the laying of the foundation-stone, and consecration, of the Memorial to King Frederick William III. in Potsdam. Later on we find notes of the journeys of Prince Frederick William to Russia, in the year 1852, which are pleasantly written, and give evidence of marked literary capacity.

When, ten years later, the Crown Prince Frederick William returned as the victorious leader from the Bohemian Campaign, he felt impelled to gather up in the form of a Diary the epoch-making events of the time, as supplied by his notes and letters from the scene of action.

If the illustrious author herein proved his marked capacity for the graphic description of severe and terrible scenes of war, the later notes of his journey to the East, in the year 1869, exhibit no less a highly developed faculty of throwing light upon the conditions and people of the countries in which he travelled, under the aspects of history and culture. With the artist's seeing eye he depicts for us landscapes of rare beauty; with fine perception he describes the works of art of a vanished age, now indeed lying in ruins, but still commanding admiration.

The effect of these lively and graphic descriptions is enhanced by a remarkably attractive style, rich in felicitous expressions. The evidences of an exceedingly clear presentation, and artistic apprehension of things seen, are again pleasantly conspicuous in the Crown Prince's diary of his journey to Spain in 1883, and make the reading of it a veritable enjoyment.

The Crown Prince also set down, as a faithful chronicler, the *memorabilia* of the year of war, 1870–71, in so far as he came day by day into personal contact with them. Herein he reveals himself as the far-sighted politician in the grand style, entirely occupied with the idea of the unification of Germany, and the resolute and liberal building up of the Empire. His measures have in many respects the character of programmes for the future, and are inspired with an imposing moral grandeur.

DIARIES OF THE EMPEROR FREDERICK

I

IN view of the preparations for war on the part of Austria, King William I. had, in the days between May 3 and 12, 1866, signed a number of orders, by which the field-armies collectively were mobilized.

While several corps were concentrating as the I. Army, and the Elbe Army, on both banks of the Elbe, and in the Lausitz, under the chief command of Prince Frederick Charles of Prussia, a second army was organized for the protection of Silesia, the command of which was given to the Crown Prince.

This II. Army consisted at first of the V. Army Corps (General von Steinmetz) and the VI. Army Corps (General von Mutius), but these were soon joined by the I. Army Corps (General von Bonin), and the Guard Corps under Prince

B

August of Wurtemburg. A special Division of Cavalry was formed out of different regiments of the V. and VI. Army Corps, Major-General von Hartmann being appointed Commander.

The appointment of the Crown Prince to be Commander-in-Chief of this Army, with his simultaneous promotion to the rank of General of Infantry, took place on May 17; on June 2 the military government of the Province of Silesia was further entrusted to him.

The Chief of the General Staff was Major-General von Blumenthal; the Quartermaster-General, Major-General von Stosch. Captain von Jasmund of the Leib-Grenadiers (I. Brandenburg), No. 8, and First-Lieutenant Count zu Eulenburg of the 1st Foot Guards, acted as personal adjutants to the Crown Prince.

On July 15 followed the declaration of war against Saxony, Hanover, and Electoral Hesse, after these states had rejected the Prussian offer of neutrality. On June 18 King William published his war-manifesto.

On the evening of June 20 an order from the King was received in the Head-Quarters of the Silesian Army, directing the Crown Prince to send a message on the morning of the 21st to the commanders of all the Austrian outposts opposite, to the effect that "through the bearing of Austria at Frankfurt-on-Maine, the state of war had practically broken out, and that the Prussian troops had instructions to act accordingly."

On the same evening the Crown Prince issued an army-order to his troops.

On June 22 a telegram was sent from the King to the Head-Quarters of the Crown Prince, commanding him, in conjunction with the I. Army, to take the offensive in Bohemia by concentrating in the direction of Gitschin. It was calculated approximately, with regard to the enemy, that, at the time of the entry of the II. Army into Bohemia, it was improbable that its bulk would already have advanced far enough on the left flank to present any organized resistance to the isolated columns of the Crown Prince as they debouched from the mountains.

The junction with the I. Army could only be effected by the right wing of the II. Army. The Crown Prince ordered, accordingly, that the I. Army Corps, followed by the Cavalry Division, should form the Advance-guard in this movement of the right wing, while the V. Corps was to take possession of the Pass of Nachod from Reinerz, so as to cover the movements of the army against the main strength of the enemy, expected on this side. The Guard Corps was directed to make use of the roads between the two Corps above mentioned, so as to be used as a reserve by the one or the other in case of need, or to occupy the third exit from the mountains, the Pass of Eypel. The VI. Corps was to remain at Glatz, on the look-out for divisions of the enemy who might show themselves to the south of this fortress; as soon as possible it was to be removed from there, and to push on the Hoffman Brigade of this Corps to effect junction with the V. Corps at Reinerz.

On the 26th, the columns of the Guard Corps, which now had to push forward from their position (the farthest back on the Neisse) so as to be available as an immediate reserve on either hand, crossed the Austrian frontier at Tunschendorf and Johannesberg, amid the cheers of the troops, and under the eyes of the Crown Prince. Detachments of the 3rd Regiment of the Uhlans of the Guard had on this occasion a successful skirmish with the Austrian Windischgrätz, and Mexico-Uhlan Dragoons. The corps bivouacked between Politz and Braunau.

The V. Corps had pushed the 9th Infantry Division toward the frontier, in the direction of Nachod. The frontier town of Schlaney was

occupied by the enemy with some sixty infantry-
men, two squadrons, and two guns : the bridge
over the Metau was destroyed. Two guns of
the 5·4-pounder Foot Battery of the Field
Artillery Regiment, No. 5, were brought up
against them, and the first firing from the II.
Army took place here. The enemy were forced
to surrender, and by the evening the pass and
town of Nachod were also occupied by the
Prussians.

After these preparatory movements on the
26th, June 27 opened the succession of brilliant
and arduous days, in which the II. Army effected
its *débouché* from the mountains.

FROM MY DIARY IN THE CAMPAIGN OF 1866

FREDERICK WILLIAM

*(Compiled by the Crown Prince after the war, from
various notices and letters to his wife, all political
and higher military considerations being omitted.)*

On June 26 we passed the Austrian frontier.
My Head-Quarters on the day before had been at
Eggersdorf, with Count Magnis, and I went from

there on the morning of June 26 to the Braunauer Strasse, by which the Guard Corps set out on its march to Bohemia.

When we reached the Austrian frontier, there was great jubilation. Every division * cheered, the bands played, many companies sang their national melodies; wherever the people recognized me, they gave me a hearty greeting, as, for instance, when I reached the town of Braunau, at the same moment as the Regiment of Guard-Fusiliers. All the villages were deserted by their male population; only old men, women, and children looked anxiously through the half-open doors as we passed, but as soon as they found we did nothing to hurt them, they brought water to the soldiers, to whom one could not grudge the luxury in the fierce heat of the sun.

About a mile and a half † beyond Braunau we threw up outposts, and I waited here, with the regiment of the Queen's Guard-Grenadiers. On the march we met three men of the Third Guard-Uhlans, who had had a skirmish with the Win-dischgrätz Dragoons, in which two of the latter

---

* The word *Zug* as applied to infantry, is translated as *division*, of which there are two in each company. The large unit of troops is distinguished by an initial capital letter—*Division*.—Tr. (From War Office Report.)

† The German mile is about 6½ English miles, or 7½ kilometres.—Tr.

were severely wounded, and one was taken
prisoner; one horse belonging to our Uhlans was
cut down, but they promptly curbed an Austrian
steed with a Prussian bridle and saddle, and rode
off gaily.

In Braunau I was greeted with loud cheers
by the Second Battalion of the First Regiment
of the Guards; then the Abbot of the Benedictine
Monastery made his appearance, and later on I
returned his visit, at the same time visiting the
fine Church and Cloisters.

June 27, 1866.

We marched forward to-day in the direction
of Hronow, over steep and difficult mountain-paths.
Part of the Infantry baggage had to follow after,
which extended the columns enormously. Every
one was in good spirits. I sent Major von der
Burg and Captain Mischke to the I. Army Corps,
in the direction of the Pass of Trautenau.

Not far from Hronow we heard the firing of
cannon, and also met a detachment (*Zug*) of eight
Dragoon Regiments (Second Silesian), which
established our communications with the V.
Army Corps. I rode off at once in the direction
of the firing towards Nachod, where one could

already hear in the distance the cheers of the
columns that were crossing the frontier. At the
customs-house of Nachod lay a dead infantry-
man, who had been left on the field last night
after a short engagement, in which the Ninth
Division had taken possession of this important
defile.

It was sultry and frightfully dusty; cannon-
balls fell round us, yet no one believed that the
enemy would make any serious resistance at this
point, the more so as the Pass, with its high and
very commanding castle, was not occupied.

The town was like a deserted place : a wounded
officer of the Dragoons lay in the market-place;
just then an orderly came hurrying by, to call up
the light field-hospital of the Division. After all,
the fighting was in earnest, and slightly-wounded
men were already coming towards me. Riding
further along the *chaussée*, I saw a steep hill on
the left, with fir-trees growing on it ; the artillery
were going up, and shells were bursting in the air.

Making my way, not without difficulty, between
the guns and the ammunition waggons, Captain
Fassong (Fifth Artillery Brigade) overtaking me,
I was speaking to some of the artillery-men, who
were rejoicing with me over the beginning of a
fight, when a shell whizzed over us. A non-

commissioned artillery officer riding near me said with a beaming face, "That was a good one!" Just at that moment we stumbled at the very edge of the wood, into musketry fire; some ammunition waggons, on which the wounded had been laid, came wildly towards me; it was not easy to get out of this confusion, especially as the path was a hollow way. I looked round for a better place, which would give a general view, and tried to get to another hill, but was suddenly caught in a detachment of the Fourth Dragoons, who tore over a hill-top in mad confusion, hurrying out of the battle, with loose horses and riders of different arms running off in all directions. To resist the torrent was impossible, especially as I found myself between this wild rout and a column of infantry, as well as the artillery and ammunition waggons; in fact, just in front of me, and in my path, some guns had been dismounted. It was only the almost total block of the road that checked the Dragoons, whom I ordered peremptorily into arrest, while loose horses crushed me between the wheels of the waggons. At this moment I perceived at my side Captain von Plötz, and Lieutenant Baensch (Sixth Artillery Brigade), with drawn swords, expecting a hand-to-hand fight with the enemy's cavalry. It did not come to that : and indeed the worthy dragoons seem to have been overcome with panic, the Lord knows why, in this attack (which otherwise would certainly have succeeded), when their detachment fell in, and advanced with one of the wings. I was raging, but could do nothing, so I shouted to the infantry column of the 46th Regiment that there was a pretty fight ahead of us, to which they replied with enthusiasm. Major-General von Stosch manœuvred the infantry columns with great circumspection, to bring them into action by the shortest possible route. Eventually I reached my hill. Thence one saw the cavalry stationed alongside of the half-battalions of infantry, changing their position at every moment on account of the shell-firing. Lieutenant-General v. Löwenfeld, came a message, had been drawn late into action with the bulk of the Ninth Division, so that he could no longer maintain his position.

While I was deliberating with Blumenthal and Stosch what would be best to do, the Tenth Division had already advanced and mingled in the *mêlée*, and the news came shortly after that the day was going as well as possible, while the cheering could be heard from our own side.

Captain von Jarotzki, from the Staff of

the General-Commando of the V. Army Corps, announced to me that a standard had been taken by the Second Silesian Dragoon Regiment, No. 8. I fell on his neck for joy, and passed the news on at once to the troops standing round me, who broke into loud shouts of satisfaction. The instant before, Colonel Walker had pointed out to me that there were corn-flowers all round us, and I had just plucked one for my wife. This seemed to be a good omen, and must be added to the manifold significances of this flower for us. Shortly after, another standard was announced as taken by the First Regiment of Uhlans (West-Prussian).

I now rode down, to express my acknowledgments to the brave fellows. Two soldiers were carrying off Count Rittberg, of the 58th Infantry Regiment, who was severely wounded in the lower abdomen; but he was still conscious, and recognized me, rejoicing in a touching manner over the standards we had taken. I soon reached the cavalry. The Second Silesian Dragoons, No. 8, had halted on the *chaussée*. Lieutenant-Colonel von Wichmann, Commander of the regiment, whose face was covered with the clotted blood that had streamed down from a sword-cut, informed me with a beaming countenance of the deeds of his regiment. The men, looking as proud as they were happy, responded to my congratulations with a "Hurrah" that I shall never forget.

Half the corps of officers was unfortunately *hors-de-combat*. I went on to the West-Prussian Uhlans, and found the same scene. The Commander, who was wounded, was missing. In order to shake hands with one at least, I gave my hand to the standard-bearer. General von Wuuck, who had taken over the Brigade the day before, had joined in the attack, and had unfortunately received a cut on the back of his head; luckily the brain was not injured, and the wound was harmless. During this exchange of greetings the shells whizzed over us, and a dragoon, turning to me, christened them the "Austrian bees."

We went into a neighbouring farm to water our horses. Here I met the 47th Infantry and the Fifth Battalion of Jägers together, the men all in good spirits and happy. At the same moment a drummer from the First West-Prussian Grenadiers, No. 6, brought me a flag which had been captured, or rather, in the hand-to-hand tussle, had been taken away from the fallen ensign. A wounded Austrian infantry-man appeared to be wearing a uniform similar to that of my own Austrian regiment; asked by a musketeer who spoke Polish, he replied, "Crown-Prince-of-Prussia's Infantry," so that my own name was fighting against me. This is a singular coincidence.

I now rode on to a height, and a shell exploded just in front of us, upon a dead horse, which was blown into quarters.

Shortly after, we saw the West-Prussian Uhlans make an attack on the cavalry, in which attackers and attacked were mixed up together; the regiment captured two guns.

I sent Leopold Hohenzollern off to look for Steinmetz, and get exact information as to the state of the battle, since its successful issue seemed no longer doubtful. Shortly after I met Steinmetz, whom I embraced, and greeted as the victor, for we now saw the enemy drawing off on all sides in the direction from Skalitz to Josephstadt.

After discussing the principal matters for the next day, and exactly repeating the orders already given for the forward march to the Elbe, we decided to give the name of "Battle of Nachod" to to-day's achievement. Telegrams were sent to the King with news of the victory that had been gained.

After that I rode over the different points of the battle-field; at the station of the right wing lay a young Austrian officer of the "Kaiser's Cuirassiers," who was severely wounded in the leg, dead horses and the corpses of Austrian cavalry lay around him. In a brook lay an over-turned Austrian gun, said to have been taken by the 6th Brandenburg Regiment, No. 52. Here I met the West-Prussian Uhlans, and made them my acknowledgments for the capture of the two guns. Further to the left we were confronted by a gruesome field of corpses, covered with Austrian infantry sacrificed to our percussion-guns. Every-where wailing and groaning—whilst our men carried the enemy to the ambulance station, or shot off the arms they had taken from them, so that one ran some risk of being hit by our own people. Here I met Adalbert, who had been much under fire to-day with the In-fantry. Lieutenant-General v. Kirchbach described to me the decisive moment for his Tenth Division, who lost many brave officers here, their corpses, as those of a Captain v. Heuduck, and Lieutenant Walter, being borne away before my eyes. I shook hands with many of the wounded; they accepted their fate with quiet resignation, and without audible murmuring.

Near Skalitz the ground fell away steeply, and here about eighty guns were posted; these, although exposed to the enemy's fire, had suffered little, because the Austrians had to aim from below, and could get no direct effect.

I spoke words of recognition to many of the soldiers, and as I was shaking hands with a non-commissioned officer and the corporals of a battery, which had had much to do, and had suffered considerable loss in its station on the left wing, all the gunners ran up to me and pressed me by the hand. At one part of the wood our infantry of the Ninth Division had had a sharp fight; here again the Austrians were lying in heaps, the wounded crying out for water, one on the other hand was quietly lighting his pipe.

Further on we found the body of Major v. Natzmer of the 8th Dragoon Regiment, who had fallen in the cavalry attack; his *perruke* had dropped under his head, one glove was half drawn off. Most of the dead Prussians had a peaceful expression.

On the left wing the infantry had fought along a hollow path, and then by the walls of a church, where the Austrians lay in heaps, the Kaiser's Jäger piled three high, again the result of our percussion-guns. On the way I met many brave

Battalions to whom I spoke grateful words, and I also met Lieutenant-General v. Löwenfeld. Major-General v. Ollech was severely wounded. Lieutenant-Colonel v. Walther, the commander of the 46th Infantry Regiment, was wounded in the head.

We had been thirteen hours in the saddle, evening was coming on, and it behoved us to think of turning homewards, seeing that my Head-Quarters were still two miles off.

Passing two ambulance stations, I further visited an officers' hospital, near which was a shed for the wounded men. What a scene of misery! A sergeant of the 52nd Infantry called to me, stretching out his hand, and wanting to know the issue of the fight. On hearing my account of our achievements, he exclaimed, " Now, thank God, I will gladly bear all my wounds ! "

Many of the captured officers and men of my Austrian regiment now came towards me, and I made myself known to them as their commanding officer, on which we shook hands—a strange meeting !

In Nachod itself we found the Commander of the regiment, Colonel Baron v. Wimpffen (whom I had known in 1852 in Petersburg), lying wounded in the arm, and many other officers of the regiment were with him. Many of our Dragoon officers suffered severely, but were in good spirits at our victory, and the prowess of the regiment. Major-General v. Ollech was fairly comfortable, though heavily wounded in the thigh, otherwise the same good fellow as usual.

I ordered that the Castle of Nachod, which is many stories high, and belongs to a Prince Lippe-Bückeburg, in the Austrian service, should be turned into a hospital. Prince Pless was busy all day, rendering' St. John's ambulance aid to the wounded.

I must also mention that as I was making in the morning for the height above described, I ordered a battery to come up, which was not accomplished without difficulty, on account of the steep slope ; the Infantry of the 1st West-Prussian Grenadiers, No. 6, had already occupied the summit. I further ordered the opposite hill-top to be occupied also, because our left wing appeared to be threatened from the side of Neustadt—the more so, as the wood shut out any distant prospect. The troops had already done three miles before they came into battle, and were in some cases so exhausted that the men lay down in the trenches of the *chaussée*. I then gave the order to discard the baggage, which some of the Advance-guard had already done of their own accord, and the relief to the men was obviously very great. Such a measure is, indeed, open to the objection that many of the men might not find their knapsacks again, or even that, in the case of losing the position, these might fall into the enemy's hands; but in the scorching heat it was imperative to give alleviations of this sort.

At sunset I left Nachod, thanking God from my heart that He had been pleased to give victory to our troops, and thus, on the first day of the campaign, to show the world what was meant by our officers and soldiers. During the day we thought many times that, as on the appointed days of prayer and intercession, petitions were going up to Heaven in the churches of the Fatherland for the success of our arms. A heavy weight must have been thrown into the scales this day for the future of Germany, under the leadership of Prussia.

June 28, 1866.

Late in the night of yesterday, Major von der Burg and Captain Mischke returned from the I. Army Corps, to which I had sent them. There has been a sanguinary battle at Trautenau with the Austrians, under Gablenz. In this encounter our brave East-Prussians took and occupied the town of Trautenau till four in the afternoon. Then, however, Gablenz came up with fresh troops, and Bonin had to evacuate the position he had gained. So that at night a retrograde movement of the I. Army Corps was to be expected, the more so as single bodies of troops had already retired in disorder.

It was at once clear to me that the important position of Trautenau must, at all cost, be re-occupied, so I immediately dictated the order for the Guards to march on Trautenau, so as to get to the rear of Gablenz' right flank by Eipel, and thus repossess ourselves of Trautenau; * in this way giving enormous relief to the I. Army Corps. In Blumenthal's room, we four wrote the orders

---

* This order ran as follows :—

"As the issue of the action of the I. Army Corps at Trautenau is undecided, the Corps of Guards will continue its march in the direction already ordered as far as Keile; if the action at Trautenau be still going on, it will then march on the latter place and engage the enemy immediately. The Corps will set off as early as possible. '

"(Signed)   FREDERICK WILHELM,
"*Crown Prince.*"

In this connection Sybel remarks, in his book, "*Die Begründung des Deutschen Reichs*" (p. 143), in order to show the activity which characterized the Crown Prince, "Such important and at the same time incomplete intelligence would have incited many strategists to greater and more stringent precautions; in the Crown Prince it merely called out an instant determination to move forward with accelerated and redoubled energy."

for the respective Corps, so that it was half-past
one before we got to bed.

Early on the 28th, I rode with the whole Staff
to Kosteletz, a mountain village, three-quarters
of a mile from Nachod, close to the Josephstadt-
Schwadowitz railway, where I found myself in
the centre of my army, and could operate in the
direction of Nachod or Trautenau, as required.

Albrecht (son), with the heavy Brigade of
Guards, the Guard-Reserve Artillery, and several
columns, were bivouacking here. Steinmetz asked
for reinforcements, as he was out-numbered; I
could, however, only send Albrecht to him, by
withdrawing the latter from the Guards, since
the Guard Corps had to be kept together in its
full strength for the important events of the
day. At 11.30 there was heavy firing of cannon
near Skalitz, the smoke of which we saw, without
being able properly to overlook the operations.
Steinmetz was obviously engaged in a sharp fight:
of course I felt very anxious, since I had been
obliged to refuse him the desired reinforcements,
and felt sure that he would not have asked for
more troops without pressing necessity. Forwards,
towards Eipel, we could also hear and see that
the Artillery were engaged. Towards 2 o'clock
such a tremendous dust-cloud was moving in the

direction of Nachod, that for some time we took for granted that the V. Army Corps had been forced to execute a retrograde movement. Hence it was a vast relief, as evening drew on, to see the Austrian fire retiring farther and farther in the direction of Josephstadt, followed so closely by our men that it was evident the day was ours, and that the brave Steinmetz and his gallant corps had won another victory.

This was speedily confirmed by Major von Gaffron and Captain Kroseck, whom I had sent to the V. Army Corps; and to-day's engagement must have been even more severe than that of yesterday. Adalbert was fully exposed, especially when he was in the thick of the fire with the King's Grenadiers, and lost Lieutenant von St. Paul of the 3rd Foot Guards, who was acting as adjutant for him, in place of his sick brother.

I also visited our wounded of the 3rd Uhlan Guards, who made a splendid attack yesterday, at Czerwenagora, upon the Austrian Mexico-Uhlans, and then rode to Eipel, to spend the night there. It was a magnificent ride along the south side of our beloved Riesen-gebirge, whose snow-summits, yesterday as to-day, stood out as the witness of our victory. The Guards were bivouacking in Eipel, and it was here that I received the first intelligence of the sanguinary combat in which most of the Berlin and Potsdam Infantry Regiments had taken part; many of our dear friends had also fallen.

Hardly had we arrived, when it was evident that Eipel lay fairly open to the enemy, and my Head-Quarters appeared to be insecure; nor did I find the general atmosphere more hopeful, in spite of our definite successes. Just then came Lieutenant v. Rosenberg from the Posen-Uhlans, to announce that the I. Army Corps had retired last night without a halt over the frontier to Liebau, and was bivouacking there with Hartmann's Division of Cavalry. What had happened to Trautenau had not been ascertained.

Some painful moments of deliberation as to what was best to be done ensued, whilst the dawn was already breaking. Then Major von der Burg, whom I had sent to the Guard Corps, arrived with the announcement that everything was going splendidly; the fighting had indeed been very severe, but the results were brilliant to a degree. Trautenau was in our hands, the Prince of Wurtemburg was already quartered there, and Gablenz, entirely beaten, was in full flight. I immediately ordered Bonin to march beyond Trautenau to Arnau, and make himself master of the passage of the Elbe at that point; and gave orders that the Prince of Wurtemberg should go to Königinhof, and General von Steinmetz to Gradlitz, to occupy the defiles in either direction respectively, while General von Mutius was to follow the V. Corps. I myself went immediately with my two personal adjutants, and von der Burg, to Trautenau. The ride in an unforgettable moonlight night, enhanced by the fragrance of the air from mountain and pinewood, was wonderfully beautiful.

Shortly before reaching Trautenau, these enjoyments were dispelled by the stench of corpses and dead horses' bodies, and the general havoc that characterizes a battle-field glittered eerily in the moonlight. At the gate we were received by our own pickets of the Elizabeth Guard-Grenadiers; their company took a flag to-day. Not a single inhabitant was to be seen, only soldiers here and there; on the picturesque market-place, surrounded with stone arcades, were bivouackers, canteens, prisoners, arms taken from the enemy, slightly wounded men, all viewed in the moonlight, and the rays from the canteen lanterns.

We took up our quarters in the best room of the "Hotel," where the Prince of Wurtemberg was established, after ordering out a tipsy Austrian soldier, and then slept soundly, for it was again 2 a.m. before we got any rest.

June 29, 1866.

The Prince of Wurtemberg was in high spirits over yesterday's victory, and praised the gallant exploits of men and officers in glowing terms. The Second Battalion of the Guard-Grenadiers (Kaiser-Franz) in particular suffered heavy losses, Lieutenant-Colonel v. Gaudy and Captains v. Witzleben and v. Wittich being killed. I rode out to the bivouacking troops, who greeted me with loud acclamations. When I gave my hand to some of the Kaiser-Franz men, they all flung themselves upon me, and tried to take my hand, which moved me deeply. A grenadier planted a birch-pole in front of me; I gazed at him, wondering what it meant. "Just look at the point of it," they said. It was the head of the flag, with the Iron Cross; the staff had been broken in the hand-to-hand *mêlée*, and could not be found, but these brave men had saved the tip, and brought it to me thus. I could not help kissing the head of it; honour to all those gallant fellows who have fallen!

Bonin now came in with his Army Corps. The strain on his brave troops during the fight of the day before yesterday, as well as the exhaustion of the men, must have been extraordinary. I ordered the corps to defile before me, my East-Prussian Grenadiers at the head of the Advance-guard, and commended the men for their brave conduct. They looked fresh and energetic, in spite of the African heat and the grinding dust. Many of the officers wounded the day before yesterday, among them Captain v. Lettow, Lieutenant v. Loellhövel, Ensign v. Borbstädt of my East-Prussian Regiment, lay in Trautenau. I went to see them. The Austrians kept them prisoners for one day, and even took their swords away. The whole town stank of blood, and it was so crammed with wounded and prisoners, that many Austrians had to lie under the arcades, - not a single Austrian surgeon with them! Three Prussian surgeons had been made prisoners, and were only left with our men on giving their word of honour not to carry arms against Austria in this campaign! To be sure, Austria refused to subscribe to the Convention of Geneva.

In the afternoon the Head-Quarters were moved to Prausnitz, a friendly village lying back on the Elbe, between Gradlitz and Königinhof. The

way led over a great part of the battle-field, where
the Guard Corps had been in action yesterday.   It
presented a ghastly appearance, for along with
those who fell yesterday lay the rotten corpses
of the Austrians who were killed on the 28th,
with heaps of arms and uniforms, like the
front of a military depôt.   This was apparently
the place where the Austrians had rested, or
formed up, or where they had been taken prisoner.
Nothing is more awful than a battle-field on the
day after the fight!   No one who is not wanting
in sensibility can look on it without profound
sorrow.   Happily our men only lay there for a
very few hours, for ambulance-bearers and comrades
hastened to carry wounded and dead alike to the
bandaging-station.

Some firing was reported; but at this stage
every door that bangs sounds like a shot to one's
excited nerves, and no one would believe it until
I satisfied myself that it was a fact.   The news
soon came that the V. Corps had been engaged
in a heavy cannonade, while the Advance-guard
of the Guard Corps had taken the passage of the
Elbe after some easy fighting at Königinhof, and
the 12th Company of the First Foot Guards had
taken a flag from the Coronini Regiment.

My quarters were at the Priest's house; he,

with his flocks and the greater part of the inhabitants, having fled into the forest. Since no authorities were in the place, and our troops had to live while bivouacking in this neighbourhood (our provision column not having yet come up), we were obliged to resort to commandeering. Many poor families had perforce to give up the little live-stock left them by the Austrians, but this was unavoidable. The Kaiser's troops, indeed, had not spared their countrymen, before our arrival on the scene.

After some hours the Priest, a Jesuit of the purest water, came in, and bade us welcome. With him was a pert and dressed-out lady who had "fled" from Trautenau to her friend the *Pastor*; lastly, the Chaplain, trembling like an aspen leaf, and using so many words in his terror, that one had to help him to finish his own sentence. At last we all got off early to bed, our meal having been a late supper rather than dinner.

June 30, 1866.

In the night Captain v. Hahnke, whom I had sent to Steinmetz with orders, waked me to say he could not go by the nearest way to the General, because the enemy were still on this side of the Elbe; he would have to make his way by riding some considerable distance round. This was uncomfortable, as we might be nicely caught in our Head-Quarters. Soon after 4 o'clock, Jasmund waked me, to say that a lively cannonade had begun, and seemed to be coming nearer. To jump up, dress, saddle, and breakfast, was the work of a moment in the firing. As we were riding off, however, Hahnke, who had ridden all night, came back, and announced that the cannonade meant nothing, but only concerned the baggage of the V. Army Corps, which the enemy was bombarding from the opposite bank, so it was all "much ado about nothing." I rode to the Guard Corps partly in order to hear Wurtemburg's report, and subsequently to reconnoitre Königinhof for myself along the high banks of the Elbe. A sharp storm had at last cleared the air. The town was in our hands; the enemy's Jägers held the opposite bank with some inconsiderable defences, the high walls of the valley were mounted with guns and batteries, so that a passage here would be dearly paid for. Hiller, Kessel, and still more Obernitz had much to relate. From here I rode to the gallant V. Army Corps. On passing the bivouac I was greeted heartily by the soldiers of every regiment, and was touched when they smiled at me with proud and happy faces. In the King's Regiment of Grenadiers there are still ten sound officers.

I embraced Steinmetz, and told him that I had begged his Majesty to send him the Order of the Black Eagle, which visibly delighted the old hero; a great happiness had befallen him in the late evening of his life, and he rejoiced that my military experiences should be inaugurated under such favourable auspices. He ought to reckon in yesterday's affair, when he fought hard at Schweinschädel, along with the two battles of Nachod. This morning there was a sharp cannonade, and a great barn with the enemy's granaries caught fire. The flames blazed up not far from his house, and that in which Adalbert was quartered. A reservist of the 46th Regiment, by name Mersiewski, took another flag yesterday, and was at once promoted to the rank of non-commissioned officer.

The bivouacs of the V. Army Corps were collectively within the range of the enemy's fire, which I objected to. Steinmetz, however, would not alter the place he had once taken up, and accordingly in the afternoon the enemy threw shells into the bivouacking troops, happily without wounding many of them.

The Austrian General v. Fragner had fallen at Skalitz: in his pocket we found important papers. In the first place, Ramming's report to Benedek of the Battle of Nachod, in which he begged for reinforcements, as in all probability he would be attacked again on the morrow, and had been obliged to retire to-day, with serious losses. Next, Benedek's order in consequence of this despatch, that Archduke Leopold should proceed to the VIII. Corps next day, and take over the command. Finally, a long proclamation, to be distributed " on crossing the Prussian frontier " ! Steinmetz handed me over these papers, which I at once made known, and then forwarded to Berlin.

Sunday, July 1, 1866.   *Head-Quarters at Prausnitz.*

A day of rest, and no thundering of cannon, a thing unheard-of !

I sent the Catholics to mass ; the priest seems to have prayed for our King as " the present Sovereign "—he deserves to be hung !

Alexander arrived ; in the evening I rode round the bivouacs of the Advance-guard, where the

Guard-Fusiliers, in particular, who had also taken a flag yesterday, greeted me with the greatest enthusiasm. Helldorf, of the 1st Foot Guards, was proud of the exploit of the 12th Company, and would not admit that the Guard-Fusiliers had accomplished the same thing. He wanted to fling on to Vienna in his usual go-ahead manner.

Anton Hohenzollern was whole and sound, and had led his column all day with the greatest fortitude and devotion; his men adore him.

I returned with Colonel Walker. I cannot insist enough on the extent to which this amiable, intelligent, and experienced officer has won my heart and confidence. Everything he says is practical, and hits the nail on the head, and his interest in our army and its future must attract every one who comes across him.

To-day Count Schweinitz, the Chief Justice (*Ober-Appellations-Gerichts-Präsident*) from Posen, leaves us: as an old tourist he had kindly offered to show us the paths over the Riesen and Glatzer mountains, which I had accepted. We owe him the indication of many marching routes, which we should not otherwise have discovered, on the advance to Bohemia.

Fürst Pless and Herr v. Salisch visited the hospitals at Nachod and Skalitz, and were pleased

with the arrangements for the wounded. Un-
luckily, the Cavalry Division bivouacking in our
vicinity had committed some excesses; certain
individuals even penetrated into the quarters of
Leopold Hohenzollern and Colonel Walker.

July 2, 1866.   *Head-Quarters at Prausnitz.*

On establishing our Head-Quarters at König-
hof we saw plainly how sharp the fighting must
have been in the streets of the town, and how many
dwellings had been damaged. Whether, however,
our people alone were responsible for this, may be
doubted, since the Austrians are notoriously bad
tenants. My lodging was at a manufacturer's,
who had apparently fled in the greatest haste with
his belongings, for unpaid bills were lying everywhere, with unfinished bits of writing, and the
crockery was still covered with half-eaten food.
Some Guard-Jägers must have looked round here
before we came in; one of them had written on
a lady's photograph that there was no cause for
alarm at the Prussians, they were honest people.
Signed—"A Guard-Jäger!"

I visited the hospital in a large manufactory,
where, among others, was the badly wounded
ensign of the 3rd Battalion of the Guard-Fusiliers;

when he was wounded, Sergeant Gräser at once seized the flag and led several sections against the enemy. After this I rode over to the opposite side; the enemy had gradually evacuated this since yesterday morning, so that our Advance-guard had already taken possession of the opposite heights.

Then a Pioneer officer met me with the intelligence that he had seen some Feld-Jägers, who assured him that Josephstadt was evacuated by the Austrians. I sent immediately to the V. Army Corps, and ordered a reconnaissance to determine the truth of this news, and gave the same order to Lieutenant-General v. Hiller. The latter was not sufficiently informed from the out-posts, so that it was important that I should get definite intelligence. Steinmetz had thrown up a pontoon bridge, and some two battalions had been ordered over to the right bank of the Elbe.

We had a pretty ride to Plateau, from which we could see first Josephstadt, and in the far distance the conical summit with the castle of Pardubitz, and so came to our outposts, where, however, nothing had been seen of the enemy, hardly even a patrol. Strange, quaint figures from the Passion-story, along with shrines to the Saints, stood hewn out of the rock in the forest, and on the

D

precipices, and seemed to be the tasteless, costly expression of some soaring fancy of the seventeenth century.

On this road I met Fusilier Bochnia of the 1st Foot Guards, who had taken the flag at Königinhof. He carried the case of it over his shoulder, and is a handsome Ober-Silesian, in his fourth year's service, slightly wounded by some bayonet-cuts. Colonel Walker treated him to cigarettes, and I gave him some ducats, which I happened to have by me. On the heights we were taken round by Lieutenant Chorus, of the 2nd Foot Guards, who was well orientated. Major von Petery of this regiment commanded a portion of the outposts, and I met him here for the first time since his gallant behaviour of the last few days.

Our dinner, from want of room, had to be out-of-doors. Adalbert, and Anton von Hohenzollern were there. Lieutenant von Schleinitz in the 2nd Foot Guards, an orderly-officer from Berlin, came with positive intelligence that the King was close to us; indeed, already in Gitschin.

I was very tired, and hoped to get to bed early, but was not to be let off so easily. In the first place, Prince Friedrich Karl sent to say he wished to-morrow to make a reconnaissance, and begged me to reinforce him with the Guards, as he had intelligence that troops were collecting on his front. While I was talking to Colonel v. Kessel about the fight at Sohr, Major Count Gröben from the General Staff at the King's Head-Quarters was announced, to take part in to-morrow's reconnaissance. As yet I knew nothing officially about this reconnaissance, for First-Lieutenant Count Blumenthal, my orderly-officer, who was to bring me the order, had not yet returned with his over-tired horse from the King's Head-Quarters.

Scarcely had I gone to bed, when a fresh orderly-officer arrived from Prince Friedrich Karl, followed shortly by General v. Blumenthal. The latter had been yesterday to Gitschin, and reported that Prince Friedrich Karl laid great weight on the concentration of the enemy, nothing of which had been reported by our reconnaissances. After some hours' sleep, General v. Blumenthal and Major Count Finkenstein, the aide-de-camp, waked me with the King's order not to reconnoitre on the 3rd, but, as several Corps of the enemy's troops were marching on Horzitz, to cross the Elbe with my army, and support the I. Army, which was moving forward at 3 a.m. this night. And thus the night went by ; the night before Königgrätz.

July 3, 1866.

The Battle of Königgrätz. It had rained hard in the night. My orders, sent out at daybreak to the Corps, directed them to march off by 8.30 a.m. At this hour I joined the bulk of the Guard Corps, and with them made the excessively heavy march, in pouring rain, over the steep bank of the Elbe and the mountains lying to the back of it. The paths were obliterated, which terribly hindered the advance of all the regiments, and made the march difficult to a degree. I did not believe in the possibility of a big engagement, because I was of the opinion that the Austrians would not attempt to give battle, with their backs to the Elbe.

Far off, however, we heard intermittent cannon-shots, and at length we reached the highest point, not far from the neighbourhood in which we reconnoitred yesterday. It then became clear that a sharp artillery fight, at any rate, was in progress, for we could hear single cannon-shots quite plainly, and distinguish the enemy's from our own batteries. On this plateau the march in the sopping ground was frightfully heavy.

Then came the message, Lieut.-General v.

Fransecky was nearest to our right wing with his 7th Division; he had a difficult position, and begged for reinforcements of artillery. The reserve artillery of the Guard Corps was at once ordered out.

At the village of Zizeloves the Advance-guard of the Guard Corps went in the direction of Masloved, and after some three-quarters of an hour the battery itself opened fire, taking up its station on this side. It seemed as if the firing was rapidly increasing in our right flank, and as if a forward movement of our men was simultaneously taking place.

Half an hour straight in front of us, at the height of the village of Horenoves, stood an enormous and solitary tree. This I gave to the different corps as their main *point de vue*, for the enemy seemed to have taken up a very strong artillery position there, which jutted out hook-wise upon the I. Army. The firing indeed seemed to stop at times, only to begin again with renewed activity, and it seemed to be gaining ground in that direction. The bulk of the Guard Corps followed slowly, in particular the Second Division of the Guards, because they were all marching along one route, instead of in several columns, so as to save time and space.

The Advance-guard went forward slowly, but decidedly gained ground, whilst in our right flank the artillery fire steadily retreated; the enemy's battery at the big tree fired once hotly, then the guns were silent; the enemy must have felt us within their flank.

On reaching the plateau, especially on halting at Zizeloves, I at once recognized that my task was to surround the enemy's right flank and dislodge them. I shouted this order to the single columns, as they defiled before me, and many a sturdy answer from the sections assured me that I was understood.

General v. Mutius with a portion of the VI. Army Corps must now—it was about 1 o'clock— have attacked the rear of the enemy's right flank, for, on further advance towards the aforesaid tree, I could discover nothing of the VI. Army Corps, and yet I heard firing in the left flank. The ground was shocking, hindering all rapid movement, and only too easily tearing the shoes off the horses' feet. Nowhere could one get a good point of view; the wet and rain, moreover, deceived us very much as to the distance, so that the big tree never came any nearer.

The wounded were carried by, the dead lay round, several villages on our right were in flames, and the thunder of the cannon continued in the same place. We often looked round for the I. Army Corps, which had to march some two and a half miles, but was due on the field at 2 o'clock. Major von der Burg went to meet it, but brought the unwelcome news that General v. Hartmann with the Cavalry Division was behind the I. Army Corps, and could not move his position on account of the columns. At length the heads of the Infantry columns appeared, and my army was now complete.

General v. Steinmetz, whom I had directed to follow to-day with his V. Army Corps, as the reserve, had orders to join the VI. Army Corps immediately. I met their Infantry and Cavalry columns ; and was greeted with loud cheers, when I informed them how serious was the day's work, and informed them that our King was present, and to-day commanded the army in person.

As soon as we heard the significant firing of the cannon, General Blumenthal at once said to me, " This is the decisive battle," and we became more convinced of this every quarter of an hour. The advent of my army had broken the enemy's right flank, and this gave the I. Army an opportunity to take the offensive. Since my arrival on the field of battle, the advance had

once more become general; soon after, it was
rumoured that the order to withdraw had been
given just before our appearance, because after
fighting for hours the I. Army had not been able
to move from its place.

When we finally reached the famous tree,
which really consisted of two colossal limes standing one on either side of a giant crucifix, fresh
hills prevented us from obtaining any view of the
fight that was raging in front of us.   We were in
the immediate neighbourhood of two battalions of
Guard-Grenadiers (Königin-Elisabeth) when some
dispersed Austrian cavalry came by us; a section
which was pretty far off from them fired and shot
them down, man for man, so that the horses tore
by riderless.

Some Guard-Hussars, who saw this from afar,
swooped down on the horses, and claimed them
as booty.   Then a considerably larger body of
cavalry came up to us.   We could not see from
their white cloaks whether they were Dragoons or
Cuirassiers; I was preparing to ride down into one
of our battalions, in case they formed a square,
but our percussion-guns once more cleared the
ground, and diverted the danger.

Reaching the height of Masloved, where
Austrian corpses of all regiments lay alongside

of the badly wounded, I heard that Colonel v. Obernitz lay here in a farm with a wound in his head.

I at once looked him up, and found him fortunately only slightly wounded in the head; near him, however, was Lieutenant v. Strantz, of the 1st Foot Guards, who had had several fingers of his left hand shot off. In the farm our own and the Austrian wounded lay in heaps; one could not, and must not, however, stop, for to-day one's thoughts had to be wholly bent on the enemy. Obernitz thought he had narrowly escaped being taken prisoner.

A few shells fell near us, and it must be said that the Austrian artillery shoot splendidly, for the missiles nearly always hit the mark at which they were first aimed.

A short quarter of a mile before us at the highest point lay the village of Chlum; musketry-fire, cheers, and infantry-salvos were being discharged there, and it was evident that the fighting was desperate in that direction. The Guards were engaged there, and though I still had no intelligence, I conjectured that the Second Division must already be beyond Masloved. The Advance-guard from the I. Army Corps, consisting of my East-Prussian Grenadier Regiment, and the 5th

East-Prussian Regiment, No. 41, came up at the
right moment to help the Guards in Chlum; it
was high time, for they were in a very difficult
position.   I sent Eulenburg to the Advance-guard
to give them the exact direction in which they
were to march.

Lieut.-General von Boyen came from His
Majesty, from Sadowa.   He had galloped round
half a mile of byways to call my attention to the
necessity of commanding the village of Chlum,
which we were apparently no longer occupying;
and he arrived at the right moment to be an eye-
witness of the final taking of the place; while
Major von Grävenitz, of the 8th Hussars, Adjutant
of the I. Army Corps, came up simultaneously
with the announcement that Chlum was taken by
the Advance-guard of the I. Army Corps.   It
must have been just at that moment that a very
exhausted and ragged infantry column came out
from Chlum, whom I even took at first to be
prisoners.   Some prisoners were with them, but
the column was going round under the shelter of
a hill by Chlum, in order to occupy the right
flank of the place more easily, since our station
on that side was still under a sharp fire.

And now at last the bulk of the I. Army Corps
came up : the advance in such weather, and many

other hindrances, had not permitted the march to be properly directed upon Chlum.

I now rode myself to the I. Army Corps, gave the direction of the march-forward to the flank-battalion, and, while many shells were bursting in our neighbourhood, greeted the troops of the East-Prussian province! It was an inspiriting moment!

From here I rode on, past an advanced battery, freshly thrown-up, which showed by what important outworks the Austrians had fortified their position, and not far from which two Prussian 4-pounders were standing abandoned, to the steep heights of Chlum. In the vicinity of a battery that was still firing, surrounded by the men of my East-Prussian Regiment, I surveyed the three miles of battle-field, and acquired the certainty that the victory was ours, and the enemy in full retreat.

Such moments must be lived through; description is impossible! Hearty thanks—I might say ejaculations—went up to God. Then it was necessary to plunge once more into actualities, to look into everything, to go everywhere, hardly daring to glance at the ground, where old acquaintances, whom one had just before seen in full vigour of life in the battle, were stretched out.

The fight was raging at our feet, round Rosberitz; but the Rear-guard was already in unmistakable retreat; while at my left flank, which was nearest to Königgrätz, Boyen was still actively engaged with the VI. Army Corps, and the cannon from the fortress had also begun to fire.

The sky was beginning to clear, and rays of sunshine fell across the bloody battle-field. Just as the heroic death of Lieut.-General von Hiller and his second Adjutant, the promising Lieutenant Theissen of the 4th Foot Guards, was announced to me, and the feeling of grief at these losses was beginning to assert itself, I heard some cheering. We thought the King must be coming, but it was Fritz Karl.*

We waved our caps to each other from afar, and then, amid the hurrahs of the troops of my extreme right, and his extreme left wing, with whom I raised an enthusiastic cheer for our King, we fell into each other's arms. Such greetings, again, must be lived through; two years ago I embraced him before Düppel as a victor, to-day we were both conquerors, and when his troops were hard pressed I had decided the day with the advent of my army.

---

* Prince Frederick Charles of Prussia, Commander-in-Chief of the I. Army and Army of the Elbe.

My thoughts were now with my wife, my children, my mother and sister. My little Sigismund, who had gone home, hovered before me, as though his death had been the forerunner of a great event in my life. Yet no victory compensates for the loss of a child; far rather does the gnawing grief first make itself fully felt, amid such powerful impressions.

But I had to remind myself that this was no time to give way to such feelings; that, on the contrary, all one's thoughts must be turned to the defeated enemy, to the proper use to be made of the victory for which we had fought. I pointed out to my Adjutants the pressing necessity of immediate pursuit of the Austrians, and sent Jasmund to Steinmetz with instructions to set out at once after the enemy. I gave the same order to the 2nd Hussars, who had just arrived upon the heights of Chlum; and directed that the command should be repeated to General v. Hartmann by Captain Count Rödern, as also by Major-General v. Borstell.

The artillery fire was still continuing, but was retiring to a distance, and there was now a little pause, in which we collected intelligence, and were able to identify the dead and wounded. Anton Hohenzollern was severely wounded;

Count Dohna, of the East-Prussian Jäger Battalion, lay shot through the breast, not far from the body of Theissen, whose scarf and neck-chain we took off for his family. Dohna charged me with greetings to his father, and was still able to say that only two officers of the battalion were left uninjured after an appalling volley from the Austrian Jägers.

Lieutenant v. Pape, of the 2nd Foot Guards, the only son of the Commander, was carried by, hit with three bullets ; I embraced him in his father's name, as I had known him from a child, while Lieutenant Chorus, of the 2nd Foot Guards, informed me that he had captured a gun !

Never shall I forget the earnest expression of Kessel's countenance, when we met here, as he was mustering the First Regiment of the Guards from Chlum. From him I received the first particulars : on our right, the 7th Division, more especially the Magdeburg Regiments, Nos. 26 and 27, must have had a desperately hard position.

Around us lay or limped so many of the well-known figures from the Potsdam and Berlin garrison ! Each had something to tell. Those who were using their weapons as crutches, or were being supported up the heights by their comrades, looked sadly woe-begone. The grimmest sight, however, was an Austrian Battery, whose entire equipment of men and horses had been shot down. And thus the most diverse sensations chased through one's brain in a second.

Now came an order from the King that General v. Herwarth was to pursue the enemy with his VIII. Army Corps, while all the rest were to bivouac on the field.

After quite unexpectedly meeting the Grand-Duke of Mecklenburg-Schwerin at Chlum, of whose presence in the army I was ignorant, I next rode to the villages, to obtain further intelligence, and to visit the King. I talked some time to the men of the 27th Infantry Regiment. They said, as out of one mouth, " We all knew that you would come to-day ; we had a hard stand in the wood at Sadowa, till all at once we heard, He is coming ! He is coming ! Then everything went well again, but it was high time that you did come."

This simple, homely account of the situation made a deep impression on me.

In Rosberitz, where the battle must have been truly desperate, to judge from the masses of dead and wounded, and where the farms were still blazing, I found Anton Hohenzollern, who was hit in the leg by three bullets. He was quite beaming, and at the same time touchingly *naïf* in the way he depreciated his wounds : he wished me luck, and said he had been under a furious fire with his detachment, had ordered rapid file-fire, was then wounded, and even thus taken prisoner, so that his sword was taken away in spite of his wounds ; but was then on our advance set free again. He was lying in a peasant's house, among dying Austrians, but was at once transported to a S. John's ambulance.

It is a gruesome thing to ride over a battle-field, and the ghastly mutilations that meet one's eye are indescribable.

War is an appalling thing, and the man who brings it about with a stroke of his pen at the " green table," little recks what he is conjuring with.

I first unexpectedly met some wounded from the 51st Infantry Regiment, among them Captain Hiebe, one of my former subalterns in the 11th Infantry, who was shot in the foot. A badly wounded Grenadier of the 2nd Guards called out to me, " Oh, dear Crown Prince, do have me taken away."

Major v. Eckart of the 2nd Guards, who seemed to be fatally wounded, passed us in an ambulance-waggon. He could only reply to my inquiries in a weak voice. Then I met the Kolberg Grenadiers, and the Blücher Hussars of my Pomeranian Army Corps : an unexpected pleasure, to find them here.

I also met Uncle Karl and Wilhelm Mecklenburg. The latter had received a slight sword-cut. Finally, after much seeking and asking, we found the King. I informed him of the presence of my Army on the field, and kissed his hand, and then he embraced me. Neither of us could speak for some time ; then he was the first to find words, and told me he rejoiced that I had so far achieved successful results, and had shown capacity for command. As I must already know by his telegram, he had given me the *Pour le Mérite* for the preceding victories. This telegram I had not received, and thus it was on the battle-field, where I had with him decided the victory, that my King and Father presented me with our highest military order.*

* The order *Pour le Mérite* had already been conferred on the Crown Prince for the 27th and 28th of June. It came, however, as a complete surprise, since the telegram intended for the Crown Prince had fallen into the hands of the Austrians. It ran as follows :—

"Victory ! Thanks to you and your splendid troops. Repeat to General Steinmetz' Fifth Corps the thanks you have already expressed in my name, and give my royal thanks to the Guard Corps for their incomparable valour, and for their prompt realization of my parting words. To-morrow I am going to the army by Goerlitz. I send you the order *Pour le Mérite*.—WILLIAM."

E

I was deeply moved, and those standing by seemed also to be touched. It had been a wonderful evening, and just while we were exchanging our greetings, the sun was setting in full splendour. Bismarck, with all the officers of the King's Head-Quarters, as well as my entire Staff, were present. I met Schweinitz and Reuss VII. again here.

I further had a long talk with the King, in which I particularly recommended Generals Blumenthal and Steinmetz to him, for these two high military authorities had taken an active part in all my arrangements. His Majesty had granted my request that he would give the Order of the Black Eagle to General v. Steinmetz for his services, and ratified my proposal to give the name of Königgrätz to this battle.

We now rode back by Chlum, to seek for night-quarters in Horenowes, but the baggage, which had been left in Königinhof, could not arrive before the early morning. After many wanderings, in which all the horrors of the battle-field pursued us into the darkness, we at length reached the above-mentioned place, where 3000 Austrian prisoners were already lodged.

The troops were bivouacking in every part of the field ; only a few of them were singing.

Here, as so often, the comic was lurking near the tragic. A number of infantry-men were following a tame pig, so as to enjoy roasting it before the camp-fire! The hunt went in all directions, till at last the revolvers came into play:—and close to this scene lay the corpses of cavalry-men from the hot fight that had raged that afternoon at the foot of Chlúm, and in which the two Regiments of Dragoon Guards, the Neumark Dragoons, both the Brandenburg Uhlans, and also the Zieten Hussars had taken part.

It was astonishing how quickly our men managed to carry off their fallen comrades, so that there were far fewer bodies of Prussian than of Austrian soldiers. The ambulance-bearers, too, conducted themselves splendidly in this respect.

We settled ourselves on straw and the like, in an entirely empty house with no furniture, and after living the whole day on bread and cognac, had to feed ourselves again in the evening on cheap ammunition-bread, which we had bought at a canteen; *à la guerre comme à la guerre*, is accomplished here in the full sense of the words. We ourselves had been on horseback from 8 a.m. till 8.30 p.m., and so slept well in spite of the impossible lodging—in as far as the excitements of such an adventure allowed one to sleep in peace.

We were not able either to feed or to water our poor horses. Whenever I met baggage-waggons I pulled out some hay, and gave it to my faithful Cairngorm to eat out of my hand. The chestnut has done me good service again to-day.

I felt that this had been one of the most significant days for Prussia, and prayed God to enlighten the King and his Council, as well as to bring about the right conclusion for the welfare and future of Prussia and Germany. In the night I had vivid dreams of my wife and children!

July 4, 1866.   *Head-Quarters at Horenowes.*

One of our Feld-Jäger lieutenants (Krieger) who had already been useful to us yesterday evening, from his zeal and discretion, discovered a coffee-canteen. The rest of yesterday's canteen-bread still held out, and so we had a successful breakfast; coffee out of beer-glasses, and the spoons each man made for himself out of twigs. Then I visited our wounded in this place, among them Colonel v. Zychlinski, Commander of the brave 27th, who insisted on returning to his regiment, until I formally forbade it;

further, Captain Count Groeben of the Guard-Hussars, whose horse had been shot, v. Fabek of the 3rd Guards. None of our men were repining, to-day as little as yesterday; the Austrians, on the contrary, murmured a great deal. A captured Hungarian spoke half in German, half in Danish, because he had been in the campaign of Schleswig, in 1864. At length our things arrived, and I was able to have clean linen. Then Captain v. Wrangel of the Guard-Hussars announced that he had ridden to Königin-hof, had demanded entrance in my name, had been led in with his eyes bound, and had demanded a capitulation in my name, which was not refused unconditionally; so that a written demand would very probably be successful. I at once sent Major von der Burg on this errand, and Captain Mischke on a similar errand to Joseph-stadt. The latter, however, in spite of beckoning with the flag of truce, and signalling by trumpet, was fired at, his own and the trumpeter's horses being wounded, and this happened indeed some half-mile from the fortress. Burg was more fortunate, for he brought a written acceptance of capitulation with him. The Commandant asked to have till 12 at noon to-morrow to consider and make enquiries. I refused.

In the afternoon, Prince August of Wurtemburg announced to me through his Orderly-officer,
Prince Croy, that Lieut.-Field-Marshal von
Gablenz was with him, and urgently desired to
speak with the King and myself. I ordered that
he should be brought with bandaged eyes to the
King's Head-Quarters at Horzitz, and at once
rode off myself by a nearer way to His Majesty.
The King, however, had already gone off to the
bivouacs, met Gablenz on the way, offered an
armistice, and sent him on again to Horzitz, to
Roon, Moltke, and Bismarck. It was accordingly
there that I met him. After an embrace and
exchange of reminiscences from 1864, he told us
quite openly that the Austrian army was totally
destroyed, and was in a most melancholy condition. All this had been clearly and openly stated
to the Kaiser; he, Gablenz, came on his own
responsibility, only authorized by Benedek to
appeal to the King's feelings : a three days' truce
could not do us any material harm, and would
also give them no advantage; in the mean time,
however, much might possibly be arranged.

I told him quite openly that as a soldier I
never could entertain such propositions. If
Austria handed over the fortresses of Josefstadt
and Königgrätz, along with the Elbe, to us as the

lines of demarcation, we might certainly give a three days' armistice, otherwise not. He did not feel himself authorized to accept this. He then told us that the Arch-Dukes Wilhelm and Joseph were slightly wounded; Count Festetics badly wounded in the leg, Count Thun in the head. Colonel Binder was dead. The loss through our percussion-guns was enormous. Even at Trautenau he had conceived a vast respect for our brave troops; yesterday, however, I had come up quite unexpectedly in his flank, and when he heard the firing of my batteries, it became clear to him that the day was lost for the Austrian army. This whole embassy I took to be a *ruse*, without, however, feeling sure what lay behind it; the Austrians either wanted to gain time, or to get some information as to our disposition of troops. Both physically and mentally Gablenz was the picture of exhaustion, but he must indeed have been tired out, as he had ridden over from a place two miles behind Königgrätz.

The King only returned at 11.30 at night; Gablenz had to wait till then, and only to depart without having effected his business. Bismarck invited me, with my Adjutant, and General v. Stosch, to dine with him. As it was midnight before His Majesty allowed me to depart, I could not do the two miles back in the darkness with my tired horses to Horenowes, especially in the hostile disposition of the inhabitants, so I spent the night in the quarters of the Duke of Coburg, who had just arrived. In the King's Head-Quarters the most essential things were still wanting, seeing that there was a lack of food and drink. The King, namely, had not gone back to Gitschin, his Head-Quarters of yesterday, but had taken up his quarters after the battle in Horzitz, with Prince Friedrich Karl, while the baggage was still in Gitschin. A few wounded officers came in late yesterday evening from the battle-field, among them Colonel v. Wietersheim, Commander of the 6th Pomeranian Infantry, No. 49, who is said to be very severely wounded.

July 5, 1866.

Early, at 6 a.m., I went back from Horzitz to Horenowes, and went to bed by daylight. I now learnt for the first time, from Captain v. Frankenburg of the Guard-Landwehrs, the Orderly-officer of Mutius, how splendidly the brave VI. Army Corps on my left wing had worked, and how materially their prompt surrounding of the right Austrian flank, where, among others, the Black-

and-Yellow Brigade was fighting, had aided in the result. Through Frankenburg I conveyed to General v. Mutius my sincere wishes for his success. He well deserves the *Pour le Mérite*. In the afternoon I rode with the Staff over the field of battle to Opatowitz, our night-quarters.

Horrible sights at the burial of half-dressed corpses, or rotten and mortified bodies, were to be seen in appalling variety; never shall I forget the corpses from which the head had been torn off or mangled. The very horses shrank from these cadavers. The Commandant of Königgrätz, who had doubtless spoken with Gablenz during the night, had changed his tune, and gave no answer, so that for an hour he had to be talked to with field-guns. I rode to the bivouac of the 2nd Division, where I received hearty greetings, and was able on the way to convince myself of the confused flight of the Austrians, since at every moment the overturned waggons, discarded knapsacks, and similar traces, showed how hurriedly the troops had departed. The suburbs of Königgrätz were burning; the Commandant had tried to raze them to the ground. Not far from a railway-crossing at the friendly village of Opatowitz, we were met by a captured gendarme of Benedek's Staff-Watch, who, however, could only speak Italian. I talked brokenly with him as best I could in his mother-tongue, and ascertained that he had deserted because they had nothing to eat nor drink. In the place itself I found Colonel v. Pape, Commander of the 2nd Guards, who was just returning from the funeral of his only son, the same whom I had found wounded at Chlum. I also spoke to a non-commissioned officer, who had just come out of captivity. In effect, seventy men of different regiments were made prisoners the day before yesterday during the battle, and were at once conveyed by the Austrians to Königgrätz. These prisoners, therefore, had to accompany the entire flight, which this sub-officer called a regular rout, and were compelled to swim through the inundated environs of the fortress, as well as through the Elbe. At Pardubitz, Benedek saw our men, shook his head, and ordered their release, because the Kaiser's people had not enough for themselves, let alone the feeding of prisoners. An Austrian officer said to another non-commissioned officer, with his revolver at his breast, " Confess, fellow, that you were led by French officers in disguise, for of yourselves you would never have succeeded in getting such results ! " No one could have paid us a greater compliment.

I found some badly wounded Austrian officers

in a peasant's house, in which I was looking for the wounded Prince Windischgrätz, the son of the Field-Marshal. He had, however, already been transported. The others lay upon straw, longing for hospital comforts. An Austrian surgeon, who had apparently been taken prisoner, wished to go after his troop, and was not to be persuaded to remain with his countrymen, although not a single Austrian surgeon had stopped to take care of the Kaiser's men. Of course I did not let the fellow go. The officers would only sign a bond "not to serve against us in this war," with the inclusion of the clause, "until after the exchange of prisoners." Our night's quarters were in a friendly mill.

July 6, 1866. *Head-Quarters at Pardubitz.*

Uncle Ernst * met us in the act of marching off; we rode to-day to Pardubitz, being much delayed on the way by the marching troops. Once more we crossed the Elbe on pontoon-bridges, in place of the permanent bridges that had been burned by the Austrians. Here I learned what a splendid charge the Neumark Dragoons had made, the entire officers' corps being wounded. I further

* Duke Ernest II. of Coburg.

heard how boldly Prince Krafft of Hohenlohe had joined in with the Reserve Artillery of the Guard Corps at Maslowed and Chlum, and that he had effected important results. Men of the VIII. Army Corps were looking for their companies. A painter of stained glass, from Cologne, a reservist, had succeeded in taking fifty-four prisoners to a Prussian ambulance station, after they had made him prisoner in the first instance. I told him he should some day work at the window of Cologne Cathedral, which we have designed for the main entrance. In the evening the King arrived, and I brought him the flag captured at Schweinschädel by the 46th Infantry, which was handed to His Majesty by Mersiewski, who had actually taken the flag, and had been promoted to the rank of non-commissioned officer in recognition; and by Fusilier Schellin of the First Guards.

July 7, 1866.   Head-Quarters at Chroustowitz.

Rode to the charming Thurn-and-Taxis hunting castle of Chroustowitz, where we made our night-quarters. The neighbourhood was infinitely picturesque. Wheat land is here in perfection. The castle is of an imposing size, in the earlier rococo style, with the corresponding arrangements of garden. The stables are splendid, and a real treat for our horses.

July 8, 1866. *Head-Quarters at Chroustowitz-Hohenmauth.*

This morning, at 4 a.m., I was awakened by the rattle of a carriage. Gablenz had come back again! He brought conditions of armistice, based on Moltke's idea of the evacuation of the fortresses of Josefstadt and Königgrätz. I sent him to Pardubitz, with the Kaiser's aide-de-camp, Count Fratzavari, a knight of the Theresien Order, who escorted him (evidently Baron v. Fejervary). I went to the King by another route. Gablenz brought papers to Moltke; these were the signed "instructions" from Mensdorff, at Zwittau, to Gablenz, to hand over the above fortresses, after the previous free and honourable withdrawal of the garrisons, military stores, and war material; further, an eight weeks' armistice, with fourteen days' warning of re-commencement of hostilities; and, lastly, a new line of demarcation, to be hereafter regulated more precisely, behind which the Austrians might retire without any danger! A victorious conqueror could not have dictated other conditions to the vanquished. The King, of

course, declined to receive Gablenz under these
conditions; on the contrary, he was politely conducted away, with a document from Moltke to
the effect "that we were ready to enter into
direct peace negotiations with Austria." The
newspaper reports of the cession of Venetia are
fully confirmed. Henry VII. of Reuss has gone
to Paris with an autograph letter from the King
to express our willingness to consider negotiations for peace. But that we remain in marching
form is, of course, understood. Schweinitz was
sent to Petersburg. On the return journey, one
of my black horses fell, and I had to take a
baggage horse from the first good waggon we
met. Returned to Chroustowitz. Gablenz was just
leaving. He stopped my carriage, took me aside,
and said he hoped to be in Vienna to-morrow
morning, and that peace would soon be arranged. After a few remarks on the singularity
of the cession of Venetia to France, he repeated
his professions of ignorance. "But," said I,
"Mensdorff is with you in Zwittau; he must
surely know it; and the fact has been known
since the 4th of this month!" "Mensdorff has
been there since the 5th," he replied, "but I
have heard nothing; for the rest, your Royal
Highness must not forget that Bismarck has also

been treating with Italy." Upon this we parted with all our old cordiality and friendliness. Wrangel appeared. In the evening I reached our Head-Quarters at Hohenmauth on horseback. A nasty, dirty little hole.

July 9, 1866. *Head-Quarters, Leitomischel.*

A little rain; a ride of some $2\frac{1}{2}$ miles, to Leitomischel; sunshine on the way; met a few Saxon prisoners. Leitomischel was the famous seat of Wallenstein, adorned with a magnificent castle with three rows of open arcades one above the other, recently squandered by the worthless heirs of the great name. In the castle were 5000 Austrian wounded, without a single Austrian surgeon, or any instruments. Isolated cases of cholera have occurred among them. .. . . Benedek had lodged in my room, and related with great depression that he had led the infantry columns himself at Chlum, but they refused to do any more—so he had been forced to retire. We heard that Anton Hohenzollern's wound was very severe, as the thigh-bone is said to be splintered above the knee. He is in Königinhof, under the care of the excellent Dr. Middeldorpff, who has offered his services gratuitously in this war, as already in 1864. . . . .

July 10, 1866.   *Head-Quarters, Mährisch-Trübau.*

We marched off on horseback in pouring rain, 4½ miles to Mährisch-Trübau. High boots and rain-cloaks were in request to-day. As we crossed the steep passes of the mountain, Mähren lay charmingly in the sun before us; the rain kept to Bohemia. The Second Division met us, and I marched with the Infantry to Mährisch-Trübau. In the afternoon I convinced myself that whole companies in the I. Army Corps did not know that I was leading them, the talk being still only of Prince Karl and von Wrangel.

July 11, 1866.   *Head-Quarters, Mährisch-Trübau.*

At last a rest-day! Intercepted Austrian letters describe in plain language the disorganization of the army during the flight. The initiated write that the generalship was miserable, and " even surpassed that of Solferino " ! There was a strange concurrence in the sense of being fully beaten, which turned high and low alike to their homes. One hears rumours that Count Alexander Mensdorff, who undoubtedly has a close enough acquaintance with the army to instruct the Kaiser, as an eye-witness, as to its real constitution, is to be Benedek's successor. . . .

From the Bürgermeister with whom I was lodged, I heard that the Austrians had withdrawn the day before yesterday, in the afternoon, with the Saxons, under the Crown Prince of Saxony, Benedek, and Mensdorff. In the evening we sat in a Bier-Garten with the garrison.

July 12, 1866. *Head-Quarters, Mährisch-Trübau.*

Still here on account of the march towards Olmütz; the enemy will certainly entrench themselves there, and wait for us. The V. Army Corps marched through—the King's Regiment of Grenadiers, with more than half its officers killed or wounded, so that an ensign had to act as Adjutant. The men looked at me with proud self-consciousness. Steinmetz messed with me, and I drank his health as "the Hero of Nachod and Skalitz." General v. Hartmann followed the V. Corps with the Cavalry Division. The condition of the horses in the West-Prussian Cuirassiers was more especially excellent. The 2nd Landwehr Hussars looked very smart. Hartmann has unfortunately been able to do nothing so far, and looked extremely crestfallen. At Chlum he only received my orders to follow the enemy in the night. Steinmetz has not yet

F

received the promised Order of the Black Eagle, and feels a keen desire for it, as he knows through me that His Majesty has granted it to him, at my particular request, for his three victories. In the evening back to the Bier-Garten. The day before yesterday, the 2nd Pomeranian Uhlans, No. 9, had a nice little fight at Zwittau, when two Bülows were wounded. The King's Head-Quarters are moved to Brünn, where Fritz Karl has already arrived. It will depend upon the results of the reconnaissances and the subsequent intelligence whether I shall have to remain with my army before Olmütz, or follow the I. Army with two of my Corps to Vienna. We have been without any home-letters or papers since the 8th of this month, and our tobacco has quite given out. At length a belated and uninjured packet of four days has turned up to-day, so that we have plenty to read. Four letters at once from my wife! Coburg is occupied by the Bavarians, and will be administered. At Schmalkalden, as previously at Dermbach, Falckenstein and Groeben have had successful encounters with the Bavarians, but at the penalty of considerable losses. It is said that the intervention of France is to the advantage of Austria.

July 13, 1866. *Head-Quarters, Opatowitz, Count Herberstein's Schloss.*

We marched painfully out of Mährisch-Trübau in the sweltering heat, because the Guard Corps, co-operating with the Columns of the V. Army Corps, blocked the exits. Quartered in the charmingly situated, exceedingly spacious, and many-roomed little castle of Count Herberstein, who also has properties on Glatz. I inhabit the *Boudoir de Madame.* We sat long in the shade, and dined *al fresco.* M. Lefèbre, of the French Embassy in Berlin, has betaken himself to the Austrian outposts, there to treat of proposals for an armistice.

July 14, 1866. *Head-quarters at Konitz.*

Again a sweltering heat, and terribly steep paths; met Kirchbach's Division, the gallant 1st West-Prussian Grenadier Regiment, No. 6, and the 46th Infantry Regiment. The latter in particular had many fagged out, who remained behind. The stiff close collars are no good for mountain and summer marching; I always permit the neckcloths to come off altogether, but heard to-day that Steinmetz had expressly forbidden this on the march, but ordered it, on the contrary, in action. The mountain pass we came over resembles the Thüringerwald. I heard to-day of the death of Colonel v. Wietersheim, Commander of the 6th Pomeranian Infantry Regiment, No. 49, who has died of the wounds he received at Königgrätz. The loss of such a talented Commander in my Pomeranian Army Corps distresses me very much. Quarters in the market-place of Konitz, in the ruined town-hall. Benedek, Mensdorff, Arch-Duke Ernest have come through. The Infantry are still marching in disorder. The gardeners say the taxes were becoming unbearable. The Government was doing nothing to help the increasing poverty. . . .

Major von der Burg is to assist to-morrow in Bonin's expedition, which is to go south to Olmütz by Tobitzschau, while General v. Hartmann is to push forward to Prerau. We hear, indeed, that the Austrians have already left Olmütz, and are retiring upon Vienna; this must absolutely be put a stop to. As the I. Army is to march upon Lundenburg, it might perhaps be possible to cut off a portion of the Austrian army. Lieutenant v. Wintzigerode, of the 2nd Regiment of Leib-Hussars, rode while reconnoitring right up to the redoubts of Olmütz, without encountering a single shot. He was even able to ascertain the march-off of an important number of columns towards the south. I immediately sent him my approval. In the evening rode to Steinmetz, to invest him, on the part of His Majesty, with the Order of the Black Eagle, for which I had asked the King, since it has been conferred so long without the old hero actually possessing it. Steinmetz kissed the star, and then my hand, before I could prevent him. "Would that I could thank my King thus also; the greatest wish of my life is fulfilled." Two very gracious autograph letters from the King moved him deeply. Afterwards I read these aloud to the Staff, as well as to the Secretaries, Watch, etc., and all rejoiced at the well-deserved distinction of the valiant leader. The evening was unprecedently beautiful for the homeward ride. I have sent Mischke to Brünn to His Majesty.

July 15, 1866. *Head-Quarters at Konitz.*

The reconnaissance has succeeded; Bonin led the engagement at Tobitschau with great success. Major-General v. Malotki distinguished himself in it. A *sortie* from Olmütz was driven back, many hundreds being taken prisoners. A Brigade of the enemy, said to be that of General v. Rothkirch, which had not fought with us till now, has been intercepted on the way south. The West-Prussian Cuirassiers took fifteen guns; the Silesian Cuirassiers, No. 1, three dismounted cannon; Hartmann went as far as Prerau, where, notwithstanding that the place was still occupied by the enemy, he managed to damage the railway. The 2nd Leib-Hussars, as well as the Landwehr Hussars, had broken into the squares, and captured many men and horses; but they also suffered heavy losses. Colonel v. Glasenapp, the Commander of the Landwehr Hussars, fell, covered with sword-cuts. Yesterday evening the Silesian Cuirassiers fell on a square of Saxons in the darkness, but unfortunately lost three officers in the action. To-morrow Steinmetz is going to Prerau to reconnoitre, and will be supported by the I. Army Corps. Hartmann, too, is ordered to the front.

July 16, 1866. *Head-Quarters at Prödlitz. Countess Kalnoky's Schloss.*

Pouring rain; mounted march to Prossnitz, in the hope of joining in the action at that place. On the way we met and stopped some men with blackened faces, who seemed to us to be deserters in disguise. The reconnaissance of the V. Army Corps came to nothing, for Bonin, who was nearest to Prerau, only marched off in the afternoon, owing to a misunderstanding. The two Divisions of the V. Army Corps therefore marched back to their cantonments. The men looked in splendid condition, especially the gallant King's Grenadiers, No. 7. In Prossnitz our arrival excited a great commotion among the very courteous inhabitants; sultry heat had succeeded to the rain. In the Hospital of the Barmherzigen Bruder, our officers and men were being very well taken care of. Most of them had been wounded with the sword, from which one could see that it had been a hot encounter. Among others of our officers, we found here Lieutenants v. Estorff and v. Blumenthal of the 2nd Leib-Hussars, also v. Rothkirch of the Landwehr, who had six sword-cuts on the head, and two in the neck, without, however, being dangerously wounded. Many officers of the 1st Leib-Hussars, too, were being tended here. From Prossnitz we had to do two miles further to the pretty rococo country-house of a Countess Kalnoky, whose eldest son was an attaché in Berlin, but is now in London. A Herr von

Wattwyl did the honours. The Countess had withdrawn with her daughters to a neighbouring forester's house, leaving us in possession of everything, even the beds, adorned with innumerable pictures of Saints, wreaths of roses, consecrated tapers, etc. Herr v. Wattwyl at first took me for General v. Blumenthal, and almost collapsed when he afterwards heard my name. In Vienna people seem to be expecting our speedy advent, and the Empress has already retired to Pesth.

July 17, 1866.   *Head-Quarters at Prödlitz.*

A so-called rest-day, in which at least we did not have to march. The troops, and notably the horses, required rest. The boots of the infantry need repair, otherwise the whole of this important section of our army would go to pieces. The heat is African. The I. Army Corps is going in a direction south of Olmütz; I ordered the V. Corps to prepare to march to Lundenburg along the March; the Guard Corps and VI. Corps are to march to Brünn, in a straight line by Biskopitz. The Commissariat, thank God, seems to have been well managed so far; for this we have to thank, along with the wise arrangements of my

Army-Intendant, the Cabinet Minister for War, Köllner. I paid a visit to Countess Kalnoky, whose husband has been out of his mind for ten years. The eldest son is attaché in London, and known to the Berlin Embassy; the other four sons are fighting on the opposite side, one as Adjutant to the Arch-Duke Joseph. All the ladies are living together bivouac fashion in the little forester's lodge. In the evening I went with the Uncles and most of the Adjutants to an adjacent hill, the central point of Moravia, to look in the direction of Olmütz, which, however, was invisible. It appears that the Emperor of Austria has proclaimed that Vienna is to be treated as an open town, not as a fortress. Further, that the Austrian army is to march off to Hungary, there to be organized anew, so that in two to three months it~may be ready to take the field again.

July 18, 1866.   *Head-Quarters, Brünn.*

We wanted to transport our Head-Quarters to the Castle of Austerlitz, so as to be about in the middle of my marching corps. Since, however, it appeared possible from the intelligence we had received that the Austrians might attempt

a desperate attack upon us, and then upon
our centre, from the side of the Carpathians,
Brünn seemed more prudent. In the midst of
our discussions of the *pros* and *cons*, came a
telegram from Bismarck, expressing a wish that
I would not delay too long in coming to Brünn.
I at once got ready, and did the journey of four
and a half miles by carriage, one of the maddest
sorts of high-road that I have ever seen, from
the point of view of being unpractical; it went
steeply up and down the mountain, instead of
using the valleys that lay half a mile away.
Kaiser Joseph once ploughed this road, and the
deed has been immortalized in a memorial. The
battle-field of Austerlitz is partially visible from
the *chaussée*. Brünn makes an imposing appearance from afar, with its notorious Spielberg, its
high church towers, and many luxurious dwellings, corresponding with its industrial prosperity.
In former times the nobility of Moravia resorted
hither for their winter season; these times are
over, and the richly decorated palaces stand
deserted. On arriving, the first thing I heard
was that His Majesty had just ridden off half an
hour before with Bismarck to the Dietrichstein
Schloss at Nikolsburg. So there I sat without
any intelligence, and only heard quite casually

from Count Frankenburg, one of General v. Mutius' orderly-officers, that it had been known since yesterday evening that, after a battle won by our side, General v. Falckenstein had entered Frankfurt-on-Main with flying colours, and drums beating, demanding from the rich and anti-Prussian city an indemnity of 25 millions. Thus our success endures! God keep us from reverses! Reports from Vienna say that the proffered truce has been rejected, so that we may well come to a fresh encounter before the capital. Austrian levies, especially from Croatia and in the border-districts, have been commanded; it is moreover said that 50,000 men are already on their way from Italy. It is thought that Benedek has been deposed, and Arch-Duke Albrecht made Generalissimo in his place. Burgermaster Giskra, a well-known liberal delegate to the Vienna Reichstag, greeted me, recommending the town to me, as it had conceded whatever had been demanded, and would soon be entirely exhausted. I discussed the state of Austrian affairs with this clever lawyer.

July 19, 1866. *Head-Quarters, Gross-Seelowitz.*

This is a family place of the Arch-Duke Albrecht, and his brothers and sisters; they seem to care very little for air or cleanliness. The style recalls Schönhausen, but otherwise only an oil-painting of the famous Arch-Duke Karl Ferdinand and his wife are remarkable. The truce is in the air; Benedetti has gone from Brünn to the King's Head-Quarters at the castle of Nikolsburg. They are talking of renewed negotiations at the out-posts, through M. Lefèbre of the French Embassy. Reuss VII. travelled through here on his way to Nikolsburg. On the way between Brünn and this place we encountered two showers, which resembled water-spouts, the like of which I have never seen before. In a train column a horse was drowned, and a man was only saved with difficulty. We fled with the carriage into a sheepfold. The cooling was wanted!

July 20, 1866.   *Head-Quarters, Schloss Eisgrub.*

At night came the news that Austria had agreed to withdraw from the Confederation, and that an armistice was requested. I drove to the King's Head-Quarters at Mensdorff's, formerly Dietrichstien's, castle of Nikolsburg. On the way we found the bridges over the Thaya burned; the Pioneers were restoring a sunken temporary bridge just as I came up, and in order to help me over, a number of the men undressed at once, in the cheeriest way now working in the water, now showing off swimming tricks, so that both bodies and clothes obtained a much-needed refreshment. A merry humour is so easily induced in our good people! Nikolsburg, on a dominating cone of rock, restored in the style of the Thirty Years' War, will, when finished, be very habitable; the view is more extensive than beautiful. Austria consents to payment of an indemnity to us, and also to the evacuation of the frontier; further, to the founding of a North-German Union, as far as the Maine, with Prussian military supremacy; finally, to the annexation of Schleswig-Holstein. On our side it is proposed to conclude a truce with Austria, to be shortly followed by peace; then to conclude peace with the German opponents also, reserving the partial annexation of their territories. I saw the French Ambassador Benedetti, and the Italian Ambassador Count Barral, at the King's dinner. In the evening, late over Felsburg, with a thousand difficulties (as we did not know the way nor the place), to Eisgrub, the reception-rooms of which are much like English castles. My bedroom is in the library. Duke Wilhelm of Mecklenburg was here before us, and had a merry time with his officers.

July 21, 1866.   *Head-Quarters at Eisgrub.*

Papa came here to the early breakfast, looked round the charming English grounds, and went with me all through the splendid deer-park, which is stocked with the finest herds of red- and roe-deer, and also contains wonderfully beautiful glades of oak.   Already to-day there have been conjectures as to the conclusion of peace, *in re* the establishment of a line of demarcation, and the fulfilment of the conditions of the armistice. And late in the night came Major Verdy, who had been sent in the direction of Lundenburg, where Major-General v. Podbielski was to establish the line of demarcation with the Austrians, with the intelligence that a fifteen days' truce was to come into effect at noon to-morrow.   Major Wright, Moltke's lieutenant, was in Vienna to-day, with a letter to the Duc de Gramont; he was taken to the Hofburg, and thought people were sniffing after war again.   Others, indeed, think just the contrary.   The cholera is everywhere announcing itself.   Even here two men died last night from my watch of the Grenadier Guards (Königin-Elisabeth).

July 22, 1866. *Head-Quarters, Eisgrub.*

A rest-day. Beautiful ride over the innumerable villas and grounds of the enormously extended park, through which, sixty years ago, the Thaya was diverted in order to make pretty situations with lakes.

The intelligence about the demarcation is correct. There are rumours of a fight at Presburg. A Division was certainly sent there (probably Fransecky's), to take the town by a *coup de main*, before the defeated Corps which are said to be coming down, by way of the Carpathians, from Olmütz, could arrive. The thing may miscarry for us, if, as I suspect, we stumble upon a superior force there—that would be an affair before the armistice! It is said that Count Karolyi (ambassador to Berlin), Lieutenant Field-Marshal Count Degenfeld, and Baron Brenner are on their way to Nikolsburg.

July 23, 1866. *Head-Quarters, Eisgrub.*

Ride of half a mile to His Majesty at Nikolsburg. The three gentlemen whom I mentioned yesterday have really arrived as commissioners from Vienna, and propose the above-mentioned terms. Austria only stipulates for the geographical integrity of Saxony, because it is a point of honour with the Emperor not to let his allies suffer. Another envoy is expected from Bavaria, to make an offensive and defensive alliance with Munich.

II

In the summer of 1869, invitations were sent from the Khedive of Egypt to the King, the Crown Prince and Princess, and the Federal Chancellor Count von Bismarck, to take part in the function of the opening of the Suez Canal. His Majesty felt compelled to refuse the invitation on account of his age, and of the fatigue of the journey. Count Bismarck excused himself likewise on the score of his official duties. With regard to the invitation sent to the Crown Prince, the King sought the advice of Count Bismarck; he had scruples in view of the great expenses that would be incurred by such a journey. Count Bismarck, however, overcame the hesitation of the King, by pointing out the good effect which a visit of the Crown Prince to the Emperor of Austria on the occasion of this journey must result in.

It was accordingly communicated by telegraph to Vienna, that the Crown Prince had accepted the invitation of the Khedive to take part in the ceremony of inaugurating the Suez Canal, and would visit the Emperor and the Imperial family in Vienna, if agreeable to His Imperial Majesty. Kaiser Franz Josef at once replied that it would be a great pleasure to him to receive the visit of the heir to the Prussian throne.

DIARY OF THE CROWN PRINCE ON HIS JOURNEY TO THE EAST, 1869.

After Ismaïl Pasha, Viceroy or Khedive of Egypt, had visited our Court in June, 1869, with his youngest son, and had been received with great distinction by His Majesty, he addressed the following letter to me on July 16 :—

" MONSEIGNEUR,

"Je viens de réitérer à Votre Auguste Père et Souverain la prière que j'ai pris la liberté de Lui addresser à Berlin. Je sais, Monseigneur, que Sa Majesté ne peut pas accedér de Sa personne à ma prière ; mais il a eu l'extrême bonté de me promettre d'autoriser un des Princes de son Auguste Famille d'assister à l'ouverture de l'Isthme de Suez.

"Votre Altesse a été si gracieuse à mon égard, Elle a été si pleine de bontés que je prends la liberté de Lui demander encore, comme une faveur, de vouloir bien honorer l'Égypte de Sa Présence.

" C'est un pays bien intéressant, Monseigneur, j'ose le dire, le passé et l'avenir s'y trouvent répresentés par tout ce qu'il y a de plus ancien et de plus moderne. Il mérite de fixer les regards de Votre Altesse Royale.

" J'espère, Monseigneur, que le Roi Votre Auguste Père et Souverain agréera ma prière et autorisera ce voyage que j'appelle de tout mes vœux. Si Son Altesse Royale, Madame la Princesse Royale, daignait accompagner Son Auguste Époux, alors mes vœux seront comblés, et l'Égypte pourrait témoigner à Votre Altesse Royale combien elle Lui est reconnaissante pour les faveurs dont Votre Altesse Royale a bien voulu me combler. Je prie Votre Altesse Royale de vouloir bien agréer les hommages.

" de Son dévoué

" (signé)   ISMAÏL.

"Eaux-Bonnes, le 16 Juillet, 1869."

Upon my announcing the arrival of the above despatch to the King, His Majesty replied that he must first ascertain Count Bismarck's wishes.

While the great autumn manœuvres of the

II. Army Corps were going on at Stargard in Pomerania, the Chancellor arrived at the King's Head-Quarters, and on September 11, I received the order to prepare for a journey to Turkey and Egypt. I was first of all to pay an official visit to the Imperial Court of Vienna with the object of establishing friendly relations after the events of 1866; next to return, at Constantinople, the visit of the Sultan to our King at Coblentz, 1867; and lastly, to represent our Fatherland at the opening of the Suez Canal. A visit to Greece, as well as to Palestine and Syria, was in addition permitted me. Since the opening of the Canal was fixed for November 17, there was not much time before that date to become acquainted with these countries; for the journey must be over before the function, in order that I might subsequently visit Upper Egypt, and be back with my own people by Christmas.

During the King's review, which was in East Prussia, the preparations for the journey were arranged with Admiral Jachmann, who had been summoned to Königsberg, the all-important point being a squadron for my escort. With this object, the corvette *Hertha*, which had just started from Kiel to go to her station in the Pacific Ocean, was telegraphed to make arrangements in Plymouth for the accommodation of my person and my *suite*. In addition, the corvette *Elizabeth*, which had only just left the Dantzic dockyard, and had as yet made no trial-trip, was commissioned for service. The corvette *Arcona*, as well as H.M. yacht *Grille*, received orders to go to the Mediterranean, while the gunboat *Delphin*, which was stationed on the Sulina-estuary, was ordered to the Grecian Archipelago.

It was only on September 23 that the answer came from the *Hertha*, and that from Portsmouth, because she had been obliged by contrary winds to cross the North Sea; accordingly the projected embarkation at Brindisi could not be thought of before October 15, and thus I parted from my wife and children on the evening of October 3.

My travelling-suite consisted of—

1. Prince Ludwig zu Hessen und bei Rhein.

2. Major-General von Stosch, Director of the Department of Military Economy in the Royal War Ministry.

3. Court-Marshal Count Eulenburg.

4. Lieut.-Colonel Count Lehndorff, Aide-de-camp to His Majesty.

5. Captain von Jasmund ⎱ Personal Adjutants.
6. Captain von Schleinitz ⎰

7. Surgeon-General and Body-Physician Dr. Wegner.

8. Lieutenant von Zitzewitz, appointed to my personal service, during my stay on board ship.

On the 4th I went to Baden-Baden, to say good-bye to my parents, and brothers and sisters. Here I saw my cousin, Karl von Hohenzollern, Prince of Roumania, for the first time since the beginning of his reign. A few days after, he was betrothed to Princess Elizabeth of Wied, whom in November he brought home as his wife.

The further journey was undertaken by way of Munich, without halting there, and on October 6 I crossed the Austrian frontier, received by Lieut. Field-Marshal Count Huyn, Major and Emperor's Aide-de-camp von Groller, Captain Count Wallis of the Prince Friedrich Karl Hussars, and a Guard of Honour.

Guards of Honour greeted me at many stations, as well as in Vienna itself, where Kaiser Franz Joseph in Prussian uniform was waiting for me on the platform,* and led me from thence to the

---

* According to the account in the *Debatte*, the Kaiser said on greeting the Crown Prince, " You are heartily welcome " (*Seien Sie mir herzlich gegrüsst*) ; on which the Crown Prince answered, ";A long-cherished wish is now fulfilled, inasmuch as I respectfully greet your Majesty upon Austrian soil."

Castle. Here, to my complete surprise, I was greeted by the beautiful Empress Elizabeth, whom I believed to be still in Ischl, and their two Majesties then conducted me to the magnificent rooms prepared for me.

I spent October 7 and 8 in Vienna, the first day being taken up with visits, followed by a dinner and *théâtre paré*. On the next day I received the Generals and Staff-officers from the garrison, the Diplomatic Body, and some of the Ministers. The remaining free time I used to see the new buildings, besides the Arsenal, the Belvedere, the Votiv-Kirche, and the grave of my unfortunate friend, Arch-Duke Max, the Emperor of Mexico. A gala-dinner, at which all the Ministers as well as the Chief-Bürgermeister of Vienna appeared, and which was again followed by a performance at the theatre, concluded my visit.

I look back with pleasure to the days I spent in Vienna, for they recognized there the good intentions that prompted my visit, were on that account friendly and courteous to me, and, in short, failed in no external marks of honour. After the events of 1866, it could not be easy for any Austrian to see the arrival of a representative of our King, such as I was, but no one allowed me to perceive this only too comprehensible feeling. The Kaiser was unchanged in his manner towards me, and any one who knows him as well as I, could not have a moment's doubt that he received me with genuine warmth.

The Arch-Dukes greeted me with no less friendliness than the Kaiser, and all, according to our closer or more distant acquaintance, exchanged with me words of old friendship, which were not altered by 1866.*

It was no less a surprise to me, and as I thought to the Viennese also, that during my

---

* In his book, " The Founding of the German Empire " (*Die Begründung des Deutschen Reichs*), pp. 112, *et seq.*, Heinrich von Sybel further tells us that Arch-Duke Albrecht asserted, as an expert, to the Crown Prince, that he (the Crown Prince) had done his duty as a soldier, and that every one must recognize this. The Liberal minister Giskra expressed his satisfaction at seeing in this visit the precursor of a significant *rapprochement* ; the results of the mission would make themselves felt gradually. Count Beust, too, thought no more of revenge, but took what was past as past. In fact, Beust protested vigorously against Bismarck's accusation, that he influenced the press in a direction inimical to the interests of Prussia, adding the remark that, with regard to the South German Question, he was by no means opposed to its development. As Austrian Minister, however, his first duty was to watch over the welfare of the Austrian Crown lands, and hence he was obliged to keep a sharp eye upon any *dénouement* of the South German Question that could endanger this welfare. With this statement, as well as with the condition of affairs in general, corresponds the fact, that both at this time in Vienna, and later in Egypt, Kaiser Franz Joseph had no political talk with the Crown Prince. Giskra, however, had correctly summed up the attitude of this monarch in regard to the future. A first pregnant step towards a reconciliation between the former antagonists had been taken, hereby opening a new outlook for the maintenance of peace in Europe.

stay in Vienna the rumour suddenly arose, and was afterwards confirmed by the Kaiser and Count Beust, that the former was going to Suez for the ceremonial Inauguration of the Canal.

Vienna is so altered by the demolition of the old walls, that one can hardly find one's way about in the new quarters ; these are so exactly planned after the Parisian Boulevards, that they seem to have changed places with them. The new Opera House is in particular an ornament of the highest rank to Vienna.

The further journey, in the first place by the Semmering-Bahn on October 9, afforded splendid views of the scenery, which were the more agreeable inasmuch as I had last traversed these parts in 1862, on a dull December day.

After parting with the Austrian functionaries, who from General to the lowest servant had been full of attention for me, we crossed the Italian frontier at night, and with sunrise Venice rose from the lagoons. Here nothing is altered—in contrast to Vienna, which, with its razed walls and magnificent new buildings, has become quite another city.

Here the presence of Count Usedom afforded me especial pleasure ; I went round with him daily, and devoted myself to all that was worth seeing. Only the Palazzo Morosini was new to me; it still stands unaltered in its brilliant surroundings, and is rich in memories of the famous General of the Republic, Morosini. In addition, the Church of Santa Maria ai Miracoli, with its romantic charm, was previously unknown to me.

I was obliged to accept a theatrical performance in San Carlo, which was lit in my honour *al giorno*, and was filled with an elegant audience; otherwise I preserved my incognito, and this led to entertaining scenes, since the very curious Venetian public (especially of an evening, when the music was playing on the illuminated piazzetta) took Count Lehndorff and then Count Eulenburg for me, surrounded them, and accompanied them with "*Evvivas*," while I was lost in the crowd, and looked on at the sight.

The Sindaco was determined to make use of my presence, to honour in my person the King's representative; for, said he, since Venice had *fêted* the Empress Eugénie on account of Solferino, it was the duty of the city to do the same on account of "Sadowa" (as Königgrätz is always called outside our own country)!

Ravenna, which I visited on continuing my journey, is richer than I could have conceived possible in its undamaged relics of Byzantine buildings, from the fifth and sixth centuries. Here one fully understands this style for the first time.

Bari, October 16, 1869.

To-morrow we embark, and are bound first of all for Corfu, in the hope that H.M. corvette *Hertha* will pick us up there on the 19th.

My fifth visit to Italy! I look back with delight to one of the most beautiful autumn weeks that can be granted to any traveller. After the dull skies of Vienna, the weather altered in Venice, so that no cloud was to be seen, and moonlight and starry nights succeeded to the brightest, warmest sunshine.

Corfu, October 18, 1869.

At the end of our visit to the wonderful anti-quities of Ravenna, which took me back to the times of the Christian Art of the fourth and fifth centuries, and which are unequalled in the colours of their mosaics, and the purity of style of their basilicas, we took the train to Bari. The railway nearly always follows close to the sea-shore, and the journey, especially in the neighbourhood of the miniature state of San Marino, as also at Pesaro (Rossini's birthplace), was particularly charming.

In Bari we again met with an enthusiastic reception, reminding me of my welcome in Upper Italy, in 1868. The Russians venerate S. Nicholas of this place, as their patron.

On the 17th we left Brindisi on board an Italian passenger-steamer, and reached the much be-praised island on the morning of my thirty-eighth birthday. Jasmund and Schleinitz had been unable to resist the rocking of the vessel, which, indeed, for some time was horrible. Unfortunately, rain came on ; and we could only get an approximate idea of the charms of Corfu when, towards evening, the sky cleared up. The place itself, which lies in a picturesque bay, is surrounded on all sides by high rocky mountains, with charming valleys clothed with olive-woods. The town has no definite character ; the hotels and public buildings still show many signs of English comforts, particularly with regard to their furnishing ; in other respects, all that is English has quickly vanished, to the great sorrow of the inhabitants. The fortifications that had been brought from England at enormous cost were all blown up when the island was handed over to Greece, so that only the old castles from the

Genoese-Venetian period of the Middle Ages remained standing.

The Greek population, who come into the town from the country round, are strikingly beautiful in face and figure, and wear with much natural grace the well-known tasteful costume of the Albanian people—one of the most beautiful and picturesque in Europe.

Hunting-weapons, a beautiful bronze frame of the period of Frederick I., along with a riding-whip, flowers, and cakes with candles, all packed up by my wife's care for to-day, come as a greeting from home, and from my dear ones, and most agreeably soften the pain of separation.

On the 19th, we hired the little Austrian-Lloyd steamer, the *Lario*, to take us as quickly as possible to the Bay of Lepanto, and thence to Corinth, so as to save the *Hertha* the *détour* by Corfu. The commander of the *Hertha* in effect had announced that he would reach Corfu on the 20th at earliest, and as we wanted to lose none of our time in Athens, we proposed to save the two days it would take him to get round the Peloponnesus, by making the straight journey across Corinth.

Hardly were we two hours under way, and rolling about as never before, in sight of the beautiful Albanian coast in brightest sunshine, when a corvette came into view. After looking for some time, my brother-in-law Louis was the first to discover that it carried the North-German standard; it was the longed-for and expected *Hertha*. As our rocking little Lloyd-pirate carried no sort of signalling-flags, we had to steer straight for the unsuspecting *Hertha*, and endeavour to make ourselves known by every form of arm-telegraphy. Our attempts at last drew the attention of the sailors to us, and we were able to make ourselves understood. As regarded boarding her, however, we were dissuaded by Captain Köhler, who advised us on the contrary for the sake of gaining time, and still more on account of the favourable weather, to remain on our nutshell, and keep to our arrangements for the rest of the voyage. The *Hertha* profited, inasmuch as she escaped the further voyage to Corfu.

And now began one of the strangest of sea-voyages. Although we rolled about in every direction, no one felt ill, or even uncomfortable. Indeed, we leaned over the edge for hours, rejoicing in the fine panorama that unfolded before us, first in the rays of the setting sun, then in the twilight, and lastly, in the clearest silvery light of the beams of the full moon.

Never before have I experienced such pleasure

at sea, enhanced by the marvellously mild air, like that of an Oriental dream. So we fared past the sharp rocky walls of Ithaca and Cephalonia, at whose names the Odyssey, with all the childhood's memories that link themselves with the glamour of these ancient tales, rose vividly before my mind. And if we were not yet on classical ground, the rocking element was well calculated, by the environment of its shores, to excite our soul and emotions powerfully. At length the waves went down, as, with Patras, we reached the proper entrance to the Bay of Corinth.

Delphi and Missolungi are the first spots that meet one's eye. Yet here the name is everything, for one sails uninterruptedly between the beautiful, but quite uninhabited, and strangely overgrown rocky mountains of the Morea and Rumelia. The eye can seldom detect even a wretched village or a sailing-boat.

The sunrise which we witnessed to-day must be lived through, in order to realize what we felt as we saw the highest peaks of Greece glow in the rosy dawn, and felt we were approaching the mighty rock of Acro-Corinth.

In an historic land, in which the scanty vegetation of the soil, and the want of all culture (once so rich) almost saddens one, the eternally new

and beautiful impressions of the sunrise and sunset, the silver light of the full moon, supply the
want, and, like faithful travelling companions,
make good that which is missing. Most keenly
did we feel the want of everything that the
traveller's eye seeks upon classical ground, when,
at midday, we landed at Corinth. Here almost
nothing is left—not a tree, not a vestige of building! Only the seven columns of a temple, round
which picturesquely-clad peasants were working
with their horses, indicated that here there had
once been a sacred hall, whilst nothing but the
strangely tall and picturesque cone of rock, on
which the town is throned, now stands out in
the eternally-smiling blue ether as a landmark
of long-vanished days. What the hand of man
once accomplished here of astonishing value, the
hand of man has again destroyed, and what
remained over has been ruined by earthquakes.

The new site, although it bears the famous
name of Corinth, can hardly claim the designation
of " village " ; some excuse for so much disillusion
is, however, provided in the variety of the rich
and picturesque national costume, which is proudly
worn by a marvellously fine race.

In forty minutes we had traversed the Peninsula
of Corinth, and, with greetings from the Prussian

gunboat *Delphin*, and from Dr. Köhler, legal adviser to the Embassy, and a distinguished archæologist, as well as from the Greek escort who came to receive us, we went on board our ship at Kalamaki, and made across the Bay of Ægina for the Piræus. Ægina, Megara, and Salamis passed before our eyes, but as proud names only,—otherwise the same mountain forms we had seen early in the morning, the same lack of inhabitants and buildings. Unfortunately it was already dark when we neared the Piræus, for night falls suddenly here with the sunset, only the lights and illuminations from the other ships anchored in the harbour showing us that we had almost reached our goal.

The King received me here with his wonted cordiality and friendship, in the midst of an enthusiastic crowd, who had collected round a number of triumphal arches, adorned with Greek inscriptions relating to the events of 1866. In ten minutes the railway took us into an Athens illuminated with Bengal lights, where all were on their feet, and a constant "*Ittah*" was heard. All the ministers, dignitaries, and officers had gathered at the station to meet me.

The Queen, in all the brilliancy of unaltered youth and graciousness, received us in the most

H

amiable manner, in the well-lighted, magnificently appointed, high, and spacious halls of the Palace, which resembles the Königsbau at Munich. The Acropolis looked down with high dignity in the light of the full moon upon the gay traffic of the modern town below, and wove its stupendous glamour around us; for this aspect is of all the most imposing, in that the columns still standing of the Propylæa, the Parthenon, and the Erechtheum are seen clear and transparent, while the rubble-heaps, on the contrary, are obliterated. That proud Acropolis in the moonlight must have given much the same impression as of old, in the flower of its prosperity.

Athens, October 22, 1869.

The perfect moonlight night of which I wrote last, lent to the Acropolis the aspect of a still uninjured structure from the old Greek world; even by daylight, however, the great height of the ruins prevented one from seeing the full extent of the damage. It is only on ascending the rocky hill, and climbing the steps that lead to the Propylæa, that the beholder is deeply grieved at sight of the horrid heaps of ruin, strewn by human violence in the place of the finest art-creations of the world. And yet, despite long centuries of destruction, the Propylæa, Parthenon, and Erechtheum still convey such wealth of noblest grandeur, such unsurpassable beauty of form, that I could not gaze my fill of the ruins. The Propylæa are much smaller than I had imagined; the Parthenon, on the contrary, is larger, and reminded me of the Temple at Pæstum; no temple ruins present such splendid reliefs as those which stand here, notwithstanding the thefts of the archæologists.

The Erechtheum worked the same charm upon me, with its caryatids still partly standing in their original place; while its unique ornaments, in their perfect proportions and splendid execution, have been the types of pure architecture from all antiquity. Here man's hand has, indeed, brought perfection into being; here the spectator feels what vast gaps he needs to fill in his layman's education in art. The simplest description of what here meets the eye must seem overdrawn; and, on the other hand, no heights of speech could convey the real impression of the magnificent as one here finds it. The sea of rubble, with which the ground is covered, conceals an incredible wealth of beautiful art-forms, many bearing inscriptions. Each stroke of the spade brings new relics to the light ; the inhabitants, unfortunately, show very little interest in the excavations, and when foreigners are willing to undertake the work, the export duty upon the treasures discovered is prohibitive.

And yet I must admit that this regulation is fully justified. England, France, and Bavaria despoiled the Acropolis some forty years ago, by plundering whatever is finest in their museums, with little less effect than did the rude peoples of antiquity by their gross destruction. King Louis I. of Bavaria and Lord Elgin did indeed endeavour to replace what they carried off by copies, or facsimiles in different materials, and yet this only seems to have increased the evil, since new patches upon the crown of ancient art offend the eye unpardonably.

The Acropolis Hill is surrounded by several magnificent amphitheatres, among them that of Dionysus, discovered and excavated some eight years ago by Curtius and Strack. This theatre is of peculiar interest, inasmuch as a great part of the marble seating is not merely intact, but is even inscribed with the names of the seat-holders.

To-day I am constantly thinking of my dear tutor Curtius! It was his brilliant disquisition upon the Acropolis, more than twenty-five years ago, in the Wissenschaftlichen Verein, that first attracted the eyes of my parents to him, and led to his appointment as my tutor.

As to the other antiquities of Athens, there remains, firstly, the Temple of Theseus at the foot of the Acropolis, which is in perfect preservation; next, the colossal dozen pillars of a Temple of Jupiter; then the charming memorial to Lysicrates (familiar to us all, since it stands as the cornice to the open pavilion of Glienicke on the long bridge); and lastly, the Tower of the Four Winds.

All the famous parts of Athens are gone, yet one can trace with certainty the seats of the Assemblies of the Areopagus, where once Paul preached; and the Pnyx, at whose rostrum Demosthenes gave his powerful discourses.

The bald mountains of the neighbourhood, and more particularly Hymettus, are picturesque in their shapes, but present a melancholy aspect on account of their total lack of green vegetation. In the prime of the Greek age this was quite different; but when attempts are made in the present day to cultivate the soil, which in itself is inexhaustibly fertile, they all fail on account of the inhabitants. These picturesque and well-grown people, whose proportions are fine as a statue, will not take the trouble to plant young olive trees for the sake of future harvests, but content themselves with using what is to hand, because it is less trouble to live from day to day than be at the pains of providing for the future. They are peculiarly apt in external and gracious marks of respect.

The entire external appointments of the Court are very dignified, and coupled with a judicious splendour. The *personnel* for the most part wear the picturesque national costume; the military uniform is very like the Danish, only somewhat Franco-Italian. The Infantry at first reminded me involuntarily of the Danish Infantry in the campaign of 1864.

Near the Royal Palace is a shady garden that Queen Amelia has laboriously contrived out of the waste arable land, and which afforded us grateful refreshment in the fierce heat; a late Roman mosaic of 100 feet in length, which was discovered in excavating, forms the principal ornament of the place. Lions and monkeys entertain the public, who are admitted there every afternoon. An olive wood, situated some half-mile * beyond the town, is otherwise the only shade in the whole neighbourhood.

* The German mile = about $6\frac{4}{2}$ English miles.—Tr.

Constantinople, October 25, 1869.

And so we are really in Stambûl, guests of the commander of the *Faithful*, and personally received by him, as only high princely guests are honoured after European fashion; and on Asiatic soil, for the Beylerbey Palace assigned to me lies on the Asiatic side.

One must give up all attempt at description on reaching the Bosphorus, seeing the Golden Horn, and making caïque-journeys in the radiant sunshine and silver moonlight. For, little as one's highly strained expectation is gratified in the first moment, so much the more powerful is the impression, when one gazes at the lines of towns and estates that stretch for miles along both shores of the sea, and give to Constantinople its character of a totally unique city.

Here again we have been favoured by quite exceptional weather. The clouds that threatened several times dispersed again, to show us everything the eye can desire. After a last look at the Acropolis of Athens, whose impress is indelibly stamped upon me, we made an incredibly quick voyage, in a perfectly calm sea, on board the *Hertha*, from midday of the 22nd to the morning of the 23rd October, when we reached the

Dardanelles. We were, however, little edified by the contemplation of these Straits, for here on the flat shores there is nothing at all to see; this applies more especially to Troy, the name which naturally calls up the highest expectations from one's memories of early youth,—which, however, find no realization.

The Sultan's Master of the Horse, Raouf Pasha, who proffered us one of the imperial yachts, as well as the Governor of the Province, with Count Keyserlingk, received me here, whereupon we were very agreeably surprised by permission to enter the Bosphorus on board the *Hertha*. As it turned out later, we owed this to the fact that I, as His Majesty's representative, making a return visit for the Sultan's journey to Coblentz, was entitled to the highest consideration; otherwise, according to treaty, no corvettes could pass the Danube, since war-ships are not allowed in the Bosphorus. So we went on past Gallipoli into the Sea of Marmora, where a fresh northeast breeze was blowing.

Early on the 24th we arrived in sight of Constantinople, at the Princes' Island, but could not enter the Bosphorus before 1 o'clock, partly because we had to reckon that the thick fog that unfortunately concealed everything on this morning would last till then, but also because the Sultan was to receive me first at that hour in the palace destined for my dwelling.

A very edifying and brief Service took place on the gun-deck; immediately after its conclusion, a large steamer crammed with Germans arrived, who greeted me enthusiastically, and gave escort. We accordingly boarded the imperial yacht, and entered Stambûl, escorted by the *Hertha*, *Grille*, and *Delphin*. The fog slowly lifted, but the air was cold, and we agreed among ourselves that we had really expected more from the approach.

Passing the old Serai point, the magnificent panorama unrolled before us in greater and greater splendour at every splash of the waves, while the guns saluted . from all sides, and the shouts of the men on the rigging was audible. Thus we passed the Sultan's residence, " *Dolmabagdsche*," leaving the Golden Horn to our left, and steered toward the Beylerbey Palace built by the late Sultan, and kept up in the Renaissance-Corinthian style. Directly we had anchored, the Grand-Vizier, Ali Pasha, and the Turkish Ambassador to Berlin, Aristarchi Bey, came on board to greet me, and conduct me in a gilded caïque to the steps of the aforesaid palace.

Here stood the Sultan in the open air, in an embroidered uniform, adorned with the Order of the Black Eagle, surrounded by the picturesque and rainbow-garbed officers of his body-guard, who are selected from among the many populations that own his sway. A band of music played the *Borussia* of Spontini, and a company of Infantry was posted as a Guard of Honour. The Sultan gave me his hand, and we passed silently through the rows of bowing officials, all making the well-known *salaam*, into the interior of the palace.

Beylerbey is constructed with an indescribable profusion of space, colour, and costly ornament ; every conceivable manner is employed here, so that the eye nowhere finds a resting-point, but sees before it a constant dazzle of many-coloured splendour. In one of the countless saloons, and in front of the porcelain portrait-vase presented by our King to the Sultan, the latter took his place, and invited Louis and myself to seat ourselves, while the Grand-Vizier acted as interpreter. During his inquiries after my parents, the Sultan mentioned his visit to Coblentz with evident pleasure, and I heard many times that he particularly liked to think of that reception.

After the Sultan had left us, with the same

formalities with which we had been received, he got into a charming caïque, decorated with gilding, and served by two oarsmen; opposite to him sat two Adjutants, who remained immovable, bowed, and with crossed arms, their eyes cast down.

Soon after we went to Dolmabagdsche (in German something like " cabbage-leaf ") to pay our respects to the Sultan. The sun had now penetrated through the mists in full splendour, so that we could at last admire the picturesque aspect of the shores and cities of the Bosphorus in their splendid amphitheatre-like succession.

The Grand-Signior's residence is quite European in its *tenue*, and consists in a series of palaces of different sizes, which are built in a sort of Louis XIV. style, with many-pillared halls, but with no trace of Oriental magnificence. Within, the halls, as in Beylerbey, are extraordinarily spacious, and magnificent of their kind. Here the order of the reception was repeated; the Sultan stood at the threshold of the palace when we left the caïque.

We used the rest of the daylight to make excursions in a little steamer on the sweet Asiatic waters; then came a dinner, served French-fashion, illuminated by hundreds of wax-lights in every room, after which the imperial stables belonging to Beylerbey were shown us by gas-light. The internal arrangements are so wonder-fully contrived with the application of all the latest Anglo-French inventions, that one could easily live there one's self. The moon now shone out in a cloudless sky; well-conducted European music was heard; while we wandered in the air on the terraces, and admired the Kiosk, with its many stories, shining in the light of tapers.

At length a caïque-ride in the moonlight brought the close of this richly occupied day, which had seemed to me like an Oriental dream!

Constantinople, October 26 *to* 29, 1869.

I have now explored Constantinople on every side, sometimes on horseback, sometimes on foot, but more especially in the twelve-oared caïque, and favoured throughout by magnificent weather. My constant companion was the very learned, clever, and meritorious scholar, Dr. G. Busch, Dragoman to our Embassy, who is a master of the Turkish language, and whose local knowledge is comprehensive.

To the man who is permitted to enjoy the splendours presented by the Bosphorus in peace and tranquillity, the view from Constantinople, from the entrance at the Serai point to the opening into the Black Sea is one of the most magnificent pictures to be found upon this earth.

From without, the great Mosques only present the aspect of wide whitewashed buildings, rich in cupolas ; their slender minarets, however, are exceedingly pretty, and give the chief characteristic of these Oriental cities. Aja Sofia still presents internally the appearance of a splendid Christian basilica, along with an inconceivable wealth of costly marble, and mosaics to any extent. On entering, I felt myself overwhelmed by this magnificent wonder of architecture.

The Mohammedan Mosques have nothing peculiar inside, and seem to be a mixture of the Oriental and European rococo-styles. ´ Everywhere in the entrance halls are little saloons with comfortable cushions, and invitation is not lacking to make one's self comfortable there. The invariably latticed upper-galleries, designed for the exclusive use of the Sultan, are similarly fitted. I assisted in comfort from one such, at the exegetical discourse of an Ulema ; clad in white, his feet crosswise on a divan, and a little marqueterie-table in front of him, he spoke quite naturally and without emphasis to his hearers. The elder among them, who were all attired in the old Turkish fashion, listened devoutly; the modern youths, on the contrary, looked curiously at each other.

The remains of the old Sultans' residence, situated on the beautiful Serai point, with its wealth of cypresses, present a quantity of historically interesting fragments of walls.

A single kiosk among the many here has preserved the pure and charming Oriental taste, even to its least details; and as it affords a splendid view over the Bosphorus, the Islands of the Princes, and the Sea of Marmora, this otherwise little-regarded spot of earth has made a deep impression on me. The kiosk in which the Sultans formerly gave audience to the foreign envoys is interesting; but one must not expect anything magnificent, for it contains nothing but a small dark saloon, in one corner of which, exactly opposite the visitor, is an old covered divan, adorned with a metal gilded baldachin, all set with turquoises and other precious stones: that is all. Nor do the now empty courts present anything remarkable, while they remind one forcibly of the European cloisters.

In considering the landscape of the Bosphorus, the eye everywhere falls upon what seem to be enormous palaces; a nearer inspection, however, invariably reveals them to be barracks, which, from their great extent and strikingly beautiful situation, are a real ornament to the neighbourhood. Nor are the actual residences of the aristocracy less effective. Along with these are the imperial country-houses, called Kiosks, whose name is legion.

The Imperial Stables are very well kept, and have recently been thoroughly rebuilt. The coach-houses contain some ancient gilded coaches, otherwise only European carriages.

As regards the troops, I saw twelve Battalions, one Cavalry regiment, and two Artillery regiments. The uniform, which was formerly European, has during the reign of the present Sultan been imitated from that of the French Zouaves. These, again, are known to have borrowed their uniform from the old Turkish pattern. The result is strikingly beautiful, and looks very martial; the artillery, as regards arms, material, and regulations, is remarkably like our own. The Cavalry garrisoned here are drawn from the much-discussed, exiled Russian Tcherkesses, who have retained their national costume.

During a four-hour ride all round Constantinople, we came upon the old Byzantine city-walls, which are still in preservation, along with the breech through which the Turks forced their entrance under Mahomet II. in the conquest of 1453, when the Emperor Constantine IX. fell. The way led past the great cemetery. Later, we came upon sundry quarters of the city, rigidly separated from each other according to their creeds, in which it was quite apparent how thinly populated were the Mohammedan, in comparison with the Christian and Jewish quarters.

The palaces of the Foreign Embassies make a striking effect, while several Legations from smaller states have recently established themselves also in pretty buildings.

I received the Corps Diplomatique officially, and thus made the acquaintance of the amiable English Ambassador, Mr. Elliot; the Russian General Ignatieff was already known to me from former years. The Persian Ambassador was so captivated by the Prussians that he sent me a costly Persian carpet on the day after the Reception, for which I had of course at once to make him a return present; and he then invested the officer who took it, and the midshipman from the *Hertha* who accompanied him, with Persian orders.

Yesterday the Emperor of Austria arrived from Varna; the *Hertha* was the first ship that saluted him. Immediately after the salute of the *Hertha* came the thunder of the land-batteries, and of the ships lying in the Bosphorus. When, with Louis, I visited the Kaiser, he expressed himself with much satisfaction as to his first impressions.

As the Sultan allotted him the state-rooms in the Dolmabagdsche for his abode, the former himself withdrew into the Seraglio. Here, accordingly, the Grand-Signior received me for the farewell visit.

The day before yesterday the Sultan drove with us and with Prince Amadeo of Italy to a kiosk, situated high above the Bosphorus, with a glorious view. I was with him and Raouf Pasha, his Master of Horse, in a carriage, and the conversation flowed cheerily; then we got on our horses, and rode, seated on over-richly decorated velvet housings, through new scenes to another kiosk, for a breakfast in which all my *suite* participated; then we again took horse; till we finally parted from the Sultan in the charming valley of the " Sweet Waters of Europe." Here we found richly decorated caïques waiting for us, which we boarded, to traverse the entire Golden Horn, favoured by the most beautiful evening sunshine. Steamers, caïques, war-ships, and traders of all kinds were crossing to and fro, decked with the gayest fashions of the East, and manned most picturesquely. On the whole, it must be said that the dense population in these countries presents a cheerful aspect, because even where the national costume does not predominate, the red head-coverings, known as the "*tarbûsh*" or fez, which are worn by all the Faithful, suffice to bring variety into the crowds of people, while with us nothing but black hats or dark caps are *en évidence*.

The Sultan's Friday ride to the Mosques to-day was exceptionally charming; because on this occasion the mass of spectators, apart from the above-mentioned gay crowd, was augmented by a large number of women, who, clad in flaring colours, and wrapt in quite thin veils, had taken up their station under the old plane trees, exactly opposite the windows allotted to us as spectators. The Sultan's son, Izzedin-Effendi, who has grown a great deal since 1867, stood at the head of his regiment, which formed the Guard of Honour for to-day's function! Apparently a new custom in consequence of the Grand-Signior's visit to Europe! The Grand-Signior himself wore undress uniform, over which was a kind of long *paletôt*, rode a mare, and replied to none of the greetings made to him, this being the etiquette.

Only when he perceived the Emperor of Austria and myself at the window did he greet us curtly, in military fashion.

Yesterday I visited the barracks at Scutari, where I was able to acquaint myself thoroughly with the clothing and provisioning, and was astonished to find that a kind of cherry soup, with "*pillaw*," containing a great deal of sugar, was given as the principal meal. Sixty men slept in one place, which is fitted round with a wooden shelf, on which man by man arranges himself with his blanket and mattress : a grey woollen cloak was worn at the upper edge of the knapsack, and this also served as the dress in Quarters. The married men could not take their families into barracks, and were only permitted to visit them occasionally.

Not the least part of my pleasure in my stay at Stambûl was owing to the way in which our thoughtful and highly cultivated Premier Dragoman, Dr. Busch, knew how to conduct us. He speaks Turkish quite fluently, having originally learned it only for the sake of his scientific studies, and is now the life of the Embassy. The whole conduct of business depends, as is known, exclusively upon the relations of the Dragoman with the Grand-Vizier, to whom the former repairs as much and as often as the ambassadors in Europe to the Foreign Ministers. Consequently everything depends on the personality of the interpreter, who, if he be a cultured European, can certainly make greater claim to reliability than if one has to trust to the natives, as was formerly the case. Busch was extraordinarily active over the Jerusalem expedition, and also took the lead as regards all my goings and comings, since he is well acquainted with city, country, and people.

Among the Turkish officials and officers I met countrymen who left the Prussian military service many years ago for that of the Porte, and have notably been of great use to the artillery.

Aristarchi-Bey, the amiable Ambassador from the Porte to our own Court, accompanied us daily, and always occupied himself to the utmost in making himself useful.

Each time I crossed the threshold of my palace, I found a Guard of Honour, with a band of music sixty strong, who struck up, *Heil Dir*, etc.

Our Evangelico-German institutions are small, but well conducted; the Hospital, managed by the Kaiserswerth Sisters, is self-supporting, and very well organized by the Superior.

The Chapel, which stands under the wing of our Embassy, is not large, and is very simple. An Altar Bible was presented to it by the late King. The present minister, Herr Hulsen, was formerly Divisions-Prediger in Berlin. The school is very full, and Greek and Armenian children are educated there along with the Germans. Among our countrymen who were presented to me here, I found many from Coblentz. An Armenian sect, which long since became evangelical, and is directed by a " *Vekil* " and Superintendent who were a long time in America, and speak English, makes use of our church for its services.

Turkish dishes were freely mixed with the otherwise entirely French *cuisine*. Mostly, however, they seemed to me to be too sweet, as well as too fat. On the other hand, I enjoyed the Turkish coffee, the " *pillaw*," and the roast collops of mutton called " *clebab*." It goes without saying that we smoked industriously, since one cannot pay a visit, nor even enter the barracks, without at once being invited to sit down, to drink coffee, and to smoke. At my own house, too, when the Emperor of Austria came to visit me, the Turkish servants at once appeared with the paraphernalia for smoking, and everything pertaining, so that we at any rate flavoured our discourse, which, as in Vienna, was kept away from politics.

On Board H.M. Corvette " Hertha " off Constantinople, October 29, 1869.

We have just weighed anchor, and seen Stambûl vanish quickly in the evening mists; the weather seems to be turning to rain, as if it had kept fine until our departure for Jerusalem. All the forcible impressions I have received here are chasing through my brain, and I think with grateful recollections of the splendid and abundant enjoyment which we have had here.

The Sultan gave each one of us the impression that he was pleased with our visit. The initiated had seldom seen him so contented and in such persistent good temper as in the hours in which he held intercourse with us; and, after all, that is saying something, when one reflects on the difficulties of conversation with him through the medium of an interpreter only. He has decorated all the gentlemen of my *Suite*, as well as the superior naval officers, and even my valet; and has done the same for all the *personnel* of the Embassy, so that Keyserlingk is making his *début* with the Grand Cordon.

I am curious to see what comes out of the impulse to progress in the European sense, in Turkey, to which even the Sultan is not opposed.

I am rejoiced that I have succeeded in fulfilling the wishes of our King, by obtaining from the Sultan a site in Jerusalem, that once belonged to the Order of St. John, as a gift for evangelical objects. The Grand-Vizier was much surprised when I proposed this to him, as it had till then been kept very dark; but thanks to his and the Sultan's willingness to do a kindness to our King, and also to the exertions of Dr. Busch, the affair came off. We managed, during the five days of my stay in Constantinople, to bring the necessary negotiations to an end. We succeeded in getting telegraphic orders sent off to the Pasha of Jerusalem, *in re* direct negotiations with our Consul there, and finally Ali Pasha drew up in my palace a sort of "*firman*," by which I was confirmed in the transfer of the aforesaid bit of ground.

Aboard H.M. Corvette " Hertha" between Rhodes and the Coast of Palestine, October 30 to November 1, 1869.

We have already been floating three days upon the high seas, sometimes delayed by the south-east wind, as we are steering right in the wind's eye, and yet, till now at any rate, *unberufen*, in no wise the worse. To-day the sea is actually calm, which seems to us wonderful, and we hope that it will remain the same till our anticipated landing in Jaffa at daybreak on the 3rd, for with west or north wind the landing on this harbourless coast is impracticable.

Yesterday we surveyed the entire length of Rhodes, passing for hours along the picturesque and jagged island, but unfortunately making the harbour at nightfall only, so that we could form no clear picture of that once important place, now reduced to a heap of ruins by earthquakes and powder explosions. Since the weather was favourable we were advised to push on immediately; and accordingly we sailed, seeing the cypress coasts only in the far distance, towards the Promised Land,—bathed in a real July heat, that makes writing particularly difficult.

Our arrangements on board are excellent, and every one is cheerful and in good spirits. My cabin, " No. 8," is convenient, although I have the screw as my immediate neighbour. On the other side of it are the general saloon and the library. My brother-in-law Louis has the cabin next the dining-saloon, on the starboard side.

Count Eulenburg's arrangements for the journey, as well as, more particularly, for our life on board ship, testify anew to his qualifications for his post. Most of my companions, who are making their first voyage, have so far found the swaying element very comfortable ; each, however, is anxiously expecting to experience the reverse side of this satisfaction before long.

The days on board afford a welcome rest after the fatigues of Stambûl, and are particularly well adapted for writing down one's impressions, for which there was little time on dry land.

Jerusalem, November 4 *to* 9, 1869.

If I were to attempt in this, the most sacred spot of the whole world, to express how deeply I am moved at the thought of being in Jerusalem, I should endeavour too much. Each must come here for himself, for himself live through the great disillusioning that attends on the first view, and the entrance into the City, and for himself at last achieve the deep inward peace that comes when calm contemplation and reflection have obtained the upper hand, and enable one to grasp it.

It will be the happiness of my entire life to have walked in the places in which Jesus Christ lived, the places in which His foot has trod, to have seen the mountains and the waters on which His eye rested daily. This, above all, of the Mount of Olives, and Gethsemane with the Brook Kedron, as well as the wild rock shores of the Dead Sea, with the Valley of the Jordan, and the country round Bethlehem. These places have undoubtedly retained their original character of landscape and geological formation, and they may be viewed as witnesses to the actions, teaching, and sufferings of our Saviour, since by good fortune no human hand has violated the scene, and no religious zeal has presumed to replace by buildings what can only keep its historical character in the simple growths of nature. In contrast to this the "Holy Sites" have been disfigured and defaced.

The profound and pious feeling with which one approaches the Holy Sepulchre is repulsed when one learns from the Greek and Latin monks at the entrance to the church, that this portion or that stone belongs to the one or the other Confession, and that accordingly one must first come in this direction, next go in that.

On entering the great Rotunda, in whose

midst is the space, now covered over with a chapel, that goes by the name of the Saviour's Tomb, one at first sees nothing in front of one but a dark and narrow little hall. From this the pilgrim proceeds through an opening only three feet high to a little chapel, inlaid with marble slabs, in which four men could hardly stand, and in which is an oblong altar. The altar-slab itself, also of marble, covers the space hewn in the rock, in which the Saviour rested, so that one is actually at the place of the grave, but the hollow in the rock is not visible. The monks, for fear the pilgrims should break off too many *souvenirs* in their piety, or by degrees should kiss away too much of the rock, prefer that the visitor should see no more. If one is next taken to Golgotha, there is absolutely nothing to be seen. To reach it one must pass from the Rotunda of the Sepulchre through the Greek church immediately adjacent to it, climb up many dark stairs, and then penetrate into a chapel illuminated only by lamps. Here a monk lifts up a cover under the altar, and exhibits a hole in the marble slab below, through which a little depression in the rock is visible, in which the Saviour's cross is said to have been erected. An oval opening in the rock is shown as the cleft that opened in the ground at the instant that our Lord expired. The visitor can distinguish nothing in the prevailing darkness, and can hardly see down with the help of wax tapers.

The richest compensation awaits the ascent of the Monnt of Olives, after one has crossed the dried torrent-bed of the Brook Kedron and looked into the Valley of Jehoshaphat. I reached the summit of Olivet shortly before sunset, and took up my station so that the whole extent of the city of Jerusalem, following the gradual dip of the Kedron, was unrolled before me, while on the opposite side the singularly beautiful formation of the rocky walls of the Dead Sea was to be seen, mirrored in the water, with a portion of the Valley of the Jordan in its attractive grandeur. The rays of the setting sun lit up the city and the bare, grey, desolate mountains that lie round about Jerusalem, with a golden-red, so that life and warmth seemed suddenly to have come into the landscape. At the same moment the rocky walls of the Dead Sea, which remind me vividly of Loch Muick in Scotland, took on that glow from the evening sun, which always gives a special glamour to the mountains, and the waves shimmered every minute in brighter light! Now for the first time I was able to picture the Saviour, as He tarried here and let His eyes rest in compassion on these plains and buildings, as He pitied their inhabitants, in that they would not hear at the right time the things pertaining to their peace.

Every stranger should go first to the Mount of Olives at the time when the sun is declining, and then tarry an instant under the ancient trees of Gethsemane, which may not improbably have been contemporaneous with our Lord, seeing that olive trees grow very slowly, and are fabulously old. The monks have here laid out little gardens, in which each Confession points to its own as the true scene of the Passion ; speaking generally, the bare declivity presents no attractions. Close by, the Capuchins show the Tomb of the Virgin, and the Cave in which the Saviour sweated blood, where, however, a part of the rock has been removed, " to give the altar a better position " !

Never in all my life shall I forget this first evening in Jerusalem, where I watched the setting sun from the Mount of Olives, while nature fell into that great silence which has always something of solemnity, even in other places. Here the soul could detach itself from earth, and plunge uninterruptedly into the thoughts by which each Christian is inwardly moved, when he considers the great work of salvation, that here fulfilled its sublimest issues. The reading over of one's favourite passages in the Gospels in such a spot is in itself a religious service.

We paid yet another visit to the empty Church of the Sepulchre in the twilight, in the glimmer of the few lamps. I always like to see churches thus in the late evening hours with subdued light, and this unique House of God was wondrously to my liking, although it failed to call up any of the sensations I experienced on the Mount of Olives.

So far I have only pursued my feelings, and have given free rein to my fancy, but must now come back to things positive, and continue my descriptions. And here let me say once for all that I never have more than a few minutes for writing, and can perceive accordingly, to my own annoyance, how desultory my style will generally be. But on a hurried journey, touching at all the most interesting points of the world, one naturally stays little in one's room, and can therefore devote little time to the writing-table.

When, after a favourable passage of five days, in which we were only delayed a little by the south wind, we approached the coast of Palestine, every

one looked eagerly towards the Promised Land.
Yet the yellow shores afforded little that was
beautiful; it was only after rowing in the pinnace
safely through the very dangerous cliffs that
enclose the harbour, and reaching the shore, that
we attained the satisfactory feeling of being really
in the East. I had the same sensation in Jaffa,
as in 1862 at Tunis, that everything here was
different from Europe.

We were received by our Consul-General, Herr
von Alten, and by the Patriarch of Jerusalem, and
by Kiamil-Pasha, the Governor of the Province,
and lastly by the band of the Guard of Honour,
surrounded by innumerable gaily-clad Arabs,
Greeks, and Jews, and we immediately mounted
our horses. First came two standard-bearers with
the Prussian and North-German Colours; then the
escort of Turkish Cavalry and Bashi-Bazûks;
next thirty men of our naval battalion under the
command of Lieutenant Kutzen, also mounted;
and finally, our whole company on high steeds,
with the addition of the ship's surgeon, and ship's
chaplain—the baggage on mules. After a short
rest in the colony of a Wurtemberg sect under the
direction of the brother of Hof-prediger Hoffman,
we went in the burning heat, through the famous
orange-gardens of Jaffa, towards the mountains of

Judæa. As soon as we had left the environs of the town, the already scanty vegetation became more sparse; the villages looked poverty-stricken; the inhabitants, nevertheless, bore themselves with picturesque pride, the dark Syrian contrasting with the browner Arab and the shining Moor. One was particularly struck with the many camels used as pack-animals, which grunted at the traveller, with their morose and flouting faces. The inhabitants, who greeted me in gay caftans of flaring colours, made a very pretty effect. During the ride the Bashi-Bazûks executed a sham fight, called a *"fantasiêh,"* for us, while we allowed our horses to try every method of progression in turn, as was permissible on this road, which had indeed been mended, but still resembled a freshly-laid *chaussée*; and so reached our tent-camp at Bab-el-Wâd, at the entrance to the mountains, where we spent the night.

On November 4, we departed at sunrise from our very comfortable tents in the land of the Philistines. For hours we climbed the steep rock valleys, here and there perceiving the remains of Christian churches; then to Abu-Ghôsh, whence David once fetched the ark of the covenant, the place still bearing the name of Kirjath-Jearim.

An hour from Jerusalem we were met by the

Germans of that town, all on horseback, and led by the evangelical Pastor Hoffman, son of the General Superintendent, and Court Chaplain at Berlin. During a short halt we put on our uniforms, I that of the Dragoons, and then, conversing with our countrymen, most of whom were Wurtembergers, we climbed the last steep hill, whence one catches the first view of Jerusalem. The Greek Bishop first advanced to meet us, in the name of the Patriarch, then the Jewish representative ; meantime our advance-commando of marines had fallen in, saluted, and received me with cheers—certainly the first military salute of this kind in the Holy City—and still no Jerusalem, only a vast tent, surrounded by a number of men from the Turkish Watch, and teeming with a multitude of strange uniforms.

Here began the presentation of the English ecclesiastics, the Patriarchs, Roman prelates, Consuls (among them Count Potocki !), monks, and priests. At last I escaped, and mounted my horse again, and, hoping now at last to see Jerusalem in peace, attempted to withdraw from the crowd, by attaching myself closely to our own soldiers, who were marching immediately in front of me.

It was touching to see the joy of the Deaconesses from Kaiserswerth, who are attached

K

to the only Institution here for nursing and teaching, and who all shook hands with me in their joy at once more seeing their countrymen; at their head was Fräulein Charlotte Pilz, whose beneficent influence I had long heard well spoken of.

Finally, I asked our Consul, von Alten, if we should not soon be able to see Jerusalem. " It has been before you for a long time," was the reply. That is to say, the splendid Russian monastic hospital, and cathedral-like church belonging to it, are so placed that they and their buildings hide every glimpse of the town from us, and one can only see a minaret and a few walls. Thick masses of dust whirled up from the feet of the countless inhabitants running after us, to increase the sweltering midday heat, while the road wound downwards, and still I could see no city, but only walls ; so at last we came down to the Damascus Gate, in the vicinity of which Godfrey of Bouillon undertook his victorious siege, and through which no Christian Prince had hitherto been allowed to enter. At last we passed inside the town. But here the narrowness of the streets made any view impossible. Finally we came by winding streets to the door of the Church of the Sepulchre, by which, along with our attendants and the marines, we entered the sanctuary. The Greek clergy received me in rich festal vestments, with lights, and incense, and consecrated rose-water, and led me to the Holy Places.

Our dwelling is pleasantly situated, half in the evangelical Hospice of St. John, and half in the Consulate, which is connected with the latter by a little garden and platform, inhabited by Herr von Alten, looking straight across to the Mount of Olives. All the houses are vaulted inside, with flat roofs outside, and fairly good arrangements for ventilation. The water for drinking and washing comes exclusively from the cisterns, but is always cold in the morning, because the nights get very cool after midnight.

The afternoon was employed in visiting the so-called " Mosque of Omar " on the Haram, the site once occupied by the Temple of Solomon, and the precincts belonging to the latter. Two very amiable Mullahs acted as guides, and must already have had a great deal to do with Germans, for they several times attempted to repeat words which we eventually traced to the German language ; in particular, there was one expression, " *ainstain*," which we eventually discovered to mean " ein Stein " (a stone). The mosque is externally very attractive, from its wealth of exquisite coloured porcelain tiles; inside, a great rock projects from the ground—one of the original foundations of the Jewish Temple, which also played a part in the time of Mohammed.

At dinner the Armenian Patriarch (who does not know a word of French, but is most amiably disposed towards Germany) made his appearance, along with several of the Germans who live here, and some Pashas.

A serenade, with the presentation of an address from the Germans and Jewish inhabitants, brought the day to a close.

On November 5 we rode across the mountains to Hebron, accompanied by Kiamil-Pasha and Dr. Sandretzky from Bavaria, an archæologist living here. Not far from Bethlehem the road went by Rachel's grave; it soon became one of the roughest I have ever seen, for we had to ride over smooth slopes of rock, then again over interminable loose rolling stones, so that I feared every minute that my little Barbary steed would lose his footing. But these clever, tough little animals know no difficulties, and never even stumble. So we went for six hours uninterruptedly through the bald wild mountains of Judæa: we seldom saw a bush, and only twice a spring. About a mile on this side of the place, the authorities received us on horseback, and gave us a lead. Hebron is the well-known Abrahamitic place of the Scriptures to this day; the mosque, which has little worthy of notice in itself, contains the graves of Abraham, Sarah, Jacob, Leah, and Joseph—the cenotaphs, with rich hangings, standing inside the building, while the bones that have never yet been disturbed rest far below in untrodden sepulchres. The pristine fertility of the land, and its wealth of trees, have long since disappeared; only two 'oak-trees' are pointed out as contemporaneous with the Patriarchs, and are not far from the site of the former grove of Mamre. Memories of the Biblical teaching of my childhood, imparted by my first and venerated teacher Godet, surged up on beholding the places of which I had so often ˎ seen the names—how he would have loved to accompany me to the Promised Land!

Our night-quarters were in tents at the great mountain reservoir of Solomon, from which Jerusalem is supplied with fresh mountain water by means of conduits.

On November 6 we visited Bethlehem and the Birthplace of the Saviour. This was shown to us in the hollow of a rock, between the spaces occupied by the church and cloister.

A ride round the walls of Jerusalem, which led us past the Place of Wailing and the colossal corner-stones of the Temple, with visits to the evangelical German and English institutions, ended the day, the evening of which, however, I spent quite quietly by myself on the Mount of Olives.

Our marines went everywhere to see the sights, and no one can imagine how strange it seemed to me to see our men promenading in this place, just as one is used to seeing them in the garrison or barracks when their duty is over.

Sunday, the 7th, I went alone to the Lord's Supper in the sacristy of the English church, where they were holding the German service.

At midday, in the presence of the evangelical community, as well as of Kiamil Pasha, and our own marines, I solemnly took possession, in the name of our King, of the ruins of the former Hospice of St. John, and the Church belonging to it. An armorial eagle that had been painted on board was fixed up to the beautiful door, which is still in good preservation, and the Prussian standard was planted on the highest point, while we gave three cheers for our King.*

* The words with which the Crown Prince completed the occupation ran: "In the Name of His Majesty, I hereby take possession of the

In the afternoon we left Jerusalem by the same way as we had come, visiting a few remaining institutions outside the gates. These were a girls' school, named Talitha-Cumi, which is under the direction of the brave Deaconess Charlotte Pilz, and is splendidly managed; also the boys' orphanage, established by Herr Schneller out of his private means, and by voluntary contributions, for the survivors of the massacre from the Christian community in 1860.

Our night's quarters were again at Bab-el-Wâd, under canvas. Through the careful and practical arrangements of a fellow-countryman of the name of Thiel, from the Rhine Provinces, who has been many years in Jerusalem, everything here, as at each place where our caravans have stopped, was splendidly managed. Early the next morning we rode to Jaffa, and at the entrance to that place met the Emperor of Austria, who had just landed with his large retinue; after a brief but hearty greeting, I betook myself to the Greek Patriarch of Jerusalem, who was still waiting here, and at his

ancient church of the S. John's Hospitallers, of all the ruins of the same, above and beneath the earth, and of all other remains of structures pertaining to the same above and under the earth. Long live His Majesty the King, Hoch! Hoch! Hoch!" (*Die Anwerenheit des Kronprinzer von Preussen in Palästina.* By a South-German. Berlin, 1870.)

wish discussed the cession of some property next to the St. John's land, belonging to his church. We soon signed a protocol, by which the possessions of our King in Jerusalem can be still further increased.

Amid heavy breakers we went on board the *Hertha* at midday, and weighed anchor for Beyrût, which we reached in the morning twilight of November 9, and were greeted by the corvette *Elizabeth*, which I at once inspected.

Beyrût, November 9 and 10, 1869.

We had a remarkably remunerative and interesting time in Syria ; our journey took us from the romantically situated Beyrût (which was reached in a twelve-hour voyage from Jaffa) directly into the remotest valleys of Lebanon, and then again at Damascus showed us one of the " Pearls " of all the Oriental cities ; while the ruins of Baalbec—once called Heliopolis—presented the richest treasures of late Greek architecture.

Beyrût has been compared with Naples, on account of its situation near the sea, surrounded by beautifully formed mountains. My admiration does not indeed go this length, but I willingly concede that the green gardens of its suburbs present a charming appearance hitherto unseen

by us in the East ; a great part of the town is
Europeanized, or, at any rate, has a strong admixture of " Frankish " ingredients ; among these,
the Institutions conducted by the Deaconesses of
Kaiserswerth for the education of children and
orphans, as well as the Johanniter Hospital,
can hold their own with the English Thompson
school, and the French Charité.

. Most of the Sisters are from Prussia, and it
was touching to see their delight at meeting their
fellow-countrymen. The Sultan had ordered the
Governor of Tripoli, Kiamil-Pasha, and a Colonel,
to meet me here.

On the following day we undertook an excursion into Lebanon, under the guidance of our
Consul, Weber. At first we rode through the
groves of orange and sweet-pine, which grow in
rich luxuriance close to the environs, and point
the way into the mountains by many devious
turnings. After passing through the ravines of
the picturesque rock mountains, through which
at every winding of the path one sees the
splendid blue ocean, we found, in the gradual
upward ascent, places which have appreciated the
presence of green in their surroundings, a thing
we had not hitherto seen in this part of the
world. So we went with our caravan, escorted

by the gayest costumes, deeper and deeper into the savage-seeming valleys of the Libanus. The collective inhabitants of the places—half-Christian Maronites, half-Mohammedan Druses—came towards us singing, bearing palms or green branches in their hands, while the women burned incense before me, or sprinkled me with orange-water. The usual greeting is, "Allah give you victory;" but, as a great proportion of those who met us to-day were Christian Maronites, and this said to me from the mouths of the Christian subjects of the Sultan of Turkey might have been inimically construed by him, instructions had been given previously to shout, "Hail, Prince of Germany!"

Thus we went on nearly all day, until we met the Governor of Lebanon, Franco Pasha, whose sons had already greeted us with refreshments; while a spinning school, conducted by some English, sang, "God save the Queen."

Franco Pasha is a Christian, since, according to treaty, there has been a governor of the Christian persuasion here since the blood-bath of 1860. Beït-Eddin is the name of his lofty castle residence, which was the magnificent home of the family of the late Emir Beschir-Schehab, who formerly reigned here as sovereigns.

We had to traverse two large terraced courts, lying one above the other, before we dismounted from our horses. In the upper of these stood the numerous crowd of servitors in a row; a few of them were presented. The inside of the Palace is largely Oriental, and little Europeanized, and there is not much that is modern in the whole of the arrangements, so that, *e.g.*, divans and little plaster balconies are apparent everywhere.

The evening sun lit up Deir-el-Kamar, the chief city of Lebanon, as I entered the narrow mountainous streets, which were filled with a mass of men pressed neck to neck together. Here again, as in the valleys, were palms and branches, incense and orange-water; as the women were mostly on the flat roofs of the houses, I found myself under a perpetual *douche*, which indeed was not unpleasant after the six-hours' ride in the heat. Franco Pasha's Arab infantry looked martial in their white uniforms; no less so the irregular cavalry, which in the evening performed "*fantasiêhs*" in the castle-yard by Bengal light.

From the highest pinnacle of the mountain castle we watched the sunset, which was soon followed by the new moon, so that we had a

most splendid ending to this delightful day,
which I hold to be the most interesting of the
journey.

Damascus, November 11, 1869.

To-day began at 4 o'clock, in the beautiful
hours of the morning, with a seven-hours' ride
along steeply rising, mountainous rock paths.
Our way was lighted by torches until sunrise, then
the Oriental sun burned down on our heads, making
itself particularly obvious, until at 10 o'clock we
reached the French posting-road to Damascus, and
took the *messagerie* coach, in which we reached the
aforesaid town at nine in the evening. The road,
which was only built eight years ago, winds three
times up and down the stony mountains of
Lebanon and Anti-Lebanon, and then cuts through
Cœle-Syria, before it reaches Damascus.

The officials, or rich inhabitants of the place,
who appear to be extraordinarily numerous, presented the most charming variety, as, clad in
every conceivable and *voyant* colour, they accompanied us on horseback. Both yesterday and
to-day, many Arabic documents were presented
to me, which sometimes had the translations
appended; the most original of all was one in

which a gushing and bombastic enthusiast compared me to a lily !

All Damascus seemed, in spite of the late hour, to be upon its feet : all the Dignitaries, the Pasha at their head, met me at the Gate of the city. I was made to mount, and then for over half an hour we went along the streets and through the Bazaar. Torch-bearers went in front—for there is no gas, only here and there a modest oil-lamp—but an occasional triumphal arch, set with little lanterns, gave rather more light. The beautiful Arab costumes, together with the women, who were mostly clad entirely in white and wrapped in long cotton veils, made a fantastic effect in this illumination, more particularly in the vaulted halls of the Bazaar. Greek women, unveiled, and decked with jewels, peeped curiously down from the balconies, and showed their beautiful white teeth ; in all classes of the Oriental peoples I was struck with the clean and well-kept mouth.

We dismounted at our quarters with a rich Maronite. His house was splendidly arranged, and rich in marble mosaics, silk, and golden tissues ; the great court, adorned with spouting fountains, surrounded the reception hall and the scattered pavilion-like dwelling-rooms.

Amid such splendour the European misses his writing-table, and other simple and daily conveniences, while beds and divans, on the other hand, are most comfortably arranged. To-day it was quite legitimate to crave for repose.

Damascus, November 12, 1869.

Our first walk was in the Bazaar; this seems to me more extensive than that at Constantinople, and, especially in the goldsmiths' quarters, affords much more striking pictures. European clothes are hardly seen at all, and even the modern Turkish dress of the reform is not to be found, so that we feel ourselves in the East indeed! In every tiny room that can possibly be glorified with the name of a booth, sat Turks, Greeks, and Arabs, in their old national costume, gazing with half-cunning, half-apathetic eyes at the strangers, only thawing with alacrity so soon as there was question of a purchase.

My attempted incognito was really preserved for some time; at the end of an hour, however, it was discovered; the merchants then came to our house. Even in the most active bargaining the friendly side of hospitality is never forgotten, and a *tschibuk* with coffee is offered by every one whose department one enters. It is one of the dearest customs of the Oriental to seat himself in a shop, converse a little, and then again watch the crowd aimlessly. This was particularly the case to-day, because it was Friday.

The mosques were very full. At our entrance into the Omeiyad Mosque, the former basilica of St. John the Baptist, which boasts to this day of possessing his head, the police soldiers who walked in front of us turned every one out. No one took this amiss; on the contrary, most of the eyes were directed at our feet, to see if we had drawn on slippers over our shoes! As is well known, one must be careful, on entering the mosques, not to wear the foot-covering that has touched the pavement of the streets; so either one's boots come off, or one draws slippers over them!

In the next place we paid a visit to the richest houses of the city, and on horseback visited the place where Paul, fleeing by night, was let down by cords; also that in which are the ruins of Naaman's house; and at the close of the day at sunset, we contemplated the really magnificent city from the heights.

Damascus may be compared to a pearl set

with emeralds, for the white houses, the mosques, and minarets, surrounded by a mile-wide ring of green groves of oranges and citrons, involuntarily suggest to me this image. I shall never lose this magic impression.

When in the evening I returned to my quarters, I was suddenly asked to allow the marriage of the fifteen-year old daughter of the house with her betrothed in my presence. They had, so ran the message, been on the point of marrying, when a death in the family obliged them to put it off; since they could not, therefore, have any great festivity, they were anxious to take the opportunity, which was not likely to occur again, of celebrating their wedding in our presence.

So of a sudden I became best man at an orthodox Greek wedding. The ceremonial reminded me of the Russian rite, more particularly in the use of the crown, and the taking of the cup of water by the bridal pair; otherwise the ceremony consisted exclusively in long prayers, without any exchange of rings, as with us. I stood at the right near the bridegroom, while his stepmother kept her left arm round the bride. Costly diamond flowers hung over her forehead, as over that of the bridegroom's mother; the dress was pale pink, with threads of gold silk worked through it; the other women were more simply, but no less characteristically, dressed than these. The priests wore rose-coloured silk vestments, stitched with gold flowers, seemingly of the same cut as those of the Russian Popes; the whole assemblage held candles in ·their hand, the wedded pair alone excepted.

Baalbec, November 13, 1869.

On the next day, at three in the morning, we rode out of Damascus, accompanied by the whole family.

At the gate we mounted the diligence, to go to Baalbec. At the place called Shtaura, we got on our horses at 10 o'clock, and rode for five hours over the plain of the Becka‘a, which has been used from all time as the highway to Heliopolis by the hordes of Heathen, Crusading, and Muslim peoples who have passed through Syria. We were surrounded by several hundreds of mounted Arabs, who performed continuous "*fantasiêhs*," and thereby covered us well. with dust.

In Baalbec, or Heliopolis, are the ruins of the Temple of Zeus (which date from the late Greek

L

period), as well as those of the Sun-God, the destruction of which was due rather to an earth-quake than to the ravages that are unfortunately too common here. The decoration is already overdone, but the material and its application are still treated with the same exactitude as in the Golden Age of Art. Arabs, Turks, and Kurds all use the ruins to build fortresses with; in spite of all, however, eight majestic columns still carry their entablature, and the old foundations are yet standing with their corner-stones of over forty feet in length, bidding defiance to destruction.

A splendid sunset enhanced the aspect of the ruins, whilst remarkably good beds afforded us a welcome night's rest.

On November 14 we rode back by the same way that we had come, took the diligence again, and reached Beyrût in the afternoon. At the boundary of the city we were surprised to see Franco Pasha, who entertained us as his guests in a large tent, surrounded by his sons, by many officers, and his picturesque escort.

I forgot to say that both yesterday and to-day we were entertained *en route* by an escort of camel-cavalry, which had the strangest effect. Each pair of soldiers sat one behind the other on a kind of saddle, which was buckled on to the hump, and supported themselves in loading their arms. Instead of the bridle-rein, a rope went over the bumptious and ill-tempered nose of the animal, which always gives a sullen grunt when it has to kneel down or stand up again. Several regular evolutions were executed with remarkable precision, and the trot was fairly even.

Port Sa'id, November 16, 1869.

We are lying here in the new harbour of Port Sa'îd, which is at the mouth of the Suez Canal. Attempts at writing, on the way between this and Beyrût, had to be given up, on account of the horrid rolling, and because the sea was excessively high.

Even the embarkation at Beyrût was extremely unpleasant, because the surf rose so much, after a stormy night which had already disturbed our rest in Baalbec, that the waves were ten to twenty feet high. Since, however, there was no other hindrance,—the storm itself being over, and the time appointed for our arrival at Port Sa'îd at hand,—we put to sea.

At sunset we lay off the roads at Port Sa'îd,

but could not enter the harbour, because, in spite of repeated signals, no pilot appeared, and we could not venture to steer in by ourselves in the darkness, on account of the large coast traffic. We were, moreover, warned by the English Admiral and Commander of the Mediterranean Squadron, Sir John Milnes, that two of his iron-clads had already stuck in the sand at the entrance to the harbour.

Thus we had to stay all night on the high seas, which, thank goodness, calmed down visibly and sensibly. And so we came into harbour this morning at 8.30 in full state, the *Elizabeth* leading, the *Delphin* bringing up the rear. The English war-ships did not salute my standard, apparently because it was still too early to run the flags up; the Empress Eugénie, who came in immediately after, was, on the other hand, greeted with the customary marks of honour.

And now from all sides were heard cheers and firing of guns to salute us. An imposing array of vessels was closely packed together in the none too large harbour, flags were flying from all their masts, and the crews were in the rigging. The same thing was repeated for the Empress Eugénie, who, standing on the covered deck of her yacht *Aigle*, made gracious bows in answer to our greeting. The saluting and cheering now went on the whole day without intermission, as the Emperor of Austria, the Empress of the French, the Khedive, Henry and Amalie of the Netherlands, I, and the rest of the strangers present, *e.g.* Mr. Elliot the English Ambassador, General Ignatieff the Russian Ambassador, etc., went about, paying each other visits. Naturally the din began afresh each time one passed a war-ship, which had an extraordinary effect on account of the forest of masts in the harbour. The town, on the other hand, offers little, and was visited about as much as Wilhelmshaven at the Jahdebusen !

The Austrian corvette *Greif*, on which Kaiser Franz Joseph received me, was remarkably simple in its appointments, as was also that from the Netherlands, on which Heinrich and Amalie had made their passage here. The Empress Eugénie received us with a charming grace in the big saloon-like cabin on board the beautifully fitted *Aigle*, and, cheerful as ever, held a three-quarters of an hour conversation with us. Prince Joachim Murat did the honours on board, and previously came to pay me a visit. In the *suite* of the Empress were, among others, her nephew, the Spanish Duque d'Huescar with his two sisters, the Demoiselles d'Alba, also Madame de la Poëse, the Comtesse de Larochelambert.

Meantime, what interested me the most was to make acquaintance with Abd-el-Kader, who came to see me on board ship, on which occasion he wore the ribbon of the Order of the Red Eagle over his white Algerian costume. His handsome and apparently youthful face has characteristically strong features, and a highly attractive and intellectual expression. His whole appearance is that of a man to be reckoned with. I was also interested in the personality of the Hungarian Minister, Count Andrassy, whose fine, distinguished appearance was enhanced by his clever, bright eyes. He had not been in Vienna during my visit, so that I first made his acquaintance here.

The Viceroy came to see me shortly after my arrival, and was very kind and amiable. His two sons, who accompanied him, looked good and intelligent. The yacht on which he received my return visit is a floating house of the greatest luxury.

In the afternoon, at 3 o'clock, we all went on shore to attend an Arabic and Roman Catholic Te Deum. For this, two kiosk-like pavilions had been erected side by side; while in the one there was a kind of pulpit such as is used in the mosques, in the other was a Roman Catholic altar. Opposite these kiosks was a tribune with a high baldachin. Kaiser Franz Joseph led the Empress Eugénie. The Khedive took Amalie of the Netherlands, and behind us came the multitude of uniforms.

Immediately in front of their Majesties walked three Austrian workmen, a great number of whom are at present employed here, and who everywhere prepared great ovations for their Kaiser. One preceded the Emperor with the Austrian flag, walking between two fellows, who wore the fez on their heads, but were otherwise dressed European fashion, and carried arms. German-Italian "*Vivas*" for Kaiser Franz Joseph mingled with "*Vive l'Impératrice.*"

Along with these the splendid Egyptian troops, clothed in gray, *à la Zouave*, shouted at the word of command their "*Haya Padischa*" or "*Tschok-Jascha*," which I fancy means something like "Health and long life," so that one had a nice mixture of languages.

The Arab service was conducted by a venerable old Mullah, clad in a beautiful dark violet velvet caftan. Then a Roman Catholic Bishop appeared, who intoned the Latin Te Deum, after which a

French Almoner of the Empress, Monseigneur Bauer, ascended the steps of the altar, and made a very clever discourse in a resounding voice.

It was characteristic that a Christian priest should thank the Mohammedan Sovereign in the name of Christianity and of civilization for the making of the Canal!

During this function, which took place close to the sea-shore, it interested me to watch the natives, who, undisturbed by what was going on, were saying the prayers prescribed by the Koran, stretched upon the sand of the dunes, their faces turned to Mecca.

We left the scene of the function in the same order in which we had entered, and then rowed quickly, *incognito*, round the harbour, and visited the *Arcona*, which had come in yesterday.

A splendid full moon vied with the illuminated ships, while our sailors engaged in all sorts of pastimes, danced, and gave themselves up to well-deserved recreation, of which they were much in need after the not inconsiderable exertions of the last weeks.

To-morrow we must go on board the *Grille*, because the *Hertha* carries too much water for the present depth of the canal. I am sorry to leave the corvette, in which we have had such a very enjoyable voyage, and of whose captain, Kohler, I have acquired the highest opinion, on account of his prudence, tranquillity, steadiness, and insight. He rightly enjoys the full confidence of our navy.

Inauguration Passage of the Suez Canal, on board the " Grille," November 17, 1869.

And so we find ourselves upon the newest wonder of our age,—inaugurate the Canal,—and feel that we are witnesses of an event that will be of quite stupendous importance in the world's traffic, and which is the proof of what human foresight, perseverance, and strength of will can accomplish. May God's blessing rest on the sources of commerce that will spring from it, and on the new undertakings that will necessarily be its appanage. Would that Germany might shortly have to glory in similarly great undertakings in the field of commerce.

The departure was arranged for 6 a.m. First the *Aigle*, with the Empress Eugénie; next the *Greif*, with the Emperor of Austria; then I on board the *Grille*; lastly, the Netherland steamship with Prince and Princess Henry of the Netherlands, followed by the Ambassadors, and some fifty other steamboats.

But the procession was only set in motion at 10.30, because an Egyptian steamboat, sent ahead out of extreme precaution, only wired late that the through-passage was certain. Then 'we started down the Canal, the mouth of which is marked by two obelisks, constructed of brick-work.

From that moment to the arrival at Ismaïlia, the passage offers nothing but the view of a straight-drawn canal, enclosed all along by sandy banks. It was, however, instructive to listen to the information given by M. Laroche, one of the first French engineers of the work, who was our conductor. One of the Austrian ships, the *Eliza-beth*, stuck three times in the sand, and kept us back with all the other vessels, otherwise the seven-hour passage was accomplished without touching the shore; of course the steering had to be very cautious.

Ismaïlia, November 18, 1869.

Here we are on thirty ships in the great basin of water, at the newly constructed town of Ismaïlia, which lies halfway between Suez and Port Sa'îd, and consisted at first only of the houses of M. Lesseps and his employés, but is now springing up.

When we arrived yesterday evening at night-fall, we could only see the pink, shining, sandy shores, and a sea of lights,—to judge from the number of which there was an important town, whence we could distinguish hollow sounds of trumpets or tambourines. Curiosity soon took us ashore, and then we found ourselves suddenly plunged once more into the enchantments of the East. For the desert was covered with a tent-encampment of over 30,000 Arabs, headed by their Sheikhs, and gathered from all parts of the land ; every tent was illuminated, besides which lanterns were burning everywhere, while fireworks sent up their shining trail for hours into the night.

While the Sheikhs in solemn gravity, seated on their divans, received visits, smoked, or played chess, the Dervishes were praying, howling, and whirling in their tents. Syrians performed con-juring tricks with children, and danced *almén* with distortions of their bodies, and the Arab singing-women were heard chanting behind the shelter of their wooden booths. Between these moved the crowd of Arabs in gay caftans, and white or striped burnouses, each stalking along with grave pride.

It would be a hopeless undertaking to describe

the magic effect which this Oriental gathering
had upon me, and on all of us; again and again
we said, it is exactly like a dream! The picture
was almost as beautiful on the following morning,
but the darkness lent more charm to the traffic
in the camp than did the bright sunshine.

In strangest contrast with this was the ball
which the Khedive gave at night in his unfinished
palace. In spaces where perhaps some eight
hundred persons would have found room, there
were now two to three thousand guests, among
whom unfortunately but few displayed Oriental
garments amidst the sea of black coats. It was
so crammed, that after a single promenade or
polonaise which we made round the room, and in
which half the guests did not discover that "Their
Majesties" had arrived, we practically spent the
whole evening in a little *salon*. We gentlemen
were bidden to appear in civil dress, so that the
strangers were unable to discover what nationalities
were present.

Before the function we all went round the
Bedouin camp once more *incognito*.

To-morrow we go down to the Bitter Lakes,
the day after to Suez, and then I go direct to
Cairo and the Nile.

Suez, November 20, 1869.

The - Passage of the Canal has been successfully accomplished; none of the ships on which were the principal guests had any difficulties to overcome, and even where there were some dangerous rocks we passed safely over them, and avoided them by constant steering or slow progress.

The fact now lies patent to the whole world that great ships can be brought from the Red Sea to the Mediterranean, and the trade of the future will take its route henceforth with an extraordinary saving of time by the shortest path from India and the Pacific Ocean to Europe.

At daybreak we weighed anchor in the Bitter Lakes, where there was a strong wind yesterday evening, so that we were rocked by the waves. This basin, which has only been filled with sea-water since the spring, and was till then a stretch of dry land, has already the aspect of a proper sea.

Although it is surrounded by the sands of the desert, the landscape does not look sandy or bare, because there is always a peculiar rosy glow in this part, which makes an indescribably living shimmer at all times of day, and even in the darkness. Otherwise no living creature was to be seen about us here, except those who were on our thirty steam-ships.

I had already, yesterday evening, visited Their Majesties on board their ships; Kaiser Franz Joseph was very courteous, and returned my visit at a later hour.

At 12 o'clock we reached the small and quite insignificant town of Suez, charmingly situated at the foot of picturesque hills, and washed by the "blue" waves of the "Red" Sea. And so I have made acquaintance with this sea also, after being only four weeks ago in the Black Sea, and in the course of the previous summer having bathed in the waters of the North Sea. I cannot deny that at that moment my thoughts turned with a little sigh across the waves of the Red Sea to the East. Here I was close to the spells of India and to the Himalayas as never before, and as I never shall be again in the whole course of my life! But the thunder of the guns and the cheering of the crews upon the rigging of the East India transports and many other merchant vessels, dispersed all traces of sentimentality, and the prosaic reality of proceeding as rapidly as possible to the disembarkation took its place, because I was to travel the first after the Viceroy upon the railway, to take ship again this evening for the Nile journey.

The passage of the Suez Canal has no intrinsic charm ; only the' circumstance that the desert and the sand (with the homelike feelings it arouses) give out a real 'shimmer of light, which one must see to realize it, render the inanimate land-scape a little less monotonous. It might therefore be supposed that a two and a half days' voyage would gradually become monotonous ; this, how-ever, was not at all the case ; we all found it a welcome opportunity for undisturbed writing or reading, besides which our sufficiently restricted society on board ship was in no melancholy humour. To me the climax of these days was indisputably the sight of the Arab tents in Ismaïlia, and the impression I received there will remain indelibly linked with the images of the Opening of the Suez Canal. This life, so entirely different from any festival and traffic of the people that I have ever encountered on my various travels, presents a charm that is unique of its kind.

The fairy tales of one's childhood find realiza-tion here to large extent, without the necessity of any great outlay of imagination, and a few hours' wandering in this Oriental crowd give new-comers a clearer idea of the life in the East than if they had been travelling there for weeks. Hence it was a joy for us to succeed in wandering round three times without our *incognito* being discovered, so that everything went on naturally and without constraint around us. When, on the other hand, the Khedive arranged an official promenade for us all, with "*fantasiêhs*" to order, the picture turned at once to a made-up affair.

I was more particularly struck by the distinguished coolness with which sheikhs as well as vassals and slaves demeaned themselves, looking down with a certainly comprehensible contempt out of their splendid caftans upon our civilian garments. The swarthiest and most ragged Moor in this country wears his shirt or caftan, and the *Abáyeh* with as much dignity as a nobleman.

On the Nile, November 21, 1869.

After the landing at Suez yesterday, which was delayed for nearly an hour by the clumsiness of our pilot (so that we could only pay a hurried visit to the fine Dry-docks, which are of the newest construction), we took the railway, and in six hours arrived at Cairo. On the way we saw our first grove of palm trees, which drew loud exclamations from us all, as it lay shining in the golden evening sunlight. Beside them the cotton plantations presented a sober aspect, the tall shrubs with white blossoms looking like a potato-plant shot up. The villages one sees consist of absolutely flat lumps of earth, built in a square—a sort of caricature of human dwellings. Otherwise the landscape is pure desert land, bare rocks and sand.

We reached Cairo at eight in the evening, in the beams of the full moon, and a voluptuous sea of light, the streets and squares being illuminated. The Khedive received us in the Station Buildings, from which we drove in elegant carriages that were quite English in their turn-out, surrounded by escorts, torch-bearers, and runners in Arab dress, to the landing-place of the steamers.

The whole garrison lined the way, and shouted incessantly " *Tschok-Jascha* ; " but several times I heard the tune, " *Ich bin ein Preusse* " (I am a Prussian). Eventually we were conducted through one of the triumphal arches which the Austrian inhabitants of the place had erected in honour of their Kaiser, its Latin inscription giving point to it.

A French *cuisine* awaited our hunger on board the steamboat, coupled, moreover, with the greatest luxury of all kinds. My bed is protected against

M

the flies by a curtain of silver muslin, with gold stars.

On the banks we saw now groves of palms, now regular woods of this splendid and poetical tree. The character of the shore is little romantic, and so far less fertile than one would have expected from the descriptions.

The brown waves of the river resemble our mountain waters after heavy rain-flows, and desperate resolution is needed to wash one's self in this brown, coffee-coloured water. Pelicans, birds of prey, and a few eagles, which circle round us, bring life into the desert, while the inhabitants of the poor little lime-huts, for the most part clad in nothing but a turban, gazed at our steamboat. The temperature is not high. At midday, indeed, the sun is fierce, but the mornings and evenings are cool, and demand precaution in the way of clothing.

On the Nile, November 22 *to December* 1, 1869.

Already for four days we have been steaming up the Nile, without any alteration in the character of the scenery of its banks, or of the more distant bare mountains, from that described above. The temperature, indeed, becomes a little hotter every day, but at sunset gives way to very cold

hours in the night and evening. We may congratulate ourselves on approaching the .tropics just
at this time, especially as there is a north wind
blowing.

Three steamers were told off for my convoy;
two of them accommodate my numerous retinue,
while the provisions and kitchen requisites are on
the third. We stop every morning to collect the
entire company on my ship for breakfast, where
they then remain till late evening. We live much
too well on board, especially when one considers
that we go on for days without any exercise other
than at most a promenade upon the little quarter-
deck.

Up to the present we have only landed at Siût,
on the 23rd, one of the largest cities of the
country, to see the Rock-Tombs which date from
the XIII. Dynasty—1400 B.C.—but are no longer
in good preservation. The town is built of brown
bricks and inhabited by brown men, who, since
they find it hot, wear next to no clothes. As the
Nile has been falling for fourteen days, the spring
is already beginning here, and the plains present
the same appearance as with us in March, when
the winter sowing begins to come up green.

The effects of light and colour in the glorious
transparent air are magnificent, and even the stars

shine with far greater brilliancy than with us. Jupiter really illuminates the darkness, and is reflected in the water before the moon rises. The Great Bear, on the contrary, has already disappeared below the horizon, so that even the starry heavens show us how far from our homes we have travelled. Our travelling party on board ship has been increased by Professors Lepsius and Dümichen, extremely pleasant and amiable companions, who know how to impart their scientific knowledge and discoveries in the most attractive manner, without falling into any dry or dogmatic tone. It is a real pleasure to me to make this part of the journey under such guidance. Moreover, the repose on board is a true luxury after the preceding weeks. The life on the steamboat almost reminds one of the Rhine journeys.

Next came the days of Egyptian study proper, for on the 25th we arrived at the Temple of Dendera at daybreak. In the afternoon we reached the Plains of Thebes, where we visited the half-destroyed ruins of Luxor with the Colossi; then the wonderful dynastic temple of Karnak, and its Avenue of Ram-headed Sphinxes, in which almost all the dynasties have sought to immortalize themselves; and lastly, we rode far into the night along the western banks of the Nile, past the remains of the vast City of the Dead to a part of the Tombs of the Kings.

On November 26 we continued our inspection of Thebes, including the Tombs of the Kings at Bîbân-el-Mulûk, and the Temple of Medînet Habou and Alt-Kurna, along with the so-called Statue of Memnon; then we pursued our journey up the Nile past Esneh to Edfu.

On November 27 we made a thorough study of the Temple of Edfu, which has recently been excavated; it is of colossal proportions, and in perfect preservation: the pleasure was unalloyed, because here no ruins compel one to whip up the imagination; rather what is seen is clear and comprehensible to the bystander, and permits one to appreciate the marvellous works of the ancient Egyptians in their boldest architectural efforts.

In the afternoon we went on up the Nile through sandstone rocks and breaches to the First Cataract of the Nile, where we came to anchor at Assûan and the island of Elephantine. A boating party in the evening sunshine took us to the rocks, where, however, only rapids, and not, as I had expected, cataracts, were to be seen. A rich growth of palm trees lent a great charm to the landscape, which was repeated on the following day, when, after a camel-ride through the desert, we perceived Philæ in the morning hours of November 28.

On visiting the tolerably well-preserved ruins on the island of Philæ, which lies in mid-stream, we experienced the glamour of being in Nubia. Our satisfaction, however, reached its climax when in the afternoon we got to the edge of the tropics, and crossed the zone of the Crab, and we had the satisfaction of sleeping one night below 23 degrees of the northern latitude. At Philæ we were transferred to an elegant *dahabiyeh*, the name given to the usual sailing vessels on which the Nile traveller journeys, and which are comparable to a large covered gondola. Our dahabiyeh was towed by little steam-tugs, and steered by statuesque black Nubians, clad wholly in white. Our joy in the tropics could only be of short duration, for the return to Cairo and approaching voyage home across the Mediterranean Sea had to include a whole week for the Nile journey down-stream. And so we had to content ourselves with the thought that we had penetrated beyond the First Cataract, and were able to say we had been in the tropics.

On November 29, after visiting the first of the four famous rock-hewn temples of Gerf Husên, as well as a peasant's farm of the most primitive kind, we turned northwards. From the moment at which the helmsman made this revolution, and we turned our backs to the equator, we really began our homeward journey, and every one was accordingly in good spirits ; for, in spite of palms and Nile, and however great the enjoyment afforded to-day by the Nubian landscape, the longing after the Fatherland and one's dear ones left behind there, will have its way.

From Philæ a camel-ride brought us down by the Cataract to Assûan. I confess that this mode of riding pleases me much more than I had anticipated, for as soon as one gets the right balance, perched on the hump-saddle, and becomes used to the animal's step, one feels quite comfortable. After we got on board our original steamer again, the journey down the Nile was prosecuted without further stoppage.

On December 4 we hope to visit the Sahara from Pedreschin, to enter Cairo on the evening of the same day, and after remaining some days there, on account of our Oriental-Egyptological studies, to take ship on December 9, on the *Elizabeth*. Please God, we shall make the shores of Europe in a four to five days' voyage, and then land at Brindisi, Naples, or Marseilles, when, after a rapid journey through these countries, which are already familiar to us, we hope to be seasonably reunited with our dear ones before the lighting of the Christmas Tree.

I have purposely abbreviated this portion of the journey. In the first place, all correspondence must be ready at the latest by December 3, to catch the last post that leaves Alexandria before our own departure. In the second, it would be only a vain commencement to attempt any detailed description of the ancient Egyptian Temples. As memorials of this wonderful people, they resemble each other with an almost schedule-like precision. In all, the same magnificence, the same colossal proportions, the same admirable craft of builder and stonemason, but also the same repetition in the types of figures, meet the traveller, and daily cause him fresh surprise.

A certain art, or rather perhaps dexterity in art, is not wanting in these memorials; in fact, I saw relievos of charming delicacy. Nevertheless, what we call taste and æsthetic is wanting, and the eye feels itself overwearied, since it perpetually meets the same thing. Thanks to the scholars of Berlin, who have raised the study of Egyptian art and history to such a high pitch, the presentments of Egyptian structures and monuments of art, the originals of which I have been permitted to see here, are known, and even in a certain sense familiar to us. Still, it affected me strongly to see with my own eyes that which, defying centuries of destruction, bears witness to the rich history of a past age of culture, and to the capacities for work in the people who have been the vessels of such a civilisation.

Our rides to the Temples were always upon donkeys; one driver held the rein, while a second went by the side, to spring forward to help the rider, if a saddle-girth gave way or a buckle burst —which, for the rest, happened every moment!

Accordingly, our riding-parties were always merry, but reached their climax when we all mounted on dromedaries to ride across the desert to the Cataract at Assûan. On mounting the aforesaid animal it must bend completely down, an operation that takes place in three bends of the knee. Having now taken one's place on the broad saddle, consisting of two stuffed pommels, so that one leg of the rider is laid right across the animal's neck, it bellows like our stags in the rutting, and raises itself to its feet again in three leaps, when one must be careful not to lose one's balance. At first one feels quite giddy up there, but this does not last long: one soon gains confidence, finds one's own method of sitting comfortably, and in the end feels very snug. I rode the whole time on the camel, although my white donkey was led at the side, because this kind of riding appealed to me more; and the same held good for the gentlemen of my *suite*, who, in half-European dress, with the native protections against the heat of the sun, presented a sufficiently comical appearance.

The inhabitants of Egypt are distinguished from those of Nubia by marked characteristics. The Egyptian is brownish-yellow in his skin, and looks as if some vestiges of European exterior still clung to him. The Nubian, on the contrary, is dark brown, already turning black, but of much nobler build, and I must also say of more intellectual appearance. We particularly noticed this in the men who were told off to steer and to guide us. The Nubian race is said to be particularly capable and dependable, and is much sought after in Cairo for this reason. The inhabitants of Dâr-Fûr and the Sudân, on the contrary, who are frequently met with here, are quite of the ancient Moorish type.

The Egyptian fellah often goes naked, especially when he is working in the fields. He is much darker, and more earth-coloured, than the richer and superior class, and with his scanty clothing can often be hardly distinguished from the soil; a light apron, open at the sides, hardly covers his loins. The women, on the contrary, are clothed in a long heavy woollen material, that hangs over their shoulders, and falls into the most beautiful antique folds I have ever seen. These women walk about with a straight and indeed proud carriage, bearing clay vessels on their heads according to the custom of the country —one thinks to see antique statues walking before one's eyes, and every sculptor ought to spend a long time here on the study of these folds and garments. I have frequently stood in astonishment to rejoice in the sight. As the women are exceedingly shy and retiring, they are in the habit of veiling their faces, which are usually uncovered, so soon as they become aware of a stranger. Hence one can rarely tell of what material their clasps and bracelets are made. Many wear heavy silver armlets, others mix glass spangles with fruit kernels in gaudy variety in their ornaments.

The Nile people collectively are very thin according to our notions; they are tall, with square shoulders, no trace of calf. At first we took their huts for piles of bricks. Since it hardly ever rains here, palm branches are sufficient

for the roof; there are no conveniences in the
way of seats, and four posts carrying a straw
mattress serve for a bed. The inmates always
look clean, thanks to the Koran, which enjoins
daily ablutions. Here in the country, more particularly, one sees that every Mussulman fulfils
the external precepts of religion with the greatest
fidelity. The sailors of our ship went three
times a day to the paddle-box, where, turning
to Mecca to make their obeisance, they knelt
down, with their foreheads touching the ground,
and their hands raised, a ceremonial lasting each
time for nearly ten minutes. On shore one sees
the people in rows fulfilling their form of orison,
and should any one be interrupted by his duties,
he seeks in every free moment to make up the
appointed tale once more.

In parts where the intercourse of the people
with strangers has already sharpened their wits,
one is often addressed in a jargon of German,
English, French, and Italian, and that with a
vigour of gesticulation and expression that often
reminds one of Italians' vivacity.

Innumerable Old Egyptian objects are everywhere offered for sale to the traveller. The
scarabs are always the prettiest, while the remains
of mummies disgusted me. The latter are

beginning to diminish considerably, since the graves have been plundered by speculative lay-people, who have carried off everything they discovered there.

The smuggling away of the larger works of art is, indeed, forbidden now by the customs-prohibitions; but how many Tombs of Kings and Temple ruins show gaps and empty places, the former ornaments whereof are now on view in the principal Museums of Europe!

On the Nile, December 2, 1869.

We have been travelling down the stream of the Nile for days, and expect to reach Cairo to-morrow. All the colossal ruins we visited on our journey up are flying past us again, "smiled on" by the eternally blue sky and unbroken sunshine.* The air has, however, changed materially since we turned from Nubia, for a stormy north wind blows upon us continually, making the nights, mornings, and evenings extremely cold, and compelling us to prepare warmer clothing. When, on the other hand, the sun

* *Von dem stets blauen Himmel und ununterbrochenen Sonnenschein* "*belacht.*" A punning reference to the double sense of the verb "belachen"—as in the catch, "*Wer lacht über Griechenland?*" "*Ein ewiger blauer Himmel.*"—Tr.

shines, or one finds shelter from the wind, the refreshing warmth is the same we have become familiar with.

A voyage up the Nile is perhaps among the most pleasing experiences of a journey, but it takes a terribly long time; at least, it leaves me with the feeling that, in spite of all its enjoyments, I have no desire to undertake it a second time. Everything in Upper Egypt interested me, but more, as I said above, on account of its novelty than because I thought it beautiful. In spite of its palms and rocks, there is a great monotony in the landscape, while in Italy, *e.g.*, I never could gaze my fill. There everything is life, variety, and change; in the Valley of the Nile it is all just the contrary.

They lie behind us now—those temples, whose towers and ruins we mostly learned to know at break of day, and in the rays of the rising sun. Vanished are the Colossi of Memnon, which we first saw shining in the evening light, and then in the rosy dawn; vanished the Rock-Temples, and Chambers of the Tombs, over which soar eagles, vultures, and other birds of prey. Pelicans and herons tempt the bloodthirsty to futile shots at these rare birds, which seldom appear in flocks.

We shall soon be again in the centre of one

of the capital cities of the East, which is indeed engaged in throwing off its national character for the most rapid artificialities of modern life, so that shortly it will only resemble Paris or London.

The Pyramids look down gravely on this European movement.

Cairo, December 4, 1869.

We interrupted our journey down the Nile to Cairo, on the afternoon of December 3, to disembark at Sakkâra, and thence to visit the Serapeum with the Tombs of Apis, along with the tombs and pyramids in the vicinity. The monotony of the journey was broken near Minyeh by some Coptic monks of a mendicant order, who begged from us in a most original manner. These swarthy men sit quite naked during the whole day on the rocky shore, and as soon as they see travellers coming (since they are able to calculate with great accuracy the exact speed of any steamer), jump into the stream, climb up into the small boats, and will not budge from the place until they have compelled one to give them alms.

Under the guidance of the most distinguished

of the French Egyptologists, Professor Mariette, we visited the tombs of Apis discovered by him,—the name of the Bull, under which people living here thousands of years ago worshipped the divinity. Nearly a hundred burial-chambers hewn out in the rock, each containing a granite sarcophagus in which eight persons could be seated comfortably, are to be found here deep under the earth. One asks one's self in amazement how those colossal sarcophagi could have been prepared and transported into the vaults in those days of little mechanical contrivance! Nor is less astonishment excited by the fine *relievos* of the private tombs, which must date from a period at least three thousand years before Christ. The Pyramids—in a very damaged state—stand in the midst of the desecrated Plain of the Dead at Memphis, which city itself has vanished from the earth without a trace, and on whose ruined heaps the palm trees are now growing.

Late in the evening we got to Cairo, and sought rest in the Palace on the Ezbekîyeh.

Early on the 4th I received and paid visits to the Khedive, the Heir Apparent, etc. The former spoke fluent French, and did the honours in the most amiable manner, a certain distinguished reserve being noticeable in his bearing.

He is a man with insight into the troubles and needs of his country, and is earnestly engaged in raising it by the introduction of European culture.

The Heir to the Throne received me in a house near the desert, where his father possesses three or four palaces close together.

The tombs of the Khalîfs which we inspected to-day, and which contain the bones of the rulers of this country from the epoch of the twelfth and thirteenth centuries, are famed for their fascinating display of Arabic cupolas and many-coloured marble slabs.

On the hill on which the citadel is seated, Mehemed Ali built a splendid mosque, with two slender minarets entirely constructed of Oriental alabaster, in which he placed his tomb. Hard by is the modest dwelling, in a pleasant house, in which he died. From here we enjoyed the view over the mighty city in the finest evening sunshine, and I could understand why Cairo, along with Damascus and Constantinople, is rightly called the Pearl of the East.

This was the first day of the Ramadân—the fast that lasts for four weeks, in which no Mussulman from sunrise to sunset may eat, or drink, or smoke; even the odour of edible things must be avoided during this time.

N

What we have to-day seen of Cairo gives one the impression that, by some process *à la Hausmann*, a European city had everywhere been constructed in place of the old town; I have, at any rate, seen hardly any but European houses outside the Bazaar.

Cairo, December 5, 1869.

To-day, Sunday, was celebrated by an open-air service, in which we united for the laying of the foundation-stone of the German Evangelical Church here. Pfarrer Luttke, from Alexandria, gave a simple discourse in good taste, and the whole function was conducted in proper German fashion, with the assistance of the entire German colony of Cairo, who yesterday honoured me with a serenade and torchlight procession. Nudar Pasha, the present Foreign Minister, as well as my two Egyptian companions, appeared in gala-dress. We collectively attended the function in uniform.

The church will have to be built by degrees, although a substantial contribution from our King was announced to-day by telegram. It will soon be surrounded by modern buildings, representing the new Cairo. The church is to be erected on its own ground and property, given for this object by the Khedive. At present the community only possesses a hired hall for its ecclesiastical necessities.

Excursions in the neighbourhood to-day comprised the "Petrified Forest," the "Virgin's Tree," and the ruins of "Heliopolis." At the tombs of the Kalifas we let ourselves be photographed, to leave to our contemporaries and to posterity the exotic picture of the camel-riders of our race. But neither camels nor the universally prized donkey did credit to their reputation to-day, for at each instant one of the four-footed creatures declined his duty, nor could the carriages be moved from their places.

The stone forest is a place in which the ground is covered with vast remains of petrified tree-trunks. Under the Virgin's Tree, according to the legend, the Blessed Virgin rested with the Christ-Child and Joseph after the flight to Egypt. It is a very old and gnarled sycamore, with knotted trunk and green branches, standing in the midst of garden ground. Tradition sees in the present tree the descendant of one that died many centuries ago, and had been regarded as historically sacred. There was formerly no wood in its vicinity.

A few steps from the Virgin's Tree was once

the city of Heliopolis, known already in the books of Moses as " On," but to-day vanished from the earth without a trace. Only a single obelisk, dating from the earliest times of history, and of importance to Egyptologists, is still standing as an index to the buried splendours.

We returned to Cairo covered with dust. In the evening we attended quite a good performance of the Italian Opera, in an imposing and tasteful theatre, built in six months by the Viceroy.

Cairo, December 6, 1869.

We began to-day at three in the morning, because we wanted to ascend the oldest and largest of the Pyramids of Gîzeh.

The imagination can form no adequate picture of this stone edifice, which the Kings built for themselves as their burying-place, and one asks once again in astonishment, how the Egyptians managed, in their total ignorance of machinery, to execute such structures. Beautiful I cannot indeed call the Pyramids when one gets near them, because on close consideration the devastation strikes one more than the total effect of the still-existing intact structure. In the landscape, on the contrary, the Pyramids look very picturesque, especially when their summits are illuminated by the morning or evening sun.

The ascent of the Pyramids belongs to those things that one undertakes for the sake of saying one has done them, but which otherwise makes no claim to utility or pleasure. A couple of Arabs place themselves in front of each stranger, and draw him step-wise from stone to stone, for the external covering of the Pyramids resembles a staircase built of irregular disintegrated square stones, each step being often three to four feet high. One's knees gradually refuse to work, one's breath goes, and at last one arrives, shaking in one's whole body, at the summit. Thence a wide view is, of course, obtained. The ill-fortune was, however, in store for us, that just to-day the sun quite exceptionally did not rise, and the morning illumination therefore was also wanting.

The descent presented almost as many disagreeables as the ascent, with dizziness added on to them. To complete my enjoyment, I went inside the pyramid with Lepsius. This expedition is quite indescribable, as any mine would be easier to crawl through than these holes. Every conceivable position and flexion of the human body was employed to get forward, in addition to which one had to take two or three men who help by pushing, dragging, or carrying the visitor forward. We went uphill and downhill; sometimes we slid, or had to crawl on all-fours. At length we reached the burial-chamber with the stone sarcophagus, inspected the granite blocks of the greatest regularity masons can achieve, and sweated like a Turkish bath. It was so hot, that we had to take off our coats, and were dripping.

The Pyramids are surrounded with remains of tombs and temples, that were for the most part discovered by Lepsius; and since his name is universally known here, and to the mind of the inhabitants is inseparable from all the Egyptian discoveries, they showed him to-day the tomb of Professor Lepsius, vastly to his own and our delight !

The Khedive has built a pavilion, roads, viaducts, and dams, to facilitate the expedition for strangers, and the approach through the moist surroundings of the Nile—a grotesque object in contrast with the structure of the Pyramids built three thousand years ago.

We went to the Museum instituted by Mariette at Bûlak, and admired its unique treasures. Certain statuettes and gold objects in the Museum convinced me that the Egyptians had a real and even exalted notion of art.

We then visited the latest creation of Ismaïl Pasha, the Palace of Gezîreh, which is built throughout in Moorish style.

To pluck Mandarin oranges from the trees, and eat them in the open air, and that in the beginning of December, was a most agreeable and unwonted treat for us Northerners.

Cairo, December 7, 1869.

Our stay in Cairo was brought to a close by a ball at the palace Kasr-en-Nîl, preceded by a dinner in Gezîreh. Madame Ferdinand de Lesseps, a nineteen-year-old Creole, who in youthful enthusiasm had married the sixty-five-year-old Creator of the Canal immediately after the conclusion of the Inauguration Ceremonies, was the chief guest of the evening.

On the morning of December 8, the Khedive and his *suite*, as well as our countrymen, escorted us to the station, while the Heir to the Throne went on with me to Alexandria.

Rain and wind, a rare event in this country, set in during the four hours' railway journey, and gave Alexandria a very gloomy aspect. This great trading centre has almost entirely laid aside its Oriental character: on that account, however, the view from the vice-regal Summer Palace of the great harbour lying at its feet is quite unusual, and was so much the more beautiful to-day on account of the regular forest of masts with which its space was filled. Otherwise the sights are hardly worth the attention of the traveller who brings his stay in Africa to an end here. We went through the streets and squares, the pavement of which deserves the name only in parts inhabited by the Europeans. Otherwise one has to struggle step by step through slime and puddles.

A visit to the German Evangelical Church, and the hospital which is now building, ended with a drive to Ramleh, to the country estate of our Consul Theremin, where the German inhabitants of Alexandria, who had all decorated and illuminated their houses, gave me a torchlight procession.

Late in the evening we went on board the *Elizabeth*, and parted from the Heir Apparent, as well as from the Egyptian escort.

On the morning of December 9 we weighed anchor in a strong north wind, which, more particularly as we passed by Crete and the entrance to the Adriatic Sea, rose gradually until early on the 12th. When we came in sight of the coast, it was impossible to say whether we were off Calabria or Sicily. The restless element assumed such an unfavourable character, that we were forced to turn and steer again for the high seas, to avoid the danger of being cast on the cliffs; and so we prepared ourselves for the cheering thought that we might, under these circumstances, be cruising for days on the ocean.

However, since our calculation of time had been based upon an uncertain voyage, the threatened delay did not much matter, and we resigned ourselves to our fate.

The rain, which came down in torrents, and the heavy rolling of the ship, made our stay on board really most uncomfortable, because we did not know at last where we were going.

All the same, both now and through the journey, I remained proof against sea-sickness.

By good luck the wind " veered " several times in the course of the day, so that even during the night the sky cleared, and early on the 13th the sun was struggling with the clouds, until at last we had light enough to reckon our longitude and latitude with the help of the measuring instruments. We had hardly done this, when the sun broke quite through, and brilliantly justified the calculations of our officers. We found ourselves in sight of Cape Spartivento, and were able quietly to enter the Straits of Messina.

The snow-covered Etna projected far into the blue heaven, and at its feet lay the charming outline of the Sicilian coast, recalling happy memories of previous journeys. The aspect of the Calabrian coast was equally attractive, and my companions were entranced by it, as to nearly all of them it was the first glimpse of Italy.

We made without halting for Naples, which lay before us on the morning of December 14 in all its unique splendour, and I felt an indescribable satisfaction in seeing it again. Yes, I am not afraid of saying that I would compare this view with any of the impressions that I received in the East.

The Crown Prince and Princess, who are staying here, and have just celebrated their first parental joys, received me as an old friend, and I saw the Heir to the Throne, the Duca di Napoli, who was born here, and is only a few weeks old, and also the Duke and Duchess of Aosta. I employed my spare time in revisiting Sorrento and Pompeii, as well as the rich treasures of the Museo Reale. Since 1862, when I was last here, the town has acquired quite a different and flourishing aspect.

My pleasure in staying in this splendid Naples was disturbed by the news from Cannes, where my wife and all the children were staying, that our youngest son Waldemar had an attack of bronchitis. He was, indeed, so much better as to be out of danger, but the journey from Cannes so as to arrive in Berlin for Christmas was not to be thought of. I accordingly decided to proceed to Cannes by the comfortable Rome-Florence railway, so as to take ship at La Spezzia, since there was as yet no direct communication along the coast, and then to steam on the *Elizabeth* to Villafranca, whence there is only an hour to Cannes.

We reached Florence in twenty-four hours, after I had greeted the Abruzzi and the Campagna as old acquaintances; I passed through Rome, however (where the Œcumenical Council had just begun its sittings), late in the evening, and without stopping.

In Florence, which I had last seen in its spring vesture, on the occasion of the Crown Prince Umberto's wedding, I visited King Victor Emanuel,—who, just recovered from a long dangerous illness, received me with open arms.

On the 19th we went by Bologna, where I parted from my entire retinue, and travelled to

La Spezzia. After a very rocking, but pleasant night voyage, when I dined with the officers in their mess, we landed on the morning of the 20th at Villafranca. Another short halt at Monaco and Nice, and then I finally arrived at Cannes, where, thank God, I still found my dear ones. The circle had meantime been increased by my Sister-in-law Alice, my Cousin Albrecht, and my Uncle and Aunt Frederick of the Netherlands, with Cousin Marie.

A cheery Christmas gathering united all this unusually large group of near relations under the Christmas tree, in a foreign land. We then paid a farewell visit to the *Elizabeth*, where we were greeted by the American Admiral Radford, who was lying with two war-ships in the harbour of Villafranca, and who invited us on board the *John Franklin*, which had just been dressed for a ball. All the Americans of Nice and the neighbourhood were collected there, and so finally we had also been upon the territory of the United States.

On the 26th we went, in a three days' journey, by Avignon and Dijon to Paris. On this journey I felt the moment when we turned our backs to the sea at Marseilles, to be bitingly cold.

The Emperor Napoleon and the Empress

Eugénie received us on the 29th with their wonted friendliness, amid a ministerial crisis, which had resulted on this very day in the nomination of M. Emile Ollivier.

After a last halt in Cologne, we arrived safely at Berlin on New Year's Eve.

III

On the outbreak of the war with France, in 1870–71, three armies were mobilized on the German side; the Third, under the command of the Crown Prince, consisting of—

The V. Prussian Corps, under Lieut.-General v. Kirschbach.

The XI. Prussian Corps, under Lieut.-General v. Bose.

The I. Bavarian Corps, under General of Infantry von der Tann.

The II. Bavarian Corps, under General of Infantry v. Hartmann.

The Würtemberg Field Division, under Lieut.-General v. Obernitz.

The Baden Field Division, under Lieut.-General v. Beyer.

The 4th Cavalry Division, under Commander-General of Cavalry Prince Albrecht (father) of Prussia.

The army comprised 128 battalions, 102 squadrons, and 80 batteries (128,000 infantry men, 15,300 horses, 480 guns).

The Personal Adjutants of the Crown Prince were Major von Mischke, attached General Staff of the Army, Captain Count z. Eulènburg, Reserve of 1st Foot Guards, and Captain Baron von Schleinitz, attached 2nd Regiment · of the 8th (Silesian) Dragoons.

Chief of the General Staff: Lieut.-General v. Blumenthal.

Quartermaster-in-Chief: Colonel von Gottberg.

Commander of Artillery: Lieut.-General Herkt, Inspector of the 3rd Artillery Inspection.

Commander of Engineers and Pioneers: Major-General Schulz, Inspector of the 2nd Engineer Inspection.

The army of the Crown Prince united the most dissimilar parts of the Fatherland. The V. and XI. Army Corps contained the Regiments from Lower Silesia and Posen, Westphalia, Electoral Hesse, Nassau, Thuringia, Waldeck, and the city of Frankfurt-on-Main. To these were added Bavarians, Würtembergers, and Badensers. The VI. Army Corps brought the Upper Silesians a few days after the opening of hostilities, and later on the Pomeranians of the II. Army Corps joined the Third Army as well. More than twelve German dialects were spoken in this army.

Owing to the intimate contact between the North and South German people (*Volkselemente*) which arose out of this juxtaposition, it was more peculiarly in the III. Army that the political reflections on this national war found their most lively expression within the army. On every opportunity that presented itself of speaking on state occasions either to the troops or to the officers, the Crown Prince emphasized the high satisfaction which he felt in having been permitted to unite the South German forces under his supreme command.

DIARY OF THE CROWN PRINCE IN THE WAR WITH FRANCE (1870–71)

July 11.—Thile very grave; can hardly see his way between Ems, Varzin, and Sigmaringen, whence he has to get his instructions. The Hereditary Prince is in the Alps. The French Chargé d'Affaires, Lesourd, said to the Spanish Ambassador, in presence of the Austrian, that he should leave, since no one was there to negotiate.*

---

* On July 3, 1870, it was announced that the Spanish Ministry had resolved to elect the Hereditary Prince Leopold of Hohenzollern as their King, and that a deputation had been despatched to Germany to offer him the Spanish Crown. This measure was resented by the French

July 12.—Bismarck is coming, Gortschakow and Reuss arrive.

July 13.—Talked with Bismarck, who received the news of the renunciation of the Prince of Hohenzollern late on the 12th from Madrid, from which he concludes that peace is a certainty; he wishes to return to Varzin—appears surprised at the state of affairs in Paris. Gortschakow is also for peace, although he has just received the news that France demands guarantees for the future : these must be waited for, yet this point, too, may be settled. He admires our conduct, and that of the Hereditary Prince, and of our press, and will take care that this is recognized by the great European cabinets. In the mean time, I hear from Paris that Napoleon said to one of his former Ministers that the Spanish affairs are quite insignificant in the present crisis ; it is a struggle for supreme power between Prussia and France. Some French papers blame the action of the Government; Ollivier's organs claim the fulfilment of Article V. of the Peace

Government, and although the Prince of Hohenzollern withdrew his candidature, it was made the pretext for the rupture between France and Germany.

At this time King William was at Ems, undergoing a cure ; Count Bismarck was at Varzin ; the Prince of Hohenzollern (father of Prince Leopold) at Sigmaringen. Hence the allusions of the first paragraph.—TR.

of Prague *in re* North Schleswig, and the dissolution of the Union between the South-German States and ourselves.

July 14.—Confirmation of the war news.

July 15.—Bismarck tells me that he is going with Roon and Moltke to meet the King, as far as Brandenburg. On the way he propounded his views as to the state of our relations with France with great perspicacity, and without any of his usual favourite little jokes, so that I now saw clearly that any compliance with suggestions for peace was already impossible : in his opinion, and in that of Moltke, the strength and condition of the French army were nothing remarkable. The King was surprised at our appearance, but had, after hearing Bismarck's report during the continuation of the drive, nothing essential to say against the urgency of an imperative mobilization. At the station, Thile with Ollivier's speech ; the King decides on the mobilization of the VII. and VIII. Army Corps, since it is evident that the French will be before Mainz in twenty-four hours. I pressed the immediate mobilization of the entire army and navy, because there is no time to be lost ; this was agreed to, and I made it known publicly. The King embraced me with the deepest emotion ; we both felt what was coming; he got with me into the carriage; enthusiastic reception; I drew the King's attention to the "*Wacht am Rhein;*" at that moment every one felt the solemn significance of the words belonging to it.

July 16.—Three armies will be mobilized; I am to command the South-German, and thus have the hardest task, in fighting with these troops (who have not in the least the training of our school) such a powerful opponent as the French army will prove to be, seeing that it has long since prepared itself, and will certainly fall at once upon South Germany.

July 17 (*Sunday*).—A striking sermon from Strauss, in the Garrison Church of Potsdam; then a Council of War, the South-Germans for me, with the XI. Prussian corps. Stosch is unavailable, Blumenthal the Chief of my Staff, Gottberg Quartermaster.

July 18.—General enthusiasm: Germany rises like one man, and will restore its unity.

July 19.—I received my official recognition. Opening of the Reichstag. Drove with the King to Charlottenburg, on the anniversary of the death of Queen Luise, where we prayed for a long while, with heavy hearts, at the grave of the grandparents; on the return journey, I said to my

Father, that a war, undertaken under such conditions, could not fail to be successful. Peaceful afternoon with wife and children.

July 20.—To Moltke, who advised me not to go to the South at present; Bismarck, on the contrary, urged that I should immediately and clearly announce my impending arrival, by a personal telegraphic despatch, to the South-German princes, in order to make a good impression, and should then proceed to those Courts as quickly as possible: the King agreed, and the telegram went off.

July 21.—The Duke of Coburg has come from Fiume, and begs to be employed in a Reserve Corps, or in the Elbe-Duchies, eventually on my Staff.

July 22.—The Queen arrives; touched by the enthusiasm on the Rhine; my Staff is getting organized; the Bureau, as in 1866, in my palace: most of the German Princes are coming in to offer their services.

July 23.—Rest.

July 24.—Christening in great state, the King too much moved to hold the child; solemn function: who of us will come back again? But— we shall conquer! I expect to be appointed to a reserve position, which will principally be called on to act in the flanks of the Central Army, for I should hardly be able to execute any great undertaking.

July 25.—With my wife quietly to Sigismund's grave for the Lord's Supper; I learn that I must set out to-morrow.

July 26.—Departure; everywhere enthusiastic reception.

July 27.—By Nuremberg to Munich. King Louis seems to be heart and soul with the national cause, his rapid decision is universally applauded; unbeknown to Bray he signed the order for mobilization laid before him by Pranckh. Enthusiastic reception. To my surprise Duke Friedrich is here, and that as a just-appointed Bavarian General,—a transition stage towards approximation with us. Brings letters patent; then goes back home, to regulate the affairs on his estate. Usedom and Hohenlohe ˗have no doubts as to Austria's neutrality, in spite of Beust's ambiguities. Reception in the Theatre; *Wallenstein's Lager.* The King thinks that Schiller had many democratic tendencies, and believes that on this account the Berliners will not be willing to put up his monument. Just as I was starting, I received a letter from him; the independence of Bavaria may be admitted in the event of peace.

July 28.—Stuttgart. The King receives me officially; the Queen friendly, pale, much affected. Suckow is honestly national; Barnbühler makes himself out very patriotic; said to Napoleon at the railway-station, in 1867, Germany will become united when she is attacked; begs to send an ambassador to head-quarters; recommends Prince Wilhelm, or Spitzemberg, who might speedily be appointed Major in the Landwehrs. The Chancellor of the French Embassy only departed yesterday, as also Barnbühler's son, from Paris. Reception of the other ministers; the Burgermeister, 'a delegate of the national party; the enthusiasm at our departure almost makes me uneasy; they presented me with a bouquet in the North-German colours; what responsibilities this freeing of the German people lays upon us! It would be well to respect the little idiosyncrasies of these States, *e.g.* their envoys. Gortschakow is summoned to Petersburg; Russia will keep a strict watch on the neutrality of Austria; Italy is uncertain, has no funds. The remarkable inactivity of the French points to some error in calculation.

July 29.—Karlsruhe. Our main thought is how to prosecute the liberal development of Germany after our struggles have earned peace.

July 30.—Went off to Speyer, where the Head-

Quarters are at Pfeuffer. Bavarian bivouac, capable soldiers; in this Cathedral the first meeting of the Prince of Wales with the Princess Alexandra took place, in 1867.

July 31.—Impressive service. Moltke telegraphed to me to go south, as soon as the Würtembergers and Badensers had arrived, by the left bank, and attack, in order to prevent any building of a bridge at Lauterberg. I am not yet ready for that, but the people feel safe everywhere, now that the Prussians have come.

August 1.—Question of an arm-band, as a token of recognition; vetoed, because too easily imitated. Long tranquillizing talk with the Duke of Coburg and Morier. Freytag is there; I hope that Roggenbach is also coming. We are ready for battle, and want to be beforehand; who could have expected it? Cartwright comes from Italy; opinions there are wavering, as to whom Rome may expect the most from. I have a presentiment that this war must bring a pause in the battles and the shedding of blood, but for now my watchword is, "In God's Name, fearlessly and steadily forward!" My Head-Quarters are swelling to such an extent, that I am obliged to divide it into two *échelons*, the first of which will include all the really working members.

August 2.—Order, to my army to concentrate; the Bavarians are fairly ready.

August 3.—Farewell; last bath in the Rhine; Landau quite retrograde; probably we give battle to-morrow; to-day is to be the unveiling of the statue of Friedrich Wilhelm III.

August 4.—Weissenburg. Our men made use of every unevenness in the ground, as they do in the peace-manœuvres, and our Bavarian companions let fall expressions of admiration, as much for our soldiers as for their manner of fighting. Gate of the city shot down, and the place taken, thus winning a secure position, and the command of the railways and roads leading to Strasburg. We had in all two Divisions, the enemy one, part of which only arrived on the scene at nightfall, but had the most favourable portion of the field. Great rejoicing; the dying and heavily wounded raised themselves, by a great effort of strength, to make known their satisfaction. The colours of the King's regiment were hit through the staff; three bearers fell before Sergeant Förster reached the heights at the van of the storming-party: I was obliged to press the banner thus gloriously upborne to my lips. On the southern declivity two canvas encampments of *tentes d'abri* were taken, with undisturbed dinner and provisions;

General Douai's little dog was whimpering round his corpse; the chattering French surgeon knew nothing of the Convention of Geneva, had no Red Cross band, and only cried out, "*Procurez nous nôtre bagage.*" The Turcos are the real savages; quarters at Pfarrer Schäfer's, in Schweighofen. French soldiers said to me, "*Ah vos soldats Prussiens se battent admirablement.*"

August 5.—Marched towards France; prosperous districts, deserted, terror of the German man-eaters; the grim appearance of the battle-field gets ever more horrible,—everywhere traces of hurried withdrawal. Roggenbach comes as the Major of the Baden-Landwehrs. A telegraph book found at the railway station gives important details; shows, *i.e.*, how little prepared the French are with mobilization, formation, and commissariat, and enables one to conjecture that the French army is concentrating its main force before Metz. Intelligence of a great French bivouac behind Wörth in three Divisions, who are waiting for reinforcements; a stronger position even than Weissenburg.

August 6.—Wörth. 80,000 French; I have 100,000 men. MacMahon's tough resistance, and fight as he gradually drew off, were admirable, but he left me the field. I had the entire lead.

Blumenthal and Gottberg supported me admirably. At 3.30 I was able to announce victory to the King.

The *mitrailleuses* are incredibly destructive within the narrow limits of their range. The South-German coöperation welded the different troops together; the consequences will be of enormous importance if we set to in good earnest, and determine not to let such an opportunity pass unused. A Colonel of Cuirassiers said to me, "*Ah, Monseigneur, quel défaite, quel malheur, j'ai la honte d'être prisonnier, nous avons tout perdu.*" I replied, "*Vous avez tort de dire d'avoir tout perdu, car après vous être battu comme de braves soldats, vous n'avez pas perdu l'honneur:*" on which he said, "*Ah merci, vous me faîtes du bien en me traitant de la sorte.*" The officers expressed surprise at their swords being left them. A talk with Roggenbach afforded me a welcome distraction after all the stirring impressions of the day. Intelligence of Goeben's victory at Saarbrück.

August 7.—Rest-day. At Königgrätz the fire was not near so hot and enduring; the Zouaves shot well, the others fired too early and too high; our helmets did good service. Great bitterness is felt against MacMahon; the Emperor they call "*vieille femme.*" MacMahon's papers are captured;

the correspondents of the *Gaulois* and *Figaro*, captured on the church tower of Wörth, announce themselves as enemies of Ollivier. Starvation threatens the wounded French soldiers ; it will be another fortnight before the Commissariat is ready. During the battle, trains were constantly going to Wörth with 60 or 100 men, who were sent into action without proper leaders. More profound talks with Roggenbach. I begged him to write down the matter of them for me shortly and concisely, if possible in paragraph form. His propositions are noteworthy, even though I cannot call them quite practical—rather are they often very anomalous : this is natural, in exchanging views as to the future constitution of Germany at a time when it is still impossible to see what will be the consequences of the victories I have gained. I am of opinion that it would be impossible for us, after peace has been won, to content ourselves with the mere tracing out (*Anbahnung*) of new efforts, in the German sense ; far rather are we bound to propound to the German people something whole and tangible, and to this end one must strike the iron of the German Cabinet while it is hot. Wörth is the first victory over the French in the open field since 1815.

August 8.—March - forward on the Vosges.

French Cuirassiers have shot their officers who were leading them into the vineyards. The material of the " Cuirasse " is splendid ; an Officer of the Zouaves cannot write.

August 9.—Thoroughly German impression. The inhabitants resemble those in the Black Forest, and understand no French, which has only been taught for the last twenty years. The difference in the Confessions makes itself felt. It is very remarkable that the Catholics in Alsace have long said that there would be war this year, which, after the downfall of Germany, would turn against the Protestants ; these predictions are repeated daily in each place. Quarters with the evangelical Pastor Hann, who describes the flight ; he desires peace ; we are not to blame ; the Empress and Ollivier ought to see a battle-field. In MacMahon's carriage was an accurate map of the Vosges, along with a plan of all the connections, which stands us in good stead : in the baggage of Ducrot, the Commandant of Strasburg, were the effects of two ladies.

August 10–12.—Petersbach. The Vosges here resemble the Thüringer Wald. The inhabitants are all German, and strongly Protestant. Everywhere we saw statues of the Reformers. The disorganization of the French is great ; the fugitives say they never had to deal with such soldiers. The range of our victories carries far; our officers are modest. Freytag is amiable, liked by every one, contented with everything, a diligent observer.

August 13.—Sarrebourg. Here the German language comes abruptly to an end.

August 14.—Blamont. The people are. getting over their fright.

/*August* 15.—The peasants say they were deceived in the plébiscite.

August 17, 18.—In Nancy. Fighting round Metz, feverish excitement; the inhabitants are Orleanist.

August 20.—Meeting with the King at Pont-à-Mousson; he is deeply grieved at our losses. Council of War. Moltke quite himself, clear, determined to go to Paris. Bismarck temperate, though not at all sanguine. Our conditions are Alsace, and indemnity for the war.

August 21.—Vaucouleurs. Baudricourt's castle, ruins, the chapel a wine-cellar; the Pfarrer told us that interest in the birthplace of the Maid of Orleans was first excited by the march-through of the Germans in 1814.

August 23.—Steinmetz seems to want to play the part of York, unnecessarily. Have seen the King again, who is once more cheerful. I obtained with difficulty that the Iron Cross should be conferred on those also who are not Prussians. Shifting intelligence as to the enemy's march; Moltke intends to get him into a mouse-trap (?). Gallifet writes that abdication is unavoidable, the Republic a probability. Benedetti's project has been prejudicial to us in England; without Bismarck's encouragement, no such speech would have been permitted. The eighty-seven-year-old Madame de Boullenois sent her regards to my wife, whom she admires as an excellent mother, housewife, and hostess; the life here is that of a simple *château*.

* * * * * *

September 1.—Sedan. Count Bothmer brings the intelligence that Napoleon is in Sedan; the King asked me yesterday what we are to do with Napoleon when we have caught him? The white flag is hoisted at Sedan : Napoleon is there. Bronsart has spoken with him; he told him that he was sending General Reille. An unsuccessful cheer; it does not correspond with the magnitude of the occasion—perhaps one cannot yet tell whether it is a piece of good fortune or no. A *parlementaire* is coming; the Princes present are forming with Bismarck, Moltke, and Roon, a circle round the King; I near His Majesty. Reille appears, humbled, but not without dignity, and brings the following letter to the King : " *Monsieur mon frère.* *N'ayant pas pu mourir au milieu de mes troupes il ne me reste q'à remettre mon épée entre les mains de Votre Majesté. Je suis de Votre Majesté le bon frère Napoléon, Sedan, 1st Sept., 1870.*" After a consultation with Bismarck, Moltke, and myself, the King dictated to Hatzfeld the sketch of an answer, which was written with his own hand later on. We had some trouble in finding writing materials,—my writing-paper stamped with the Eagle from the saddle-pocket, the Grand-Duke of Weimar gave ink and pen, two straw chairs made the table, on which Gustedt laid his Hussars' pouch as a board. "*Monsieur mon frère.* *En regrettant les circonstances dans lesquelles nous nous recontrons, j'accepte l'épée de Votre Majesté et je prie de bien vouloir nommer un de Ses officiers, muni de pleins pouvoirs pour traite des conditions de la capitulation de l'armée, qui s'est si bravement battue sous Vos ordres. De mon côté j'ai désigne le général de Moltke à cet effet. Je suis de Votre Majesté le bon frère Guillaume. Devant Sedan, 1st September,* 1870.*" Meantime I talked to Reille, an amiable man, distinguished in the best sense; he was attached to me in 1867, my sympathy did him good;—the Prince Imperial is not there. When he had departed, the King and I fell on each other's necks, the recollection of July 3 was upon us : extraordinary enthusiasm of the troops. " *Nun danket alle Gott* " (" Now thank we all our God "); I could not restrain my tears.

September 2.—The words, " The world's history is the world's judgment," came back to me from my childhood's lessons. Wimpffen's difficulties (*sic*) —— ; Napoleon is coming; is waiting in the potato-field not far from Donchery : Bismarck and Moltke hasten to him; he requests more favourable terms of capitulation and withdrawal of the army to Belgium ; wishes to speak with the King. Moltke believes this to be a pretext ; he no longer feels himself safe in Sedan, and is concerned about his carriages and *fourgons*. Moltke seeks for more suitable quarters, while Bismarck converses with Napoleon. The King keeps to unconditional surrender of arms, the officers will be free on *parole ;* the Capitulation will be signed at 12 noon. Moltke receives the Iron Cross of the First Class ; Bismarck arrives ; while smoking, they talked over everything, except politics. I proposed Wilhelmshöhe as a residence for Napoleon ; advised against the meeting on the heights, in presence of the troops, as humiliating ; suggested that the King should ride to Bellevue to the Emperor. Conference with Bismarck, Roon, and Moltke ; through the

Bavarian bivouac to Bellevue, where we found the Imperial carriage and *fourgons*, the lackey, and postillions powdered *à la Longjumeau*. We were received by General Castelnau; Napoleon appeared in full uniform at the entrance of the glass pavilion, and led the King within. I closed the doors, and remained standing in front of them; the French *suite* retired into the garden. Reille, Achille Murat, and Davilliers kept me company. The interview, as communicated to me later on by the King, was as follows.

The King began that, inasmuch as the fortune of the war had turned against the Emperor, and obliged him to give up his sword, he had come to ask what were his present views? Napoleon referred his future solely to His Majesty. The latter replied that it was with genuine sympathy that he saw his opponent in such a case, the more so as he knew that it had not been easy for the Emperor to decide upon the war. This utterance did Napoleon obvious good, and he protested warmly that he had only bowed to public opinion in deciding upon the war, to which the King replied, "That public opinion should have taken this turn, must be laid to the score of those whom you called to be your advisers." Passing to the immediate object of the visit, the King asked if Napoleon had now any propositions to make, which the Emperor negatived, with the remark that, as a prisoner, he had no influence on the Government. To the further question where then was their Government, he replied, "In Paris." The King then turned the conversation to the immediate personal position of the Emperor, and offered him Wilhelmshöhe as a residence, which he at once accepted; he seemed more particularly gratified when His Majesty remarked that he would for security give him a guard of honour over the border. When in the further course of the conversation, Napoleon expressed the conjecture that he had been opposed by the Army of Frederick Charles, the King informed him that it had been I and the Crown Prince of Saxony. To his question, "Where then was Prince Frederick Charles?" the King replied with emphasis, "With seven Army Corps before Metz." The Emperor stepped back with every sign of distressed surprise; a painful twitch crossed his face, for it was now clear to him for the first time that he had not got the entire German army against himself. The King praised the valour of the French army, which Napoleon willingly conceded, but he remarked that they were lacking in the discipline which so greatly distinguished our army. The Prussian artillery are the finest in the world, and his troops were unable to withstand our fire. The interview must have lasted a good quarter of an hour, when they came out again; the King's tall, fine figure looking wonderfully dignified as compared with the solid little Emperor. When the latter became aware of my presence, he stretched out one hand to me, while with the other he brushed away the heavy tears that coursed down his cheeks. He told me with gratitude of the words, and more particularly the magnanimous manner, with which the King had received him. I, of course, adopted the same tone, and asked if he had been able to rest in the night? to which he replied that anxiety for his people had prevented him from getting any sleep. To my regrets that the war should have taken such a desperately sanguinary course, he replied that this was unfortunately only too true, and the more terrible *" quand on n'a pas voulu la guerre ! "* He had had no news of the Empress and of his son for eight days, and begged permission to send them cypher telegrams. We took leave with *"* shake hands *"* (*sic*). Boyen and Linar accompanied him; his *suite* looked gloomy, in brand-new uniforms, beside ours, which had gone through the war with us.

September 3.—Donchéry. Bismarck came to see me. We retain Alsace, under German administration for Confederation or Empire: the Kaiser idea was hardly mentioned; I saw that Bismarck only favoured it conditionally, and took care not to press it, although I am convinced that we must come to it; the development tends that way, and no better opportunity can come than through this victory. Failly and Ducrot asked me if they might travel through Belgium: Napoleon has gone off—immediately after came a cypher-telegram for him from the Empress, which I sent after him by Seckendorf—the Belgians show much sympathy for him. My fear is that the results of the war will not correspond with the just expectations of the German people.

September 6.—Rheims. Quarters with Werlé (Cliquot), where I gave champagne as an exception, otherwise nothing of that sort is drunk under my command in the field. Cathedral and Coronation Hall spoiled by rococo style.

Apart from the desire for peace, there is a general feeling of resentment against Paris, that decides everything; the people are formally divided into French and Parisian; they wonder that we go among them without an escort.

" *Napoléon n'aurait jamais osé se hasarder ainsi* " is what one hears. My hope is in the serious nature of the people, the duty of a liberal building-up of Imperial and National life; if the right moment is missed now in the general agitation, the passions will be diverted, through inactivity, into byways. The King of Bavaria has conferred on me the Order of Max-Joseph, which is only given for victories that have been won; no one possesses it in Bavaria.

September 8.—Deep grief at Jasmund's death; many were more gifted, but few so faithful; I had counted much on him for the future. France is now our natural foe for all time, hence her debilitation is our task; the field of strategic action, hitherto so narrow, is made easier through the possession of Alsace. .

September 12 *to* 14.—Alsace-Lorraine. Imperial territory without a dynasty; indigenous Council of Administration; the question is how to separate them from the great body of the French State, and yet let them feel themselves part of a great Empire, and not condemned to rank with the Particularists (*die Kleinstaaterei mit zu machen*). Russell (the *Times* correspondent), who disappeared without a trace, travelled direct to England, even writing much in the carriage. Roggenbach advises that we use the time to advocate decentralization in France by our influence.

September 16.—Coulommiers. Order to the army to invest Paris; from Meaux to Head-Quarters. Favre announced through English mediation; Bismarck agrees; one must give him a hearing in order to know him. Bavaria, not inclined to a congress of ministers, had, in the first place, urgently demanded that Delbrück should come. Gortschakow against the cession of Alsace. Napoleon is astonished at his good treatment in Wilhelmshöhe! what did he expect from us? we honour ourselves by acting thus. Boyen says the behaviour of the public has everywhere been tactful; he admired our Landwehr-guards. The Republic is settling down, without making any talk; the Maire of Coulommiers says that Napoleon's position had already been made untenable through Ollivier. Isle de France is a splendid land; the country-folk make a pleasing impression, the people ask. quaint questions, and handle my star.

* * * * * *

September 19.—Paris invested. Versailles on the point of capitulating! then congratulates itself on being within range, on account of the mob. Sèvres begs for billets.

September 20.—In Versailles at the Préfecture. The news from Bavaria good. In considering the State apartments, where so much unhappiness for Germany has been determined on, and in which the scorn for its degeneration is pictorially represented, I foster the firm hope that the rehabilitation of Emperor and Empire may be celebrated on this very spot.

September 22.—To Ferrières. Comparable to a chest of drawers with its legs uppermost, inside a curiosity-cabinet of meaningless luxury. Favre is grateful for the treatment he has received; has left a favourable impression on our officers, but refuses our demands by letter. Impression made by Sedan and the Republic upon Austria; the Emperor of Russia sends Moltke the Order of St. George. Three years ago, I was walking with the Empress Eugénie in the Park at Versailles! Christening carriages, cradles of the Duke of Reichstadt, the Comte de Chambord, the Comte de Paris, the Prince Imperial! Solemn service in the open air—the French much impressed. Excursion to S. Cloud; picture of the arrival of Queen Victoria when the Crown Princess first came on the continent; the French eventually destroyed it themselves! On the Council table, where the decision for war had been carried, lay draughts of the Prussian army, lint in baskets, invitation cards of the Empress-Regent. The appointments are charming and luxurious.

September 28.—Strasburg has capitulated; I am writing to the King to prepare everything for the immediate restoration of the Cathedral, the Library, and so forth.

September 29.—Fifteen years ago to-day, I was betrothed at Balmoral.

September 30.—To Ferrières. Favourable news from Delbrück, to the astonishment of Bismarck. I talked to His Majesty about the Imperial Question, which is drawing near; he treats it as if it were not on the horizon: stands upon du Bois-Reymond's dictum, that Imperialism has gone to the ground, so that in future there can only be a King of Prussia, Duke of the Germans. I pointed out, on the other hand, that the three Kings obliged us to take the supremacy as Kaiser, that the thousand years' crown of Kaiser and King had nothing to do with modern Imperialism; at the end his opposition was weakened.

October 2.—Queen Victoria, who watches our actions with touching sympathy, has telegraphed to His Majesty to urge him to be magnanimous in regard to the Favre proposals of peace, although she has no practical measures to propose.

October 3.—General Burnside comes from Paris
—looks wise—speaks so candidly that Blumenthal
and I think him not to be talking without the
permission of the plenipotentiaries. They wish
for peace, but with no cession of territory. Favre,
on the contrary, told him he saw perfectly that
France, now vanquished, must acquiesce in the
loss of Alsace, but the present Government could
not take arbitrary steps in the matter, because
consent to our demands would mean their own
downfall. Therefore, the convening of a Constituent Assembly is necessary, because the desire
for peace expressed in the same, and in the name
of the people, might give support to the Government. I remarked that we have throughout
been unwilling to hinder the elections fixed for
October 2, which surprises the Americans. Removed to Les Ombrages.

October 5.—His Majesty arrives with the
colossal Head-Quarters; the mass of the waggons
is incredible, since every tinker and tailor has
his own.

October 6.—The fountains play: to the great
surprise of the public, the King goes about
casually among the crowd.

Thiers suggests bringing King Leopold to the
Throne of France, which Bismarck holds to be

still-born : it disappoints him to find no response in England; they seem unwilling there to recognize that German help will have to be sought in the future. Delbrück summoned, to explain the contradictions in his letters and telegrams. Bismarck wants to upset nothing, properly speaking; he disapproves of Jacobi's arrest, and is uneasy about its effect on the elections, but cannot persuade the King to liberate him. Vogel von Falckenstein is no politician, insists on doing everything, and declines legal assistance; the King cannot disavow him. Letter from Renan, asking me for a safe conduct, recalling our acquaintance of 1867.

October 9.—Service in the Palace Chapel.

October 10.—Preliminary arrangements of the siege. Delbrück arrives. Bavaria consents to the conditions of entrance into the North-German Confederation, only standing out for military and diplomatic points. The Ministers are not at one among themselves, and appeal to contradictory statements of the King, who discoursed with Delbrück for an hour and a half upon matters which for the most part have nothing to do with his mission; he is studying the Infallibility Question. Bismarck is much provoked with Schneider, who puts tactless and false statements into the Staats-Anzeiger. Duke Friedrich goes to v. d. Tann, believes it will come to nothing, and in Versailles finds the news of Artenay. Bismarck tells me that Chambord and Ollivier have written to His Majesty. The former would listen to the cry of his people, but with no territorial concessions. Ollivier owns to having advised war; warns us, however, against demanding concessions. The one can do nothing; the other is involved in everything, and both dare to give advice to the victor! St. Cloud in flames. Burnside comes from Paris again, deputed by the Government, who are pursuing the war without any plan, simply to keep in office. Bazaine is sending his Chief of the Staff to negotiate on a military-political footing. Bismarck would give him audience, Roon and Moltke not—disunited among themselves; upbraid each other for not having received any intelligence. Friedrich Karl is opposed, because he fears the capitulation might be definitively settled in Versailles.

The King of Würtemberg wants to treat with us directly, so as not to appear to be towed by Bavaria. Bismarck is grappling with the Kaiser Problem, tells me he made a mistake in treating the question with indifference in 1866, but did

not then think the desire among the German
people for the Imperial throne so strong as it now
appears to be, and only fears the development of
great luxury at the Court, as to which I reassured
him. The Duke of Coburg is for election by
Princes, who would take the place of the Electors.

October 14.——Stosch tells me that Boyer has
been in Versailles since yesterday evening; he
wants to negotiate for the free withdrawal of the
army of Metz, since Bazaine might attempt a
Restoration. Bismarck will make use of him, so
as to retain all means in his hand that could
possibly lead to a peaceful conclusion.

October 18.——This unique celebration of my
birthday shows me plainly the serious nature of
the task which I must accomplish in the field
of German politics, for I hope to be spared
more wars in the future, and that this may be
my last campaign. Evidently, many are looking
with confidence towards the task which will one
day, please God, rest in my hands, and I feel
a certain security for the performance of the
same, because I know that I shall prove myself
worthy of the confidence placed in me. The
present negotiations are difficult. Bismarck seems
to be putting his whole strength into the thing.
The King came to me early; he has granted my

request, and wears the First Class of the Iron Cross: at dinner he proposed my health, as the one "who has brought us all here." The Grand-Duke of Weimar asks my views about the German Question, and uses the expression, "a constitution unifying all the German States:" this must come, but in the first place Germany requires the Monarchical Head, and that indeed at the present time.—I have discovered that there has been some ill-feeling against England; that is over, but whether the predisposition for Russia and America will not fan the hatred of England once more, no one can tell.

Twesten's death is a loss that cannot be replaced; I met Bennigsen, who was summoned by Bismarck, and told me he had received a favourable impression. Bismarck is against an Upper House.

October 23.—Bray, Pranckh, and Suckow are with me; they do not say much, but are there.

October 24.—Rumours of Gortschakow's renunciation of the neutralization of the Black Sea. Bismarck tells my brother-in-law that at the end of the war he will stand out against Infallibility.

October 25.—The South-German Ministers dine with me. Mitnacht seems the most capable; he expressed himself favourably in a private audience that he requested, as does Suckow. Bray spoke with Bismarck yesterday about the Imperial Dignity (*Kaiser-Würde*); he, the latter, declared that an Upper House, in which the Kings would sit with the Counts and Lords upon a daïs, would be impossible, so that over this question alone the Kaiser and the Confederation would be at a standstill.

October 26.—Moltke's seventieth birthday. I brought him a laurel wreath; he is one with me in wishing to reduce Paris by starvation, and is against the opening of parallels.

October 27.—Metz has capitulated, but France is making every effort to relieve Paris, while Podbielski always demonstrated that it was incapable of doing so. I treat Dalwigk coldly— Hofmann in a friendly manner. Bismarck says he is not against the Upper House and Imperial Prime Minister on principle, and would not refuse his consent later on.

October 28.—In the Orangerie at Versailles. The trees might be twice as high. Napoleon III. did not like oranges, and presented a great many to the Comtesse Beauregard. But what was built in former times was for eternity, to-day it is mostly surface-show, and for appearance only.

October 29.—Telegram from Friedrich Karl, " Congratulations, *mein Herr General - Feld-*

marschall.'' An hour and a half later, I received my appointment. Its touching and affectingly beautiful words of recognition; above all, however, the sentence that my brave army must in this promotion, never before conferred on a Prince of the House, see a distinction for its own services, helped me over the feeling of grief that this peculiarly beautiful old family tradition had now been broken through. Friedrich Karl will have taken this appointment more as something expected.

Moltke has been made Count. I suggested to the Grand-Duke of Baden to come; Dalwigk appears very *coulant*, will make propositions as to the Imperial Minister and the Upper House. Roggenbach is and remains the only reasonable and dependable man among the statesmen who are present.

October 30.—Thiers arrives; meets the magnificent Guard-Landwehrs; avoids political topics until he has been in Paris. In Berlin, the laypeople from their warm rooms advocate the bombardment of Paris. To my astonishment Dalwigk unfolded to me the programme of the German Question. Prince Otto of Bavaria, who has suddenly been called to Munich by a weighty communication, came to make his adieus.

November 1.—Dalwigk had a conference with

the assembled German and Friesian Ministers, in order to win Bavaria to the idea of a German Empire with responsible Ministry and a States or Upper House; but they arrived at no result, more particularly since Bray made known that the question under consideration had already been discussed with Delbrück in Munich, but had fallen through owing to the refusal of Prussia! Bismarck, however, appealed to the South-German feeling against it. The King told Roggenbach yesterday evening that he looked upon the North-German Constitution as requiring revision and alteration, and in general expressed himself favourably in regard to the Imperial Question. Since Bismarck cannot get away, it has been proposed to convene the German Reichstag in this place; a forcible impression would be made, and if this could be combined with the Congress of Princes that I desire, the German Question would be settled at one blow.

November 2.—Report of Bismarck as to the negotiations with Thiers. The latter says that twenty-eight days are required to elect the Constituent Assembly,—the same to be a time of armistice, and *ravitaillement*, to which we ought to contribute. On Bismarck's enquiring for the reciprocal proposals, Thiers said in surprise, the prospect of arriving at a regular Government through the "*Constituante :*" on the refusal of provisions, the exclamation escaped him, "*Mais nous aurions donc alors la capitulation au milieu de l'armistice.*" When Bismarck blamed him for making use of the Turcos, he replied, "*Mais vous vous servez donc tout de même des Uhlans.*"

November 3.—Thiers makes his proposals in writing; three weeks will not suffice to get in the provisions necessary for the victualling of Paris. Reinforcements must be sent against the masses gathering on the banks of the Loire; the King, however, does not agree. Delbrück thinks one cannot compel a member of the Union, such as Bavaria, to come in at the present moment: I, however, assert that we do not know our own power, and in consequence can, in the present epoch-making moment, do whatever we earnestly desire—only in God's name, let us ask what we do want; and who does want anything in earnest now? Idea of assembling the Reichstag here given up. The Grand-Duke of Baden is coming.

November 7.—At last the reinforcements for v. d. Tann have been conceded by the King. The Grand-Duke finds the King more inclined to the German Question than he anticipated. Bismarck has told the Ministers it is the wish of the

Q

Prussian Government that the German Princes should seal the peace here with the pommels of their swords, to which idea the King of Saxony has already given his consent. The Grand-Duke of Oldenburg is coming, so we shall soon have material enough for a Congress of Princes. The Grand-Duke of Mecklenburg receives the chief command on the Loire. I would willingly have given him the Duke of Coburg, who is keenly anxious for service; the Military Cabinet, however, makes the undeniable nervous activity of the Duke of value in critical moments.

November 10.—Note to Bismarck about the attitude of our Press in regard to England. V. d. Tann's news from Coulommiers sounds unfavourable.

November 11.—Bismarck sends Abeken, who is full-bearded, to reply in answer to my note, that he regrets the tone of our Press against England, and has accordingly instructed Eulenburg; and Bernstein has also been written to in the same sense. The Grand-Duke of Baden has the impression that Bismarck is in earnest about the Imperial Question: the Grand-Duke has written a quite extraordinary letter to the King of Bavaria, which, however, remains unanswered. Würtemberg makes reservations about the Military Convention; the right to promotion in his Division is prejudicial to his own officers.

November 12.—The sentry will not admit me to the Villa Stern, as he has no order to make exceptions! The Würtemberg Ministers have suddenly departed, on the receipt of bad news, just as they were going to sign; this is an intrigue of Gasser—Suckow and Mitnacht are honest. Roon and Podbielski complain of knowing nothing. Bismarck is shocked that such Prussian Particularists should be concerned in this affair. Ledochowski is informing himself whether the Pope will be accepted in Prussia. Bismarck holds that the evacuation of Rome would be an enormous error on the part of Pio Nono, but his stay in Germany might be productive of good results, because the sight of the Roman Priesthood would cure the Germans. The King and myself are strongly against it.

November 14.—Odo Russell is coming; the Russian withdrawal is a fact. It is said that Palmerston remarked to Brunnow, on the signing of the Treaty of 1856, that it would not last ten years. General Annenkow brings a letter from the Emperor Alexander—Reuss only heard of it after it had been sent off—with the request not to telegraph until the King had received the letter. We telegraphed to postpone the step, but received the answer that it was too late—despatches had gone simultaneously to London and Vienna.

November 16.—Our representatives are to remain passive; the King is much annoyed, and tells me that this surprise is beyond a joke. In England this will certainly be taken as a reprisal for the export of arms. Bismarck, however, denies all cognizance of it.

Talk with Bismarck on the German Problem; he is willing to come to a conclusion, but points out the difficulties with a shrug of his shoulders: what, *e.g.*, are we to do against the South Germans? Do I wish that they should be threatened? I reply, " Yes, surely; there is no danger if only we maintain a firm and commanding attitude; you will see that I was right to maintain that; you are not yet fully aware of your power." Bismarck entirely refuses threats, and says that even in the most extreme measures, in last resort, we ought not to threaten, because that would be throwing these States into the arms of Austria. On taking office he had the firm intention of bringing Prussia to war with Austria, but was careful then, and in general, to avoid speaking to His

Majesty too early about it, until he saw that the psychological moment had arrived. So now we must wait for the fitting time to let the German Question develop itself. I replied that I could not view such delays with indifference, seeing that I represented the Future. It was not necessary to use force : we could quietly wait to see if Bavaria or Würtemberg ventured to attach themselves to Austria. Nothing would be easier than not merely to have the Kaiser proclaimed by the majority of the German Princes here assembled, but also to ratify some Constitution with a Supreme Head, corresponding with the just demands of the German people : this would create a pressure that the Kings would be unable to withstand. Bismarck observed that I was quite alone in this opinion; it would be more correct to reach the desired end by letting the movement come from the lap of the Reichstag. On my pointing to the dispositions of Baden, Oldenburg, Weimar, Coburg, he took refuge in the wishes of His Majesty. I replied that I knew very well that in such a matter his refusal would of itself be sufficient to make the thing impossible with His Majesty. Bismarck replied that I was reproaching him, while he knew that the blame was deserved by quite other people. In this respect we must remember the great independence of the King in political matters, in that he always looks through every weighty despatch himself, and even corrects it. He regretted that the question of the Kaiser and Supreme Head should be generally discussed, because the Bavarians and Würtembergers would thereby be offended. I remarked that Dalwigk had incited them. Bismarck thought my utterances must be prejudicial; he considers, speaking generally, that the Crown Prince ought not to express such views. · I at once protested emphatically, on the contrary, that speech should not be denied to me in this way,—rather in such questions of the future, I regarded it as a duty not to leave any one in doubt as to my views; in any case, it rested with His Majesty alone to point out to me in what matters I might express myself, and in what not—if indeed I were not thought old enough to judge of them for myself. Bismarck replied that if the Crown Prince commanded, he would act in accordance with his views. I protested against this, because I had no orders to give him, on which he explained that, for his part, he would be quite ready to make way for any one else whom I thought more fitted for the conduct of affairs than himself; till then, however, he must maintain his principles according to his best lights and individual knowledge of all the circumstances relating to the subject. Then we came to questions of detail; at the conclusion I remarked that I had perhaps been too hasty, but that no one could expect me to be indifferent at this epoch-making moment.

November 17.—Delbrück goes to Berlin for the opening of the Reichstag. In my opinion, the present disposition of the Third Army should be kept up in peace, as in this way I should remain Commander-in-Chief: I could then exert my influence, with the needful admixture of prudence and severity, only excusing myself the inspections, with parades, dinners, etc. The King is over-done; he is obliged to follow the operations and negotiations simultaneously, and the distractions of social intercourse are wanting, seeing that the daily guests are becoming highly monotonous. I am well; read and write from 6 a.m.; later on the time is cut up.

November 18.—Roggenbach thinks the situation more favourable than it appears to be. I am pleased with the *Times* article on my letter of thanks to Lindsay; would that I might succeed, according to the principles of my ever-remembered father-in-law, in forging a chain between these two countries, so closely bound up with one another.

November 19.—Odo Russell has come; his first impression of Bismarck was favourable; he is my old, respected, and beloved acquaintance of Rome in 1862. Meyer comes, to the general astonishment.

November 20.—Bavaria is veering round.

November 21.—Bismarck tells me our conversation of the 16th has decided him to set to work in earnest, and to take the negotiations in hand after Delbrück's departure; both kingdoms are now willing to come in, but he still has to play his trump-card. Roon threatens to break off the military negotiations on account of the external cognizances. Thus at the "green table" we remain for ever the same; in contrast, I am refreshed by the opinions in the Volks-Zeitung, which always hits the nail on the head.

November 23.—A moment of strained combinations. Moltke always brings the matter forward with the greatest lucidity, and even precision; has invariably considered and calculated on everything, and always hits the nail on the head; but Roon's shrugs, and Podbielski's Olympic security, often influence the King. Talked with Prankh, who has enough insight and knowledge to be able to help his own people, but for the moment cannot get beyond entrance into the Confederation. He attaches much importance to this result, but asks all the more that the rest should be left to time.

November 24.—Signed with Bavaria yesterday evening.

November 25.—Bismarck urgently advocates shelling. Blumenthal, in a Memorandum to Moltke, points out the senselessness of a bombardment that only involves the forts, which must be taken by regular approaches and assault. We ought to make good our lodgment there under the effective fire of the enemy—thence attack the strongly fortified *enceinte*—and lastly advance to the city itself. Bismarck has let it be known that if the offer of the Imperial Dignity (*Kaiser Würde*) is not made shortly from the side of the Princes, the Reichstag cannot be prevented longer than at latest the middle of next week from making the proposition. A prolonged conversation with Odo Russell again displayed the capability of this gifted diplomatist; he is satisfied with Bismarck, whom he finds very amenable. In the Roman Question, he foresees great trouble for the Savoy Dynasty in consequence of the occupation of Rome; he anticipates far-reaching democratic reforms within the Catholic Church from the successors of Pius, so that in time an active Pope might well succeed in uniting the spiritual with the temporal Sovereignty in Italy (?).   Prince Lynar is sent to Bavaria, Würtemberg, and Saxony, with an autograph letter from the King to invite the Sovereigns.   Holnstein has arrived, and is seeking lodging and stabling for the King in the Trianon.   Odo Russell tells His Majesty that it will be owing to the statesmanlike wisdom, as well as to the correct procedure of Bismarck, if we escape from the Pontifical Question without a belligerent conflict.

November 28.—In Berlin they are gone mad over the bombardment : Frau von B—— designates me as the culprit, quite correctly.   Nothing shall incline me to begin until all the ammunition has arrived; the mere firing could have commenced long ago, but would promptly have been obliged to cease for lack of ammunition.   The war-drones (*Schlachten-bummler*), who follow the course of the war without responsibility or knowledge, argue that our batteries can only be so disposed as to leave the Artizans' Quarters untouched—and *these* decide.   I offer the command to any man who talks to me in this way.

Holnstein has suddenly departed !   Bismarck

orders all members of the Reichstag who are on the field to set off to Berlin to vote.

November 30.—A draught from Bismarck for the King's letter to His Majesty *in re* the Imperial Dignity has gone to Munich. The Grand-Duke tells me they did not manage to find the right way of expressing it there, and begged it might be sent from us: the King of Bavaria has really subscribed to the letter, and Holnstein is bringing it!

December 3.—Holnstein has arrived; Prince Luitpold is to hand over the document to the King by special command. After dinner, report from Bismarck, who reads the letter aloud, the King finding it as untimely as possible, whereupon Bismarck remarks that the Imperial Problem has nothing to do with the campaign of the moment. As we left the room, Bismarck and I shook hands. With to-day's work Emperor and Empire are irrevocably established; the sixty-five years' interregnum—the Kaiser-less, terrible time—is now over, this proud title is already pledged; we owe this essentially to the Grand-Duke of Baden, who has been extraordinarily active. Roggenbach is sent to Berlin by Bismarck; I am writing a letter (*Lese-Brief*) to Simson.

December 6.—Odo Russell says Bismarck is

favourable to the alliance with England. The King much annoyed that Delbrück read the letter from the King of Bavaria to the Reichstag. Stillfried sends marvellous attempts at Imperial Coats-of-Arms, the Prussian with the crown of the Austrian House; he will not admit the crown of the German Kings, which I particularly wanted as the attribute of the German Imperial Sovereignty.

December 7.—Princess Frederick of the Netherlands dead; she was the most gifted of the three sisters. The Grand-Duke of Weimar told me that, as the King's brother-in-law, he had commanded his delegates to propose to the Council of the Confederation that Kaiser and Empire should be admitted to the League; Bismarck wished this. Great dinner at the King's in honour of the Russian Feast of St. George. Stosch on the brilliant victory at Bazoches; he speaks well of the Grand-Duke, who is considered to have talent.

December 9.—I received Delbrück's proposition of the Imperial Question; it is beyond measure weak, dull, and dry; it was deplorable—as if he had pulled the Kaiser's crown, wrapped up in old newspaper, out of his breeches' pocket: it is impossible to put any spirit into these people. It is asked if this Confederation is to be the result

of the sacrifice, a work that only befits the men,
for whom and by whom it has been undertaken.
I am quite aware of the endless worries and difficulties that to-day's sins of omission will bring
to my lot. Meantime I have ordered Commandant
v. Voigts-Rhetz tacitly to keep the Salle des
Glaces free. The Grand-Duke of Baden says that
the title of Kaiser, so apparently empty to-day,
will soon acquire its full significance.

December 10.—Russell complains of the in-
creasingly apparent isolation, of England. The
King is excited over Delbrück's procedure ; the
King of Saxony has expressed his surprise : he
is afraid of the deputation from the Reichstag,
because it looks as if the Imperial Question issued
from the Reichstag, and will not receive it until
he has the *consensus* of all the States collectively,
through the King of Bavaria.

December 12.—Pfalzburg capitulates, which
it has never done before. On the 16th the
Deputation is to arrive. The King of Bavaria
has been telegraphed to send off the document
which has long been in his hands.

December 14.—Anniversary of Prince Albert's
death. I remember how he always said to me,
we must give up the idea of playing any decisive
rôle without the co-operation of Germany.

December 15.—Moltke is expecting the capitulation of Longwy and Mezières, because the Commandant declares that he will only let himself be buried with the last stone ! His bearing and manner of expression in such moments are quite *impayable.*

December 16.—The King will not hear of receiving the Deputies, yet he is more alive to the thing ; it is unfortunate that Bismarck should just now be suffering in his foot. The Grand-Duke of Baden works as a good genius.

December 17.—I hear from Prince Karl's Court Marshal, that His Majesty is giving a dinner to-morrow to the Delegates from the Reichstag. Bismarck says the King intends to receive them before ; long talk with Simson, who is correct and logical. Count Perponcher said to Adalbert, " We want this Imperialism (*Kaiserthum*) to be not for every day, but for great Court·functions or celebrations ;" to which Adalbert replied, " If the King raised you to the rank of Prince, would you assume the title only on exceptional occasions ? " Boyen asks what our King will do, if the Prussian Landtag deny him the Imperial crown ? " *Du gleichts dem Geist dem Du begreifst* " (Thou art equal to the mind that thou conceivest).

Sunday, December 18.—Deeply moved by the

reception—dignified and good. Rogge's sermon proved to me that some weight was still attaching to the reception. Princes and Generals begged of me that they might be present, which I at once repeated to the King after church; he was much astonished, but ended by saying that if any of them really wished to be there he had no objection to make. Accordingly they all appeared, at which the King again expressed his surprise; only Luitpold was missing. At the last moment the Royal Adjutants were appointed. His Majesty took his place in the chief saloon of the centre building, the Princes of the House to the right, the reigning Princes (*Fürsten*) to the left. Simson's masterly discourse moved me to tears; no eye was dry; then came the reading of the address. The King's answer followed with some hesitation, for he no longer' reads easily without glasses; from emotion, too, he had to pause several times. Then followed the presentation of the Delegates. During the entire ceremony cannon were fired from Mont Valérien; outside there were crowds of people. The future position of the King's family is still dubious; *Kaiserliche Hoheit* (Imperial Highness) goes much against the grain with me.

December 19.—The Delegates are content;

their appearance has worked favourably. I dined with Bismarck; the officials sat dumb, the candles were stuck into the necks of bottles. Stosch is back; praises Wittich very much, as also Treskow.

December 24.—Christmas festivities. Great surprise on the part of the French at our purchases; Russell got an officer's *porte-épée* in the lottery.

December 25.—Properly speaking, it is an ironical travesty of the Angels' message, since either side appeals to God on behalf of its own as the just cause, and argues at each success that its opponents have been left in the lurch by Heaven.

December 27.—Bourbaki against Belfort. Blumenthal is happy over this indiscretion.

December 28.—Letter from the King of the Belgians, full of sympathy for the Kaiser and Empire, and full of great expectations for the latter. He sees in it the restoration of Order and Conscience of Law in Europe, and designates the duties which these involve as " truly splendid." He is zealously endeavouring to fulfil his duties as the neutral party according to agreement, but the advantages of such a position are not without serious drawbacks and difficulties. He accuses the foreign *littérateurs* of misusing the Belgian freedom of the Press against us; France complains of Belgium, because the latter permits the German wounded and provisions to pass through, while the fugitive French are forbidden to return to France, and are kept there.

December 29.—The King received a commendatory telegram of congratulation from the Köpenicker Strasse, on our having at last begun the bombardment. I drew up with the Grand-Duke of Baden a proclamation for Kaiser and Empire. The former succeeds to the German Kaiser, but is new in every respect, seeing that in 1848 the old Prussian Kingdom collapsed, to arise again constitutionally, while title and forms remained. A year ago to-day Napoleon communicated to me that Ollivier had been made Premier. Bismarck expressed himself as gratified with Leopold's letter, and begs me to point out in my answer the support that Belgium would obtain from a strong Germany, from whom she would never have anything to fear, nor, so long as Germany remained strong, need she fear France either.

December 31.—The King determines that he will allow no publicity to-morrow, because Bavaria has not yet consented. Delbrück, on the contrary, announces that the printed Constitution of the Empire will appear in Berlin this evening, and come into force at daybreak to-morrow,

R

proclaiming as actual the Kaiser and Empire. Bismarck, whom I found in bed, and whose room was like a rubbish-hole, declares that no Inauguration is possible without Bavaria's acquiescence. I then begged him to look at the historical 18th of January, which seemed to appeal to him. It is impossible for us to renounce Alsace-Lorraine, even if the conquest of the latter is precarious.

*   *   *   *   *   *

1871.

January 1.—The King greeted me seriously and with friendly emotion, with the wish that it might be granted me to enter into the pacific harvest sown by the present undertaking. He could not indeed think that the permanent unity of Germany would continue, since unfortunately a minority of the princes had not acted and thought as one could have wished, in spite of the noble example given by the Grand-Duke. I asked Delbrück how the marine, telegraph, tax, and postal departments were to be designated? "As Imperial." And the Army? "Ah, that is another matter." Whereupon I wished Delbrück joy of the resulting chaos. A masterly toast of the Grand-Duke to King William the Victorious—

in which he referred to the Empire as to-day, by the official publication of the Constitution, coming into force, although His Majesty would not assume the Crown until the members collectively gave in their adhesion. Great impression.

January 2.—A warm letter from Albrecht junior. " May this last and highest attainable step of our House be for its welfare, and may it succeed in being for the whole of Germany what it always has been and is for Brandenburg and Prussia."

January 4.—Roon forbids the distribution of the Volks-Zeitung. First day of bombardment. What will the wiseacres of Berlin say, if, after fourteen days, everything goes on as it was before ? Werder in a critical position. Nothing on account of my individual antipathy to war is to be spared me in this colossal war of the giants. My aversion to the bloody work is known everywhere ; indeed, they even say of me, as I read to my secret satisfaction, that wherever it is compatible with strict fulfilment of duty, I let mildness and leniency prevail.

January 8.—The burning questions are, treatment of invested Paris, armistice, and conditions of peace. His Majesty invites Bismarck and myself to debate over the Insignia of Kaiser and Empire. Manteuffel is coming, on his way to the Army of the South; praises the *débouché* of Albrecht, son, at St. Quentin. Bismarck consents to talk to Moltke in my quarters.

January 12.—I pointed out to the King that Schleinitz must be heard on Kaiser and Empire; he replied that he only saw in the Kaiser a reversion of the President of the Confederation, and would preferably style himself " King of Prussia, elected Emperor of Germany," in which I see a formal affront to the Princes as well as the people.

January 13.—Conversation between Bismarck and Moltke at my quarters. A lively debate; the taciturn Moltke was voluble. Schleinitz ordered here.

January 15.—Werder asks if he would not do better to give up Belfort now, because he thinks he could then defend Alsace ? Moltke read this, and said with undisturbed icy composure, " Your Majesty will of course agree that General von Werder will be answered that he has simply to stand still, and to beat the enemy wherever he finds him." Moltke seems to me admirable beyond praise; in a second he cleared up the whole situation. His reply to Trochu with respect to the Hospitals was that we would spare them, as soon as we came near enough to distinguish them. The King has finally agreed to the Proclamation on the 18th in the *Salle des Glaces*, but will have nothing to do with the preparations, not even as regards the Insignia.

January 16.—Werder's victory on the defensive; Manteuffel advances.

January 17.—In the afternoon a sitting in the King's Quarters, of Bismarck, Schleinitz, and myself, of three hours, in an over-heated house, over the title, succession to the throne, etc. In consulting over the titles, Bismarck acknowledged that in discussing the Constitution, the Bavarian Deputies would not admit the " Emperor of Germany," and that finally to please them, but without previously asking His Majesty, he had consented to the formula " German Emperor." This designation satisfied the King as little as myself, but in vain. Bismarck endeavoured to show that " Emperor *of* Germany " implied territorial rights, which we do not possess over the Empire, while " German Emperor " is the natural consequence of the *Imperator Romanus.* We had to submit, but the " of Germany " will come into use in common parlance; the address will be " Your Imperial and Royal Majesty " (*Ew. Kaiserl. und Königl. Majestät*), never the " K.K." Since we hereby recognize that we have no territorial rights over the Empire, the wearer of the crown, along with his heirs, is certainly taken in a manner exclusively from the Royal family of Prussia, and thus my plan that our united family should take the Imperial title falls to the ground. Next, long debates as to the relation of Kaiser to Kaiser, because His Majesty, against the old Prussian tradition, ranks an Emperor higher. Both Ministers contradicted this with me, and appealed to the Archives, according to which Frederick I., on the recognition of the Czar as Kaiser, expressly declared that the latter was never to have precedence of the Prussian King. Frederick William I. even demanded, on meeting the German Kaiser, that they should enter a tent with two doors simultaneously; and finally Bismarck pointed out that Frederick William IV. had only introduced the principle of subordination to the Arch-Ducal House of Austria from his own well-known personal sense of humility towards that House. The King, however, declared that since Frederick William III., on meeting Alexander I., had determined that precedence belonged to the latter as Emperor, he also would now accept the will of his royal father as authoritative for himself. As in the course of the conversation it was determined that our family should maintain its present position, the King again pronounced his desire to express its equality with the Imperial Houses. Nothing was finally settled in regard to this point, and the decision was put off till a time of peace, or to some future coronation. There was no talk of Imperial Minister. Bismarck was to be Imperial Chancellor, although the synonymous designation with Beust annoyed him so much that he exclaimed " that he was getting thereby into shocking company." The Imperial colours needed little consideration, for, as the King said, they had not to be picked out of the street, but he would only stand the cockade along with that of Prussia. He forbade the idea of an Imperial Army; the Navy, however, might be termed Imperial. We could see how hard it was for him to take leave to-morrow of the old Prussians, to whom he clung so tenaciously. When I pointed to the History of the House,— how we had risen from Burgraves to be Electoral Princes, and then Kings,—how Frederick I. had exercised a nominal royalty, and had then made it so powerful that the Imperial dignity was now to be ours,—he replied, " My son is with all his heart in the new order of things, while I care not a straw for them, and hold only by Prussia. I say that he and his successors are called to make the Empire now established into a reality."

January 18.—The duties of my wife and

myself are now doubled, but I call them thereby doubly welcome, because I fear no difficulty : and again, because I feel that I am not wanting in fresh courage to undertake the work fearlessly and persistently : and lastly, because I am convinced that it was not brought about in vain, that between the age of thirty and forty I have repeatedly been called on to make the most weighty decisions, and, looking in the face of the accompanying dangers, to carry them through in spite of the latter. The hopes, during long years, of our forefathers, the dreams of German poets, are fulfilled, and—purified from the dross of the Holy Roman Incubus—an Empire, reformed in head and limbs, stands forth under the old name, and the cognizances of a thousand years, from its sixty years' eclipse.

The good news of Werder's victory at Chenebières has an inspiriting effect upon the King ; just as Moltke had read the despatches, the music that was accompanying the sixty standards rang out. This spectacle cheered him. Counting upon this impression, I had ordered that a *détour* should be made, so that the procession had to pass by the Préfecture just at the moment of the audience. A ray of sunshine broke at this moment through the clouds. The ceremony was unique, its full significance will only be known to us in course of time; only Albrecht sen. and jun. are wanting, since they are in the field, and the Prince of Hohenzollern, who, being in bad health, could not attend the fulfilment of his dearest wishes. The order of the Court Marshal's announcement was, that "the Ceremony of the *Ordensfest* will take place," etc. As the command, "Helmets off for prayer," was forgotten, I had to give it myself aloud; the "simple prayer" consisted in a *critique* of Louis XIV., along with a historico-politico treatise on the significance of January 18; the conclusion again was better. After His Majesty had read a short address to the German Sovereigns, Bismarck stepped forward, and read in an even and business-like voice, the "Address to the German People." At the words, "Augmentor of the Empire," I heard a thrill run through the whole assembly, who had otherwise remained without a sound. The Grand-Duke of Baden now came forward with his own, natural, quiet dignity, and cried aloud, "Long live His Imperial Majesty, Kaiser Wilhelm!" I bent my knee before the Kaiser, and kissed his hand, on which he raised me, and embraced me with deep emotion. Then the Court. At dinner, His Majesty said to me that I must now be addressed as *Kaiserliche Hoheit* (Imperial Highness), although he did not yet know my title. In the evening, the Princes, collectively, were with me; the Versaillese took the thing as if the King had been made Emperor of France. The first time I was addressed as "Your Imperial Highness," I felt quite startled.

*   *   *   *   *   *

January 20.—During the family dinner I was called out; the Comte d'Hélicourt has been sent by Trochu to beg for an armistice, or at least, for a forty-eight hours' truce. As soon as I announced this to the Emperor he looked hard at me for a moment, for we both felt instinctively that such a step must be the forerunner of great things. I at once let Bismarck know how things were; we went to him to discuss the answer, which ran, that the outposts were to agree about the interments in the usual manner, the rest could only be arranged by writing.

January 22.—To-day, for the first time, prayed for the " Kaiser and King." The Kaiser has told his suite that he remains their King, now as before. Since there can be no Minister of the Empire, for which I had recommended Roggenbach, I would gladly see him employed in Alsace, where he knows about everything. We ought to put those who are not Prussians in office, but the Kaiser will not hear of it.

January 23.—In the evening I received a Cabinet Order about my title ; that is a side-issue, compared with its inner significance. I still feel myself German only, and know no distinction between Bavarian, Badenser, and whatever else the inhabitants of the thirty-three Fatherlands may call themselves, but will in no way mix myself up in their internal affairs, or rob them of their individuality. Would that all Germans might regard me and my wife as theirs, and not as North-German intruders.

In the afternoon, Favre appeared suddenly, and alighted at Bismarck's.

January 24.—Tremendous excitement. Bismarck announced, in a conference at His Majesty's, attended by Moltke, Roon, and myself, that Favre wanted to conclude an armistice, to hand over the forts and lay down arms ; he states that hunger prevails in Paris, and that *" une sédition a éclaté,"*—Trochu has retired, and is now only *Président de la défense.* Favre fears to return, and manifested a wolf's hunger at Bismarck's supper. Silence was imposed upon us, but Bismarck, coming from the Kaiser, whistled *Halali*, which was enough for Lehndorff.

January 25.—Favre is here again, eating, as Bismarck declares, dinner enough for three people all to himself, and yesterday took away some *Spickgans.*

January 26.—Conference with His Majesty in regard to an armistice till February 19; the Jura excepted; demarcation-lines of ten kilometres, Constitutional Assembly; the forts to be evacuated, with the exception of Vincennes, which is a State prison. The Germans are not to enter Paris before the conclusion of the armistice, which annoys the King; however, there is no help for it, because no one will stand surety for the safety of strangers while the Parisians are so embittered. The *enceintes* will be disarmed, the gun-carriages will be removed, the cannon will remain, as they are not transportable; the laying down of arms follows, with the exception of 12,000 men for the maintenance of order. Should the armistice expire without the conclusion of peace, everything is to be spoil of war. Favre excuses himself for having come without military escort— Trochu had sworn not to capitulate—Binoy could not come, after he had once resigned the Commando,—and Ducrot would not be accepted.

January 27.—To-day is Wilhelm's thirteenth birthday. May he become a clever, right-minded, true, and faithful man, a genuine German, who will carry out what is projected without prejudice.

Thank God, the relations between him and ourselves are simple, natural, and hearty ; and our task must be to maintain the same, so that he may always regard us as his true, best friends. The thought is really an anxious one, when one clearly sees what hopes are already centred on the head of this child, and how much responsibility we incur towards the Fatherland, in the directing of his education,—while external family matters and questions of etiquette, Court life in Berlin, and many other things, enormously increase the difficulties of it.

Favre is here again, with Beaufort d'Hautpoul, who was a little above himself, and made himself too comfortable, so that it was hard to negotiate, and Favre was much annoyed.

When the enemy's outposts on the Sèvres bridge learned the aim of Favre's journey, the officers and men immediately danced a *cancan* on the bridge with one another.

January 28.—Forckenbeck is with me.

January 30.—Visited Mont Valérien ; shocking dirt in the forts ; the guns are turned against Paris ; the French openly show us all their mines. Favre is entirely loyal. Gambetta must have put away millions in safety, as is rumoured from the Oppenheim bank circles.

February 2.—Bismarck says it seems to him nowadays as if he must also be in the service of France, because every Frenchman asks his advice.

February 6.—Rumours of presents being prepared at home for us, which I immediately deprecated. The Grand-Duke of Baden proposes that the German Princes should give the Kaiser a life-sized picture of the Imperial Proclamation. Werner was with us.

February 7.—Conditions of peace. Delbrück will listen to nothing about colonies and warships. Friedrich Karl with me; carries a riding-cane with a gold knob, and a black and silver tassel twisted round, similar to those carried by the Austrian Field-Marshals; but he does not display it before the King.

February 8.—Bismarck finds Favre temperate and subdued, but so unbusiness-like and procrastinating that the most important answers are often delayed for days, because he forgets half of them.

February 14.—Cardinal Bonnechose, Archbishop of Rouen, with me; highly cultivated, open-minded. After he had looked cautiously round, to make sure that his chaplain in the next room could not hear him, he brought up the question of the contribution, and then came to the position of the Pope. He hopes that the institution of the Empire will restore to the Pope the territory that is so essential to him, and will confine Italy to Lombardy and Venetia, and reinstate the King of Náples and the Grand-Duke of Tuscany. Russia will vouch for the former, Austria for the latter, while Germany, through her Kaiser, will know how to keep down the Revolution, and thus at the same time do a service to France, since it is otherwise certain that anarchy would ensue on the departure of our troops. To my question, how all that is to be brought about, he replied, through a Congress. Himself a convert, he spoke temperately about the Evangelicals.

February 15. — Fräulein von Oetzen sends reports from Stettin about the mismanagement of the voluntary nursing of the sick, that make one's hair stand on end.

February 16.—Russell deplores the present English politics. England could put a stop to the war by decided speaking; by her actual politics she will sink to the rank of a second-rate power. It is, however, to be hoped that, as England's Crimean ally turns away from her, she will seek compensation in Germany.—In Paris they are talking of the letting out of windows for our entry.

February 17. — With Eulenburg, Mischke,

Winterfeldt, and Hahnke to Orleans. There we saw Dupanloup before his departure for the *constituante* —a nice old gentleman, but somewhat parlous. Blois, a magnificent Castle in the Renaissance style: never did I see such wealth of carving, of fine stone-work, of clever devices of ciphers and coats of arms, as well as of artistic knots and festoons, and all this derives from the most sanguinary period of French history.

February 18.—Chambord,—bald within,—the portrait of a banished prince. Chaumont, belonging to the strong Legitimist Count Walsh, furnished entirely in style, hardly any cabinets of curios. Amboise. Chenonceau, which belongs to Madame Pelouse, *née* Wilson. In the evening to Tours, where Friedrich Karl treated me as a Field-Marshal; one of his Adjutants, that is, came towards me, as far as the third step, and remained standing there as a fixture, to which my cousin expressly called my attention, as I had of course not noticed it.

February 20.—Returned. Thiers has arrived.

February 21.—I think Metz might in any case be sacrificed. Bismarck agrees, but is afraid of being at a disadvantage, in view of the military requisitions. A Coronation would only weaken the 18th of January.

February 22.—I received Thiers; he declares that France is sighing for peace, but the Parisians lay great stress on our not entering the capital, while excesses and demonstrations seem to be feared. As regards the cession of territory, that of Alsace is hard enough, but no Frenchman will agree to the cession of Lorraine; six milliards would be impossible. He attaches most of the blame for the war to Napoleon III., expresses himself sharply as to Gambetta; the freely elected deputy is the true representative of the people. Flattering words about the name I had won in France; he acknowledged that the Kaiser was living in the Préfecture, and leaving the Castle for the wounded. He spoke with little modulation, mostly with his eyes cast down, resigned, tactful throughout, suave, without manner or phrases. When I spoke, he looked at me inquiringly with shining, clever eyes, through great sharp spectacles, clear, straight, and critically. His external aspect is that of a flourishing *rentier*.

February 23.—The task when peace is concluded will be the solution of social questions, which I must probe to the bottom. It is said that the King of Würtemberg is coming.

February 24.—To Dreux, the family burying-place of the Orléans: a strange mixture of the

s

Gothic and Greek styles, Louis Philippe, among others, as a saint on painted glass. Contradictory rumours about the negotiations, idea of taking Luxemburg instead of Metz.

February 25.—Coming to our accustomed conference, the Kaiser at once asked me what I said to the extraordinary events of yesterday's negotiations, which had lasted into the night? When I looked at him in complete bewilderment, since as usual no one had seen fit to communicate anything to me, he was incredulous. Thiers would not consent to Bismarck's proposition to hand over Luxemburg to us, whereupon the alternative of Metz or Belfort was proposed, on which Bismarck decided for Metz. Thiers discoursed a great deal, till Bismarck lost patience, and was not only testy, but talked German at him : Thiers complained of barbarity, Bismarck of the sending of an old man, with whom he could hardly quarrel. Bray, Mitnacht, and Jolly, as witnesses of the conversation, cannot sufficiently praise Bismarck's superiority. Thiers' ignorance of business has always been prejudicial to him. Our successes are enormous, as Russell says also.

February 26.—The Ratification. Where shall we find men with the right insight to set forth the truè principles, that must stand alongside of these results? The Kaiser brings the news that after negotiating the whole day, the capitulation was signed at 5 o'clock; embraced me, Moltke, and Roon. When I expressed my surprise to Bismarck that no communication had been made to me, he excused himself on the score of the lateness of the hour, and the utter exhaustion of his officials. He admitted that the great difficulty of justifying the surrender of Metz to our military had mainly determined him to hold out for this fortress.

February 27.—The King of Würtemberg came to smoke with me in the evening; most courteous to all whom I presented to him.

February 28.—I am to command the parade of 30,000 men in Longchamps, precisely where the French review, which followed on the attempt of Berezowski, took place in 1867.

March 1.—The Empress Eugénie telegraphed to the Kaiser in the name of all mothers and children, to delay the entry of the troops, even now, on account of the unavoidable bloodshed.

March 2.—Ratification fulfilled. Favre had already telegraphed, and had then come himself, but as Bismarck was still in bed, he could not be admitted, so that he could only repeat the communication in writing; upon which came the reply that the original document was required. The Emperor regretted that the Guards were not now to enter the city; but Moltke and Roon urged a strict compliance with the conditions. I went with the Grand-Duke through the deserted Bois de Boulogne; we lost ourselves, came suddenly upon the Arc de l'Étoile, and decided to go on into Paris. We went over the Champs Elysées, which were full of soldiers, along with the townspeople. The women were in mourning, but curious,—the statues in the city in mourning,—otherwise everything as it was.

March 3.—Bleichröder on the unbusiness-like character of the French. Bismarck very short with Rothschild, who at first spoke French to him.

March 4.—To Chartres, where the Gothic style was born into the world; in particular, the treatment of many of the figures is wonderful, their peculiar stiffness blending with the archi-tectural forms. Russell took leave, greatly touched at the way His Majesty bade him farewell. His stay here was a real blessing.

March 6.—I endeavoured to win Bismarck over to Roggenbach, as Governor of Alsace, but failed signally.

March 7.—Ferrières. Even the greatest folly cannot cancel what has been gained. I question the sincerity of the liberal construction of the Empire, and believe that only a new era, which will have to reckon with me, will see this. Experiences, such as I have accumulated during the last ten years, cannot have been won in vain. In the now united nation I shall find a strong support for my ideas, more especially as I shall be the first prince who comes before his people, honestly attached to constitutional measures, without reservation. More than ever in these days I think of the proverb, "Who fixes his mind upon the whole, has long since quelled the strife in his own breast" (*Wer der Sinn auf das Ganze hält gerichtet, dem ist der Streit in der Bunt schon längst geschlichtet*). I bring no sentiments of enmity against the French, rather striving for reconciliation.

March 8.—Rest. Took the air with Stosch. Rothschild has accumulated objects of luxury without method. Bismarck is to be Prince (*Fürst*), Moltke Field-Marshal. Granville, Triquetti, and Hyacinthe will justify my character in their letters, apart from military matters, where the moment must decide. As regards moral earnestness and political conviction, these can only be the result of inward maturity and inward strife, which must be carried on daily, and for which one must be self-sufficing. And when I see that my efforts for the oppressed in Germany and her neighbours are so recognized that they produce confidence in my future, I congratulate myself.

Napoleon is quietly trying to approach us;— moderation of the conditions of peace, in return for promises of a common war against England.

March 11.—In the Kaiser's place to Rouen. Our brave Goben is coming to Amiens. The Gothic here has already borrowed much from the English style.

March 12.—Home, after a separation of nearly nine months.

IV

In September, 1883, Alfonso XII., King of Spain, during the course of a long journey, had paid a visit to the Emperor William I., at Hamburg, where he had been very cordially received, and invited to take part in the manœuvres. At his departure, the Emperor invested him as a compliment with the command of the Schleswig-Holstein Uhlan Regiment, No. 15, then in the garrison at Strasburg. These proceedings excited a passionate outburst in Paris, where the Hohenzollern candidature for the Spanish throne, in 1870, was brought up again, and led to damaging attacks on Germany and Spain from part of the Press. These even amounted to menaces against King Alfonso, and when, on the return journey to Spain, this monarch passed through Paris, deplorable insults were directed against him. The excitement in the City of the Seine was calmed down by the rumour at once circulated in the newspapers that the German Crown-Prince was planning a ceremonial return-visit to the King of Spain. It was soon, moreover, reported officially that Lieut.-General von Loë had gone to Spain to announce the visit of the Crown Prince to the Court of Madrid. This intelligence was received with great satisfaction by King Alfonso, as well as by the Spanish nation.

DIARY OF THE CROWN PRINCE IN HIS JOURNEY TO SPAIN, 1883

In September, 1883, King Alfonso XII., after energetically putting down certain military outbreaks in different garrisons of his realm, had appeared at the review of the XI. Army Corps, conducted by the " Kaiser and King " at Homburg.

While thus fulfilling his long-cherished desire to visit our Kaiser, and become acquainted with his army, he was at the same time able to exchange greetings with my wife and myself, as old acquaintances, since we had already met at Vienna in 1873.

The daily intercourse with us led to friendly relations with this amiable and highly gifted young monarch, the more so as he was well aware of my personal interest in him, as the ruler called at the age of seventeen to the throne of his oppressed fatherland, and also as the man tried in such early years by hard blows of fate.

On departing from Homburg he expressed the wish that I, with my wife and children, would—in the spring, if possible, as being the most favourable season in Spain—pay him a visit : an idea that was extremely tempting to us, and from the point of view of a return-visit from our Court also seemed to be not impracticable.

The King took his homeward journey by way of Paris, where he encountered the most vexatious reception. The national feeling of the Spaniards was thereby irritated to the last degree, while they valued so much the more highly the attentions which our Court had paid to their Monarch.

In view of such a favourable feeling towards Germany in a country hitherto pretty well unknown to us, it seemed to our Government desirable not to delay the return-visit to the Spanish King, and I was accordingly requested to betake myself to Madrid before the close of the year, as the representative of our Kaiser.

In view of the excited state of feeling in France, the voyage to Spain by the Mediterranean was preferred to the nearer journey through France, and the following squadron was appointed for the purpose :—

H.M. corvette, *Prince Adalbert* ; Commandant, Captain Mensing I.

H.M. corvette, *Sophie*; Commandant, Corvette-Captain Stubenrauch.

H.M. avisa, *Loreley* ; Commandant, Lieut.-Captain Rittmeyer.

These were placed under the command of Captain Mensing I.

My escort consisted of General of Infantry Count Blumenthal, Commanding-General of the IV. Army Corps ; Major-General Mischke, Chief of my Staff in the IV. Army Inspection ; my Court-Marshal von Normann and my three personal Adjutants — Lieut.-Colonel Sommerfeld (of the General Staff), Captain Baron von Nyvenheim (2nd Regiment of the Leib-Hussars), and Captain von Kessel (1st Regiment of Foot Guards).

During our stay in Spain my *suite* was further augmented by Lieut.-Captain Geissler (First Officer of H.M.S. *Prince Adalbert*) as Orderly Officer, and Staff-Physician Dr. Benda (H.M.S. *Sophie*), as also eventually by Lieut.-General and Adjutant-General Baron von Loë, Commander of the 5th Division, who had been sent on by His Majesty direct to Madrid, to announce my arrival officially to that Court.

I left Berlin immediately after the magnificent

celebration throughout Germany, on November 10, of Luther's 400th birthday. It was a strange coincidence that I should leave my home under these particular impressions to become acquainted with that very land, in which, more than in any other, the Inquisition had waged a war of annihilation on the work of the great Reformer!

After a twenty-four hours' journey *viâ* the S. Gothard tunnel, I reached Genoa on November 18, about midnight. Notwithstanding the late hour, I was received by the officials of the town; and a great crowd of people were also waiting for me, and greeted me so enthusiastically, that I was obliged to appear on the balcony of the Royal Palace, in which I was the guest of my friend the King of Italy.

Genoa, November 19, 1883.

The morning hours were taken up with audiences, which I had to grant to the civic authorities of Genoa in the beautiful palace of the King. Then a Russian admiral, Tschebyochtew, appeared, who had arrived with the corvette *Svetlana*, and another, in the harbour, and whose unexpected arrival at such a moment was regarded on all sides as a remarkable demonstration of political amity.

At midday I went on board the *Prince Adalbert*, with a most cordial reception from the officials, inhabitants, and the Germans who reside here. At the instant when I stepped into the boat that was waiting for me, the Sindaco announced that the landing-place would bear my name henceforward. Under such unmistakable proofs that my sympathy for the Italy which is so dear to me found recognition, I took leave of this well-known, glorious country, to enter one that was strange to me, and that from its very remoteness promised something of the fabulous,—towards which I accordingly set forth with high expectations.

Amid the thunder of Italian as well as of Russian guns, we weighed anchor, and favoured by the most splendid weather, steered our course for Valencia.

On Board H.M.S. " Prince Adalbert,"
November 20, 1883.

A most uncomfortable day! for the ill-famed Gulf of Lyons claimed its rights, inasmuch as we were overtaken by a regular south-west gale, which reached such a pitch by midday that we were hardly able to steam forward, and were driven out of our course to Valencia. The situation

was so grave that I discussed possible altera-
tions of the route with the Commandant, and
thought of the Balearic Isles, or even of the west
coast of Italy, as places of refuge. Except for
a single brief attack of sickness at starting, I
did not suffer from this malady, and spent many
hours on deck, though I was obliged to cling on
tightly. My *suite* for the most part remained
invisible, the servants collectively, as well as a
great proportion of the sailors, being sea-sick,
so that the Commandant's boy, a jolly Pomeranian,
was obliged to wait on me, while Captain Mensing
did not leave the bridge for twenty-four hours.
The *Loreley* had to be taken in tow by the *Sophie*,
which perceptibly hindered our voyage, and was
doubly unpleasant for the portion of my *suite* who
were on board of her !

On Board H.M.S. " Prince Adalbert,"
November 21, 1883.

On this day, so dear to me, my thoughts
turned to wife and children ; even wind and
weather seemed to take it under their protection,
for since yesterday evening we have gradually
come out of the region of the storm, and the sea
from hour to hour has been getting calmer.

A short service, conducted in a simple and

dignified manner by Pfarrer Hein, united officers and men upon the deck; such a service at sea inclines one always to devotion, the more when it has a significance like that of to-day. Many a cheer went up in the course of it for the Crown Princess, for in honour of her birthday the men received increased rations, which, after yesterday's exertions, were doubly deserved, and therefore the more specially welcome!

Towards evening I espied the outlines of mountains on the horizon; and thus saw Spain for the first time on my wife's birthday. We had again resumed our course to Valencia, and now had the prospect of reaching the city of the Cid by noon to-morrow.

Valencia, November, 22, 1883.

And so I am really in Spain! Some hours before the landing a squadron, consisting of four Spanish war-ships (among them two ironclads), came towards us; they gave the Royal Salute three times, and then escorted me into the roads. By good luck there was no sea on here, otherwise with big waves the landing would have been impracticable, because a ship like the *Prince Adalbert* cannot enter the very shallow harbour.

The town of Valencia, picturesquely situated

on the flat seashore, the name of which rings
pleasantly in one's ear from childhood's tales of
the heroic deeds of the Cid, was covered with
grey clouds; but the sun broke through at the
instant when the Spanish guard of honour,
General Blanco and Colonel Cap de Pon, with
the Ambassador, Count Solm, and Lieut.-General
and Adjutant-General Baron von Loë, came on
board, and we got into the boat.

I set foot in Grao, the proper harbour of
Valencia, on Spanish soil, surrounded by the
assembled and very sympathetic population; who
at once pressed so closely around me that I could
hardly take the proffered fruit and flowers, presented to me by young ladies of the town in the
national costume, while my *suite* got entirely
separated from me. From Grao to the boundary
of the town the garrison-lined the way, and I
had to wait through their march-past before I
could betake myself to the quarters of the *Capitan
General* (the Military Governor).

The breakfast provided by the King under the
direction of the Royal Court-Marshal Sepoloeda,—
then a *défilé* of the Court in the Throne-room for
all the assembled officials,—and, lastly, my appearance on the balcony, were the order before I could
visit the sights of the town.

In the Cathedral it was already very dark, so that I had to confine myself to the consideration of its magnificent structure. On the other hand, I was able to see the splendid honeycombed and gilded ceiling in the *Casa Consistorial* or *Udienza* (Court of Justice), and to admire the old pictures in the Museo, which have been taken from the Cloisters, as well as, lastly, the *Lonja*, a kind of Exchange Hall, which is supported by splendid Moorish pillars. After that the darkness prevented us from continuing our investigations, so that we had entirely to forego the famous orange-gardens of the place.

The people greeted me with striking cordiality; I often heard my name called out by groups of the lower classes, or heard them cry, "*Viva España ᐟy Alemania*," when the gracious gestures from feminine hands delighted me particularly. After a Gala-Dinner, served by the Royal Servants from the Royal Kitchen, I had to visit the magnificent Opera-House, illuminated "*al giorno*," where the really extraordinarily beautiful bevy of ladies displayed as great a wealth of jewels as of sparkling eyes. In the Court Box I was the only one who sat, while the members of the several inland offices stood behind my chair; both when I came in; and when I left, the Italian Opera,

La Forza del Destino, was interrupted by clapping of hands as a greeting to me, and by the playing of the *Marcia Real*. A supper, provided by the city, was given in the grand *foyer* of the Opera House, at which the Alcalde was my neighbour, and proposed that our conversation should be in Italian, because he was more at home with this language than with French.

Men, houses, and streets reminded me of Sicily; but unfortunately I did not see a single national costume in the streets; even the priests had exchanged the *Basilio* hat, once so characteristic of Spain, for one of more modern fashion. Only the attendants on the magistrates were still conspicuous, as they wear red damask clothes of old Spanish cut, and carry finely worked wands of office embossed in silver from the seventeenth century.

As the King wished me to arrive in Madrid by 11 o'clock on the following morning, we were obliged to make a night-journey, and thereby had unfortunately to forego the sight of the orange plantations with their plenitude of fruit; they extend for miles like a garden.

The temperature was so mild that one's cloak was superfluous, even late in the evening.

When I awoke the following morning in the railway carriage, the arid brown *Mancha* extended

T

before us, so far as the eye could reach; rarely was a tree visible. When here and there occasional villages cropped up, they consisted of inconspicuous little stone houses, dominated by a tiny church without any style. The living landscape consisted of windmills, alternately with donkeys,— whose drivers retain a little brown hat, such as ladies used to wear with us in former years, along with a dark cloak thrown over their shoulders, as a vestige of the national costume. Often during this journey I was reminded by the windmills and donkeys of Don Quixote.

At last Aranjuez brought a welcome change in the monotony of the landscape. Its long regular alleys were parallel with the railway, while of its buildings only the castle cupola was just visible from the greenery of the Park. Then the character of *La Mancha* reasserted itself, and lasted to the first houses of Madrid. On the platform the King was waiting for me in the uniform of our Uhlans, surrounded by all his ministers, a throng of Generals and high dignitaries behind him, standing at the head of an Infantry Escort.

After a cordial greeting, and the customary subsequent presentation of the *suite*, we both got into an open carriage with four horses, whose jockeys, dressed in velvet coats, were powdered, and wore three-cornered hats, set on obliquely.

Near the carriage rode Generals with unsheathed swords, as well as the Master of Horse, and an escort of the Body-Guard; the troops of the garrison lined the streets, which were filled with a mass of people, who greeted us, and also shouted, but without any loud expression of enthusiasm, as is usual in Italy. So we drove for nearly half an hour, over a part of the *Prado*, as well as over the *Puerta del Sol*, to the imposing residential castle, *El Palacio*; shortly before we reached it, our carriage stopped, and the rest of the equipages with the *suite* passed us, so that the King and I were the last, and, as such, entered the great arch of the door, while a Guard of Honour received us with "*Heil Dir.*" The magnificent staircase, reminding one of Wurzburg and Brühl, was full of Grandees, fifty in number, who here represent the nobles of the Court, since there are, properly speaking, no Court officials in Spain. The resplendent crowd, in every kind of shining uniform, moved solemnly forward; behind them and immediately in front of us went the Patriarch of India (the Archbishop), while our *suites* followed, but to the right and left of the King and myself the Halbardiers formed a mobile barrier. So we passed on into a great Hall, where the Queen-Consort, the Queen-Mother Isabella II., and the Infantas Isabella and Eulalia, sisters of the King, surrounded by fifty *dames d'honneur*, wives of the Grandees, were waiting me.

Queen Maria Christina, a slender figure, whose Austrian features may be termed lovely, advanced towards me with friendly words; then Queen Isabella came forward, and expressed her pleasure at making my acquaintance at last, adding that she was infinitely grateful for the constant attention and sympathy shown her by us, which she never could forget. After I had greeted the Infantas, the elder of whom I had previously met in Vienna, and who made extraordinarily graceful curtseys, the Queen Consort gave me her arm, and we went into the *Camera*, the room which only Grandees, and not even the Ministers, may enter, and where she presented the ladies to me singly. The King then did the same by the Grandees, and, lastly, I introduced my *suite* to the August Personages.

The Queen Consort is uncommonly amiable and natural, and gives the impression of being a talented Princess, who knows what she wants. She talks Spanish fluently. The Infanta Isabella, widow of Count Girgenti, brother of King Francis of Naples, whose intellect had already attracted me in Vienna, is a woman of much character, who was early matured by a hard destiny; her sister Eulalia has not long made her *début*; she looks wide awake, and the expression of her eyes, as well as of her mouth, reminds me of my niece, Marie Else of Meiningen.

The King conducted me to the rooms prepared for my occupation, which lie on the side exactly opposite to his own, looking on to the Guadarama Mountains, and the Plain of the Manzanar. Of the rooms, which are not large, and furnished in modern Louis XVI. taste, my working cabinet is ornamented with little pictures by Velasquez, among which the one of his own hand, holding a letter, pleased me the most. The rooms are very liveable, and extremely practical, with every conceivable comfort for daily life.

When I left them to go to luncheon, the lackey on duty clapped his hands repeatedly, as did also the keeper of the doors of the King's apartments —a custom that is always observed when any member of the Royal Family appears.

After taking our second breakfast, to which all my *suite* were invited, the King conducted me in civil dress through the streets of the city by the *Prado* to the *Retiro*, a part corresponding in some degree to Hyde Park, where the personages of society, as well as the Queen and the Infantas, drive in very elegant carriages; we also found masses of people on foot.

Soon after our return, I received the Ministry of the State, collectively, after which came a dinner, in which the surrounding company took part; even yet the day was not at an end ;—on the contrary, we spent from eight to half-past twelve at the Italian Opera *Mefistofele*, composed by Boito, in which the Signore Teodorini and Gurgano, and the Signori Masine, Nannetti, and Battistini, sang the principal parts.

Madrid, November 24, 1883.

On waking, I could hardly realize clearly at first that I was actually in Madrid; the powerful impressions of yesterday in this entirely strange new world—above all the reception at the Court, which in its degree of splendour and magnificence surpassed all I had hitherto experienced, except at my wedding—still worked upon me so strongly that I really required some time to collect myself before I went to the day's work.

I paid a short visit to the Museo, in which is the famous Picture Gallery, and found so much that was splendid and worthy of admiration, that although I confined myself to the two first rooms, I still left it, feeling quite stupefied, to betake myself to the grand Parade on the *Prado* at midday. For the 10 Raphaels, 43 Titians, 62 Rubens, 21 Van Dycks, 21 Paolo Veroneses, which are shown here along with 46 Murillos, and 62 Velasquez, represent such a wealth of master-pieces, that my eyes fairly overflowed in the delight of actually standing before the originals of the pictures so well known to one by *replicas* of every sort.

Here I learned to know Velasquez on quite a new side, in his realistic studies from the life of the people, his achievements in landscape, and also his presentments of strange human pheno-mena. I have the impression that he gave himself with greater satisfaction to the expression of his fine talents in these directions than to the execu-tion of princely portraits and pictures of State events, for in spite of all the magnificence of these works, one is conscious rather of duties fulfilled from affection to the highly ceremonious Court, than of the free soaring of his genius.

Murillo's religious, as well as his secular pictures present only Spanish types, of which it must certainly be said, in view of the store of pictures amassed here, that they are not all of equal value, and do not all exhibit the grandeur of the master equally.

Raphael's *Lo Spasimo* seems to have been painted over, for the flesh-tones are remarkably reddish brown. But so, too, the *Perla*, and also the *Madonna with the Fish*, give me the impression of having suffered by touching-up.

At the Parade I was struck by the thoroughly French character of the Spanish troops; for the cut of the uniform and the red trousers are so exactly modelled on the pattern of their neighbours that it would be impossible to distinguish them. The materials of the equipment seemed to me to be good and lasting, and I should take the horses, which are indeed long in the leg, but strong and solidly built, for a useful breed. This is true also of the mules, with which the entire artillery is harnessed.

The *défilé* of the front lasted for quite an hour and a half, and the march past no less a time, so that, including the riding to and fro, we were from 1 to 5 in the saddle. After the Infantry parade was over, there was a pause of half an hour before the other regiments came up, because it was necessary to be careful at the street-crossings. The King led the troops past with his sword drawn; the Queens, the Infantas, and the Diplomats sat upon a tribune. Innumerable crowds attended this parade in the *Prado,* nor were the numbers less of those who thronged the streets and greeted us courteously as we went by. The Spaniard is externally much less demonstrative than the Italian, but to-day it was evident that the people wanted to show their warm sympathy with the Germans by outward signs.

In the evening there was a grand gala dinner in a fine long gallery, at which I found opportunity to admire the rich ornaments of the fair sex; for these old families have preserved enormous diadems of many kinds of precious stones, as well as diamonds. Queen Isabella possesses magnificent *parures.*

The Diplomatic Body, with the Nuncio Mgre. Rampolla and the French Ambassador at their head, along with the corresponding ladies, had been invited; further, the Cardinal Archbishop of Toledo (as Primate, and also Archbishop proper of Madrid), the Patriarch of India, who is in some sort Chaplain-General to the army and Almoner, and, lastly, a great number of Grandees. The King drank the health of our Kaiser, in remembrance of his never-to-be-forgotten visit to Homburg, and referred at the same time to the friendship which united our two families, as also the two monarchies—to which I replied in a few French words. Then came a *Cercle* of an hour, in which there was no end to the presentations; but I found occasion to talk longer with the Nuncio, a cheerful, good-looking prelate, as also with the French Ambassador, Baron Desmichels. I exchanged some military views with Marshals Concha, Primo de Revera, and Novaliches.

The immensely long table at which we sat was exceedingly well arranged, and ornamented with bronze appointments, of which the centres represented marble triumphal arches and pyramids; the service was admirably organized. Upon the State staircase, which reminds me of that of Bruhl, were arm in arm the entire *personnel* of the stables, powdered, in old Spanish liveries, with red stockings, while the Court servants wore clothes of modern cut. Everything here is in the grand style, and the splendid rooms of the Palace, which is appointed in the Versailles style, are all in correspondence.

Madrid, Sunday, November 25, 1883.

I attended the evangelical service, which was held in the justice-room of the German Embassy.

Pfarrer Fliedner, who has already been seventeen years in the service of the English Bible Society in Madrid, reads the prayers here out of good nature, but quite in his own fashion, since he declares he will have nothing to say to our State liturgy!

At midday the bull-fight which the King had ordered in my honour took place before thousands of people, who greeted us enthusiastically when we entered the Royal Box of the gigantic arena.

Both Queens, the Infantas, and the ladies of the Court wore mantillas and fans, and each of them had their special manner of wearing this charming national costume, now, alas, rapidly dying out!

Seven bulls did we have to sit through! If I had not been officially obliged to stay there, I would gladly have departed at the end of the first victim, chiefly because the unlucky animals on which the Picadores were seated are regularly sacrificed on the horns of the bull, and are only carried off when the bull is slain, until which time they remain where they fell—a repulsive spectacle!

I cannot enter into further details of this national pleasure; besides, its procedure has been described often enough. Only one thing I must remark,—that my fear, as a spectator, for the endangered human lives was dissipated as the thing went on, because I became convinced of the dexterity with which each man involved knew how to extricate himself from the danger, and saw that the pursuit, as well as the fleeing for shelter, belongs to the sport; and, lastly, that the Espada proceeds with extreme caution before putting the bull to death with his sword. The main point always is, that no one is hurt.

The entrance into the arena of all who take part in the bull-fight—Picadores, Espadas, Banderillos—called the " Quadrilla," is extremely picturesque, for the men all wear the beautiful Spanish national costume, richly embroidered with gold and silver, and come in with a native carriage, proud grandeur, and self-conscious security, first holding themselves very upright and then bowing low. I must say here that the Berlin performance of the opera of *Carmen* gives a true picture of the original, and that the behaviour of the Espada in the ballet seems to be taken from life.

As a striking proof of the sympathy shown here towards us as Germans, I may cite the fact that all signs of displeasure, as expressed in whistling and noises, which are usually indispensable when any mistake occurs, were entirely absent to-day, out of consideration of my presence, although just the classes who are particularly prone to such demonstrations appeared in great force among the spectators.

This bull-fight came near being used as a demonstration by the Conservative party. For when my visit to Madrid was announced, and received with the most widely different feelings, this party wanted to get up a *Corrida,* or loyal ovation. And then in all probability there would have been obnoxious demonstrations of the Republicans and partisans of the French. The King, however, succeeded at once, with his wonted tact, in allaying the threatened discord by the announcement that he was going to give this entertainment.

After the dinner came a short pause for smoking in the King's private apartments, and I then accompanied him, the two Queens, and the Infantas, to a solemn introductory sitting of the Academy for Jurisprudence—a sort of College for Jurists. As this function was official, we betook ourselves, escorted by Halbardiers, and preceded by lights, down the Grand Staircase. The President, a former Minister of the Interior, Romero Robledo, with all his colleagues, received us in black gowns, with wide falling collars, and red barettas. While we took our places under the canopy, the lawyers in the above-described dress made a picturesque group contrasting admirably with the mass of black coats. All parties, in which Spain is so rich, were represented in the very numerous assemblage, and even Martos, known as the friend of the Republic, was present.

After the Secretary, a Republican, had read the Report, Romero Robledo made a long discourse on the measures to be taken as to the treatment of the daily press. Although, as a Conservative, he made many sharp hits at his opponents, his words were taken in good part, and even greeted with applause, till finally he addressed the King and myself, when he was interrupted by applause.

When he had finished, the King got up, and spoke in his resonant voice to the Assembly. In the first place, he alluded to the circumstances of his country, in that he had been called to the Throne so young, that it had not been granted to him, as to myself, who had been to the Hoch-Schule in Bonn, to prepare himself for duties demanded by the exercise of his vocation as the highest protector of the realm. Then, however,

he continued, he had seen whither anarchy and
want of respect for law would lead, and so he
had determined to do all that lay in his power
to save his fatherland from the return of any
such fate, so that Spain, under the blessings of
internal peace, might rejoice in a prosperous
development. And, finally, calling on all who
were present to range themselves in co-operation
at his side, he shouted the watchword, Fatherland, Justice, Order, and Freedom! These words,
spoken with decided oratorical power, with no
striving after effect, yet energetic, and often interrupted by loudly expressed agreement, kindled
such enthusiasm that he was pursued by applause
that lasted for minutes.

It was most valuable to me to witness the
manner in which my young friend exposed his
gifts thus nobly before the representatives of
science, and of the different political parties; and
to see how they were deservedly honoured,
especially as the King came forward publicly at
a moment when the internal affairs of Spain are
awaking only too well-founded anxieties. Certainly his royal predecessors were far enough
from mingling in such a manner among their
people, and I regard it as a good omen for
the future of Spain that Alfonso XII. should

possess the gifts as well as the understanding for it !

To-day, for the first time, I heard speeches in Spanish, and thought at first I should be able to follow it easily on account of its Italian assonances, but I soon became convinced of the difficulties, especially when Romero Robledo was speaking; for his pronunciation, as that of a Catalonian born, is quite different from the Castilian, which one hears here, and which the King speaks so plainly that I understood him quite well.

The Spaniard is little skilled in foreign tongues, and even if he uses French in his intercourse with strangers, it is for the most part so characteristically pronounced by most of the natives that one's ear has to become properly accustomed to it.

Among the King's household no one understands anything except Spanish, so that it is not easy to make one's self understood by them. My people accordingly have to go about with dictionaries in their hand to avoid the most embarrassing confusions.

The King invited me to-day to make a journey through Andalusia, and to Granada.

Madrid, November 26, 1883.

A rainy day allowed me to consecrate my free morning hours to the famous *Armeria,* just opposite my windows, and preserved in the last remains of the old Royal Palace.

This magnificent collection may be regarded as a chapter in the History of Arms, because historical, as well as highly artistic armour, weapons of every age, and memorials of celebrated persons, are preserved here.

To the present Director, Conde de Valencia San Juan, who looks like an Englishman, is due the credit of having, with astounding industry, arranged the arms in chronological sequence, put them once more in working order, and determined the epoch to which they belong, with all the necessary adjuncts. The spectator, therefore, not only stands before arms and armour of the most different periods, but sees how coats of steel and iron mail were worn and put together.

I convinced myself with great satisfaction that the German work takes a conspicuous place among the productions of artistic handicraft that are here collected. The illustrated catalogue compiled in the time of Philip II. is worthy of notice, because it speaks for the authenticity of the materials present.

U

Charles V. must have possessed a large quantity of armour, and even if he did not use all that is collected here, it is at least known of one suit that he really did wear it, along with its appurtenances, at the Battle of Mühlberg, the more so as Titian's celebrated life-sized portrait of him on horseback, in the Museo, represents the Emperor in this very armour.

The Queen took me to-day to her two pretty little daughters, the eldest of whom, Mercedes, Princess of the Asturias, understands German.

In the afternoon, as the rain had ceased, I went with the King to a mineralogical exhibition, in which I became acquainted with specimens from the famous manufactory of arms at Toledo, as well as with the ceramics which have been revived from the Moorish types, and also bronze guns on the system of Lieut.-Colonel Sottomajor, recently introduced into the Spanish army.

The reception of the whole Diplomatic Corps, introduced by the Chief Master of the Ceremonies, Conde Zarco del Valle, *Attaché* in 1849 to the Spanish Embassy at Berlin, claimed a good proportion of my time.

After this reception I had a long and interesting talk with our Consul, Richard Lindau, from Barcelona, who has lived in Spain for many years, and was hence able to give me much information as to the present state of affairs, which he is watching closely.

In the evening there was a great military gala-dinner, after which the King made me acquainted with the Generals and Commanders of Regiments, while a tattoo was performed, quite after our own fashion, in the Square in front of the Palace, by the military band of the garrison. All along the side of the *Armeria* the word "Welcome" shone out in gigantic letters formed of lanterns, so that persistent attentions are really being shown us in the most agreeable manner, down to the least detail.

Among the Marshals is the Conde de Cheste, who is also Captain of the Halbardiers, whose uniform he usually wears. The Marques de Novaliches once received a shot right through both cheeks, which carried off part of his tongue, so that he has difficulty in speaking.

Don Arsenio Martinez Campos had the prime share in the Restoration of the House of Bourbon in Spain, for which reason Queen Isabella calls him "my Champion," and although he had already been presented to me, took him by the hand, and brought him up specially.

Many of the officers possess high Military

Orders, but these have not been conferred on them for actual wars, but rather on account of their victorious wrestling with circumstances, or for their gallant behaviour in the struggle with the Carlists in their own country.

In addition to these Military Orders there are many other Orders of Merit in Spain, which are always worn at Court, while no one puts them elsewhere, as, for instance, at the theatre.

Madrid-Toledo, November 27, 1883.

The King to-day accompanied me with my *suite* to Toledo, from whose churches, streets, and monuments, the Moorish ascendency on the one hand, and the Christian Middle Ages on the other, seemed to speak to us. For this ancient capital of Castile once possessed the significance for Spain that Moscow had for Russia, and is in some sense a Spanish Nuremburg. The fact that Toledo is built upon most dissimilar hills gives to its situation an aspect as picturesque as it is imposing, while its very steep and narrow streets, enclosed by almost windowless houses, take the traveller back to the early centuries.

At the railway station we found a guard of honour, formed of the Institution of Cadets in this place, while its students lined the street down to the bridge over the Tagus, and men in armour were placed at its battlemented portal.

The Cardinal-Archbishop Ignacio Moreno, with all the Authorities, received us, and we went first with salvos of cannon and ringing of bells to the oldest chapel, *del Cristo de la Luz*, in which are Byzantine paintings from the epoch when it belonged to the Order of the Templars—that is, before the conquest by the Moors—as well as Saracen ornaments, along with later Christian additions, and where King Alfonso VI. heard his first mass immediately after the conquest of Toledo in 1085. A thing I have never yet met with on entering a Roman Catholic church occurred here,—the priests, namely, offered me the Holy Water on entering as well as on leaving the church.

Our next object was one of the largest of the Hospitals here, of *San Juan Battista* or *el Hospital de Afuera* (without the city), in the church of which there is a fine marble epitaph in Renaissance style to the founder, Cardinal de Tavera. This was followed by an exercise of the Cadet-corps as a variety, which for the rest was very well executed by a pupil who was quite unprepared to do it.

In the famous *Fabrica de Armas* we were shown the forging of the now historic blades, which bear the inscription : "*No me saques sin razon, no me embaines sin honor*" ("Draw me not without cause, sheathe me not without honour ").

While our numerous retinue made a *detour* on account of the steep path, the King led me into the *Capilla Cristo de la Vega*, to see a very singular but much honoured carved crucifix. Queen Christina had particularly told me about it, because the right arm of the Saviour is hanging down, and all kinds of legends are connected with this remarkable presentment.

We then went to the church built by Ferdinand and Isabella in remembrance of the conquest of Granada, *San Juan de los Reyes*, on the outer walls of which still hang the chains which were then taken off the captive Christians. This building, consecrated as a thankoffering for the struggle waged for centuries by the Christian zeal of many generations of Kings with Islam, is of a purely Spanish character, for it represents the transition from the late Gothic of this country to the Renaissance period, and is in addition filled with a wealth of shields, ciphers, and strange ornaments. Near the church are some

Gothic cloisters, which exhibit wonderfully beautiful designs, borrowed by the stonemasons from nature; above it is a little picture gallery, in which breakfast was prepared for us.

Not far from this spot are the remains of several small Mosques, one of which, *S. Maria la Blanca,* was formerly used as a Synagogue; now, however, they are all turned into churches, of which the wonderfully beautiful Saracen ornaments accord but little with the modern adjuncts of the late Christian period. In the house of a very skilled goldsmith there is a gigantic hall of Moorish origin, where the ceiling has fortunately escaped damage, as indeed in this city there are many other such vestiges of the Saracen age, which we had unfortunately no time to investigate.

The proportions of the five-aisled Cathedral in pure Gothic style are extraordinarily magnificent. The Cardinal-Archbishop received us at the main door with the assembled Chapter, among whom was a German-speaking Canon, the Queen's Confessor. He acted as our guide, although in consequence of an apoplexy, from which he has suffered for some time, he is very crippled. The interior of the Cathedral is dark, and obstructed by a high choir built in the Middle Ages. Here the Gothic gives place to Renaissance, which is very strong in chapels, choir-stalls, and altar decorations. In this as in all cathedrals, there is a *Capilla de los Reyes* that is at the same time the private chapel of the Sovereign, at the door of which we were received by specially appointed ecclesiastics, preceded by mace-bearers, who showed the Tombs of the Kings that are to be seen here.

In the next place, the *Capilla Mozarabe* is remarkable, for here the mass is still read after the Muzarabic ritual, *i.e.* that in which the Christian service was suffered during the Saracen dominion. It is difficult in a short visit like that of to-day to get an adequate conception of the splendour of the materials in marble and gilded bronze that are lavishly expended everywhere in the Cathedral. While, lastly, the revelation of the wealth of precious stones and jewels preserved in the church's treasures strikes one dumb.

After all these ecclesiastical impressions came the visit to the old Royal Seat, the *Alcazar*. On the way to it I remarked many buildings of Saracen origin, which reminded me of Cairo and Damascus, along with other palatial houses, with iron-sheathed doors, beautiful lattice-work windows, and door-knockers. Carriages could not pass one another in the oldest streets of Toledo, and the horses of to-day's breed get about with the utmost difficulty.

The vast Alcazar, in which the Spanish Sovereigns down to Charles V. and Philip held their court, lies on the finest hill, and commands the whole of Toledo. This Renaissance palace, with its splendid courts, and a vast number of rooms, many of which conserve their Saracen ornamenting, was among the favourite residences of Charles V., and it was on its really marvellous staircase that he uttered the words that he never felt himself more King of Spain than on these steps. The wars of later times have, however, damaged its brilliancy and splendour, and the removal of the Residence to Madrid also did serious detriment to the Palace, until the present King restored the neglected structure to honour. The Alcazar is now turned into a school for military cadets. The gigantic court, as well as the rooms in which Moorish, as well as Christian, Art has perpetuated itself, have fortunately been restored by skilled hands.

A cadet well versed in the German language addressed me in the name of his comrades, and expressed their pleasure at seeing us here.

The inhabitants gave uninterrupted vent to their feelings of sympathy with us, so that here again I was convinced of the rapidity with which an interest in Germany has arisen in Spain.

At our departure the King made me notice that he was greeted with the cry of " *Viva el Colonel de los Ulanos!* " ("Long live the Colonel of the Uhlans! ")

In Madrid the evening was brought to a close by a representation of Meyerbeer's *L'Africaine.*

Madrid, November 28, 1883.

This is King Alfonso's birthday, of which, however, little notice was taken in the streets, such a day not being kept here as it is with us. It was only at the hour of the second *déjeuner* that I had the opportunity of congratulating the King, as did also my *suite,*—when I presented him, by command of the Kaiser, with a small bronze copy of the Monument to the Great Elector, and with a statuette of myself as a Cuirassier, in the same material. Immediately after the meal, at which all had already appeared " in gala," the Grandees and Diplomats appeared for the Court. The former, with their ladies, who wore trains, walked past the Royal Pair, seated in *fauteuils* in the Camera, after which the doors into the Throne-room opened, and their Majesties passed in, to speak to the diplomats assembled there.

Then they ascended the throne, and seated themselves; the Infantas took their place at the side, while the Court ranged itself to the right and left of the throne; the officers and officials, who had been smoking in the adjoining rooms, until their turn came, now defiled past their Majesties, and made their bow. I did not lose the opportunity of seeing this reception from a hiding-place, and was much pleased with the charming appearance of the Queen, who, in her white and gold raiment and diamond ornaments, moved about with a natural grace, walking like the Empress of Austria. Her manner reminded me of her aunt, the Queen of the Belgians, as well as of Archduchess Rainer, and there is something particularly sympathetic in her unconstrained cheerfulness.

In the evening there was a concert in the same saloon in which we assemble before meals; at this an aunt of the King, the Infanta Christina, as well as the aristocracy, made their appearance.

The members of the Royal Family, as also the *élite* of the fair sex, took their places as they liked, without distinction of rank, so that the King sat near the Prima Donna, Sga. Teodorini, an amusing contrast to the strictly observed etiquette of the forenoon! I thus had a splendid opportunity of studying the Spanish type at close quarters; now strikingly beautiful, now piquant, it often reminds one strongly of the Italian race, and yet preserves its own individuality very distinctly. As to ornaments, the wealth of *solitaires*, as well as the enormous stones of every variety, in no-wise falls below that of the English families. It was evident that many ladies painted, and also that antiquity wears pink gowns.

I was able to talk at length with the leaders of the two chief parties in this country, Canovas and Sagasta. The former resembles a German ecclesiastic in appearance, while the other has the Saracen type of countenance.

A part of the old Spanish etiquette is still kept up at the Court. The King, who also seems to have the clearest head among them, makes this a matter of personal supervision.

The Chamberlain's Office is fulfilled daily by one of the Grandees, who appears for the whole day in an embroidered coat, with gold cross-bands; the wives of the Grandees perform the same function as ladies of the palace to the Queen. The military officials on duty appear in uniform, while the King usually wears civil dress.

Since the whole of the Reception Rooms were open and fully illuminated to-day, the saloons, which had originally been appointed in Versailles taste, but were improved by later additions, were seen in their full splendour. Queen Christina, on her arrival in the country, found herself without any furniture, and with very few seats, so she can justly pride herself on having entirely remedied this defect, and introduced the present arrangements.

The Throne-room, though beset with blunders from the " Empire Period," for the most part bears the stamp of its original combination. The ancient velvet carpets, edged with silver embroidery, are set-off by fourteen life-size Florentine bronze figures of the finest green *patina*, some of which are imitations from the antique, others again are the products of the *baroque* period. At either side of the throne are two more than life-sized statues in bronze, which represent Justice and Wisdom, while on each of the six steps reaching up to it is a pair of lions holding marble globes. Besides these the space is further filled with bronze candelabras, many of which are originals from Gutierre, busts of marble and porphyry, costly *consoles* with marble slabs, crystal crowns, and enormous clocks, while a painting by Tiepolo covers the ceiling; so that this Throne-room is unique in its way, and gives a splendid impression, whether by day or by artificial light.

Taken as a whole, the Reception Rooms are the same height as the rooms in the New Palace at Potsdam; next to that above described, the one assigned to me as an ante-room is the most costly, with its old satin hangings, decorated with colossal Italian embroideries in relief, in the *baroque* style, while a cabinet entirely inlaid with porcelain plates and bas-reliefs from the former manufactory at *Buen Retiro* belongs to the sights of Madrid. If my wife had accompanied me, this would have been her boudoir.

Since the way from my rooms to those of the King invariably takes me through these State apartments, I am able to enjoy their treasures at close quarters.

In the early morning I devoted many hours to the Museo, and went through all the rooms, so as to see the modern French and Spanish Schools, until I found myself on another floor, with the Holbeins, van Eycks, Roger van der Weydes, and a host of masterpieces of the Old German and Flemish Schools.

Later on I visited the *Academia de San Fernando*, to see Murillo's very famous pictures, *The Dream of the Roman Patrician* and *Saint Elizabeth*, which pleased me more than the examples of this Master in the Museo. The rooms are used for public purposes, and are in parts so dark that it is difficult to recognize Zurbaran's paintings, as also a little sketch by Raphael.

After I had made some official visits, and also paid my respects to the mother of the wife of our Spanish Ambassador, Count Benomar, I spent a few moments in the family circle of the English Ambassador, Sir Robert Morier, who is well known to us. In such drives as these, as also on ordinary occasions, the lackeys perform the duties of grooms when I get into the carriage; for as we only leave the Palacio at foot's pace until the great doorway has been passed, the footmen in knee-breeches attend us on both sides to the street, where they remain standing, and bow, with their hats off, till the horses begin to trot. The same thing is repeated on the return to the Palace.

Madrid, November 29, 1883.

Again I devoted the morning hours to the enjoyment of the paintings at the Museo, and endeavoured, as far as possible, to orientate myself among the 53 Teniers, 33 Tintorettos, 55 Luca Giordanos, 58 Riberas, 35 Bassanos, etc., always, however, returning to the masterpieces of the Italian and Dutch Schools, and to Velasquez.

Lastly, I glanced through the rooms in which the newer School is represented, including the creations of Goya—celebrated at the beginning ot this century—many of whose pictures are also in the Palace. The very latest Spanish School has made an extraordinary development, and promises, thanks to the Academy instituted in Rome, to do great things.

After a pianist from Hamburg had played before their Majesties, I visited the Artillery Museum and plan-room of the Engineer Corps, where the history of the development of those weapons, as well as some historical relics, are shown in models. The Infanta Isabella, who is constantly occupied in thinking of what I ought to see in Madrid among the objects that are to my taste, particularly recommended me to visit this collection.

Lastly, I went to the Church of the *Atocha*, specially venerated for its image of the Madonna, —here the official Court and State Ceremonies take place, distinguished men are buried, and trophies are put up. Structurally, the church is of little interest; the only thing remarkable is the Monument to Marshal Prim, which is entirely made of Toledo steel, inlaid with gold.

To-day's anniversary of their Spanish Majesties'

wedding enabled me to present the Queen with some porcelain vases, executed very beautifully by the Royal Manufactory at Berlin from old rococo models, — and received with evident pleasure by Queen Christina, who is a connoisseur.

In honour of the day, our Ambassador, Count Solm, gave a dinner to the King in his pretty house, which is fitted up with valuable old furniture and his own paintings, but which he now has to leave, because the building is shortly to be turned into a Cloister. The Marshals and Ministers, with the highest Dignitaries, were invited. As the Foreign Minister, Ruiz Gomez, was my neighbour, I had a good opportunity of discussing political questions with him.

After the dinner I accompanied the King to the Theatre.

Madrid, November 30, 1883.

The Spanish *entourage* thought it very singular that I should spend my morning hours in the Museo; but I employ these leisure moments in the contemplation of treasures that I shall probably never see again in my life.

Titian, Rubens, and Van Dyck in one room, on the same wall as Raphael—that in itself sounds almost overwhelming. Still, it is not in keeping with our modern requirements to hang masses of various masterpieces on both walls of an exceedingly long gallery, lighted from the top; the effect of the pictures is thereby seriously detracted from.

Since in such a wealth of masterpieces one may be permitted to have favourites, I admit that among the Raphaels here the half-length of the so-called Cardinal Bibiena pleases me more than any of the other pictures.

Further, among the Murillos, I give the preference to a blonde Virgin ascending to Heaven over any of his other pictures, because the idealistic treatment of this appeals to me more than his many realistic, however beautifully-handled, figures.

The *technique* of Velasquez, looked at closely, often resembles a canvas covered with dashes; while at the right distance his pictures are really perfection.

Titian, Paolo Veronese, Van Dyck, and Rubens, are here so wonderfully represented that I should take Madrid as the place which possesses all their best works.

A history of painting as such is not represented in the Madrid Galleries, because the collection of paintings is more casual, and originated in the pictures taken arbitrarily from the various castles, in particular from the Escorial. Since Charles V., Philip II., and Philip IV., little more has been acquired, and till forty years ago these treasures were actually relegated to the rubbish-rooms to give place to modern stuff! However the aforesaid Emperor and his successors may have thought magnificently and acted royally in their various enterprises, in the collecting of this vast number of masterpieces alone they raised to themselves an indestructible memorial.

At midday I accompanied their Majesties with the Infantas to the unveiling of the Memorial to Queen Isabella *la Catolica* (wife of Ferdinand) by the Municipality, to which we resorted " in gala," the gentlemen in uniform.

The simple ceremony was performed in the presence of the Marshals, Ministers, the Cardinal of Toledo, the Patriarch, and others, as well as of troops who lined the way, after which we partook of a *déjeuner à la fourchette* provided by the city.

The statue, which is executed with great artistic taste, represents the still-venerated Queen on horseback, between two famous contemporaries, entering Granada, and holding in her hand a gigantic cross, which she carried on that occasion, and which is still preserved.

From here the King took me to some barracks, where troops of all arms were drawn up in the court, in order to show us the equipment and handling of the troops, and then the arrangements of the barracks. It interested me to examine more closely the excellent material in cloth, leather, and metal, which had already struck me on parade, as well as the long halls, so contrary to our ideas, which are used as rooms, without giving the soldier any locked space in which he can put away his effects, as he is only allotted a knapsack, or haversack.

The sandal-like covering for the foot is quite peculiar ; it is arranged, as is the custom of the country, so that in summer the bare foot rests on a laced sole.

The mountain artillery exercised with their small-calibre guns, which can be taken to pieces for the march, and transported on mule-back ; the men manage to put them into firing order again, at the shortest notice, with commendable dexterity.

The Spanish soldier has for the most part a swarthy complexion and black hair ; his expression is not unintelligent.

We only got home after sunset, but were illuminated by the strange, so-called zodiacal light. Just after I had received a deputation of the Germans resident here, the King suddenly came in, presented me with the highest Spanish military order of San Fernando, and stayed on some time with me.

At dinner we all appeared "in gala," on account of the ball that was to follow, although it was only to begin one and a half hours later. The customary afternoon smoke with the King came off on the ground-floor, because his rooms were to be used for the Reception to-day, and, indeed, we lingered in these rooms, in which, as usual during Court Functions, any one may indulge himself in smoking to his heart's content.

At the beginning of the ball I led Queen Christina to the State Rooms, which were, indeed, the same in which we take our meals daily, and where the Concert had been given—since there is no Ball-room in the *Palacio*. The Grandee on duty clapped his hands as a signal that the Court was approaching, and after greeting the Papal Nuncio, as well as the Patriarch, the dancing began. A *Quadrille d'honneur* came first, in which I danced with the Queen; the King was my *vis-à-vis* with his mother, and General von Blumenthal danced with the Infanta Isabella, Lieut.-General Baron von Loë with the Infanta Eulalia, Major-General Mischke with Countess Dubsky, wife of the Austrian Ambassador, Court-Marshal von Normann with the Marquesa de Lalaguna.

Queen Christina and the two Infantas also requested round dances from me ; after that the King led me through all the rooms, to make me known to a number of persons. When I was subsequently left to myself, came the not less difficulty of recognizing among the eight Duquesas, twenty-eight Marquesas, and thirty-three Condesas, those who had been presented to me on the day of my arrival by the Queen ; but the magnificent family jewels, exhibited to-day in their full magnificence, afforded in themselves a welcome and convenient subject of conversation, and, indeed, thanks to the amiability of the fair sex, the talk was never at a standstill.

At the Spanish Court, on occasions of this kind, the Grandees, when not military, wear embroidered coats, the officers appear in uniform, the civilians, however, who have no uniform, in knee-breeches, as at the English Court ; on the other hand, every invited guest who happens to be a delegate must appear in black tie and trousers. Since in Spain there are a number of

Grand Crosses, as also of Orders of Knighthood, nearly every one wears distinguished orders ; this is particularly the case with the officers, for even Captains wear several stars, and Staff-Officers display ribbons of the First Class. There are stars which designate the higher ranks of civil servants, as, *e.g.*, the Grand Cross *S. Ildefonso*, given for thirty-five years of service.

The Royal Family, with some of the Diplomats and Grandees, supped seated in the castle-halls, which are hung with great Gobelin tapestries, and thereby present the appearance of a fine saloon. When I endeavoured to devote myself to the inspection of it, I was prevented, with the remark that it was "very bad;" on the other hand, the famous collection should be hung up next day, in my honour, in all the corridors, which is only done on very special occasions.

The splendid *fête* ended only towards morning.

Madrid, December 1, 1883.

To-day began late for all of us, since we required a thorough rest after the exertions of the night ; in the afternoon a "drive into the country" was arranged for our amusement, to the villa at Pardo, which, in brilliant summer sunshine, was a great success.

After that I enjoyed a walk upon the balcony beneath my windows, which affords a wide view over the valley of the Manzanares, as well as the snow-clad Guadaramas Mountains. Below, the Castle Watch, consisting of several companies of Infantry, a Division of Cavalry, and a Battery, the strength in which it is daily stationed here, was forming up. So soon as the Relief reaches the edge of the square in front of the *Palacio*, it marches up in slow time with advance and rear guard, to the sounds of the National Hymn, which melody is then played also by the Castle Watch, who, meanwhile, stand to their arms ; then about three-quarters of an hour elapse, while all stand in form with their arms, till the whole of the formalities have been fulfilled. No soldier, however, enters the upper walks or inner parts of the *Palacio*, because the ward of these devolves exclusively upon retired non-commissioned officers, who form the Halbardiers, and wear uniforms similar to those of the " Swiss Guard " at the end of the last century, with three-cornered hats and gaiters, but . without powder or pigtail. All through the day they carry tall halbards in their hand ; at the approach of darkness these are exchanged for muskets.

When I came out of my room, a great portion

of the renowned Gobelin tapestries had already been hung on both sides of the corridors, so that I could walk between these *chefs d'œuvre* of the art of weaving, which begin with the fifteenth century, the oldest having, as is known, been bought by Joan 'the Crazy,' from the annual market of Flanders.

The wealth of splendid and well-preserved Gobelin tapestries, exhibited by the thousand at the Spanish Court, is well known to be unique. It was in the first instance Charles V. who adorned his castles with a store of gold-embroidered arrases, and his example was followed by Philip II., from whose time the canopy of the Escorial is preserved here, among others—these being at first made to the order of the several Kings, although subsequently manufactories were established. In the treatment of subjects, the motives alternate between religion, history, symbolism, and mythology, or are derived from the life of the people, arabesques being intermingled. Here one sees the heroic deeds of Charles V., there the Gospels, then adventurous groups of fantastic inventions in the splendid costume of the Burgundian Court, or scenes from the antique world of Gods and Sagas, many of which were prepared from the designs of famous masters.

A whole section of such wall-coverings belonged to Count Egmont, and came with the confiscation of his goods into the hands of the Spanish Crown.

The great bare Halls of the Palacio at once assumed a hospitable aspect; for the suspended Gobelins fulfil their original function to-day in clothing the walls and giving them an air of festivity.

After the second *déjeuner* their Majesties and the Infantas, with myself, mounted a "four-in-hand" coach, the King, next whom I sat, taking the reins, while the Royal ladies sat behind us. So we went two miles out into the country, first through the pretty parts of the *Casa del Campo* and *La Florida*, later through a grove of cork trees, in which there were deer. The Queen gave me no peace till I lighted my pipe, another proof of the delightful ease with which I am treated here!

Externally the Summer Residence presents nothing striking beyond its vast proportions; the more remarkable therefore are the masses of Gobelins, from the two last centuries, with which each small space of the hundred rooms is covered. Nowhere have I hitherto seen such a wealth of tissues, so richly squandered, for there is literally no room in *El Pardo* where the walls are hung with paper. After visiting "*La Zarzuela,*" a charming summer-house, quite in the style of the *Trianon*, we got into a little carriage drawn by six Andalusian ponies, when the Infanta Isabella seated herself on the box. She drove us with great dexterity, galloping all the way over hill, stock, and stone, while she urged the ponies on faster and faster, through oak-woods, by the lonely hunting-castle of *Quinta*, back to Madrid. We went by such roads that my *suite*, who were following in the next carriage, were unable to follow, which added not a little to the cheerful humour we were all in already.

The unconstrained intercourse with Queen Christina, whose features remind me of the wife of General von Albedyll, *née* von Alten, as well as with the Infantas, the younger of whom, Eulalia, is very attractive, with a clever, half-melancholy, half-roguish expression, gave a particular charm to this country excursion.

In the evening a sort of Gala-Opera was arranged in my honour with Meyerbeer's *Huguenots*, and to-day we were received on entering with "*Heil Dir.*" This, however, did not prevent the public from disapproving of the *prima donna* who took the part of the Queen, and the latter accordingly began to weep, so that the performance threatened to be interrupted, had we not all given her fresh courage by clapping our hands. Between the acts the Ministers, as well as our highly-approved-of Ambassador, Count Solms, came to pay their respects.

When, late in the night, we came back from the Opera, the gloomy corridors of the Palacio, all hung with tapestry, presented quite a changed appearance from that of the ·previous evening. Each lonely hall seemed indeed to be peopled by all manner of gay but silent, indistinguishable forms, while in reality only the Halbardier standing at his night-post gave a sign of life, inasmuch as—so soon as I approached him—he cried to the watch, by order thirty strong, " *Arma per Sua Altessa el Principe Imperial,*" and the latter had then to stand at arms, even if I did not pass them.

And here I must mention that from the oldest times to this day, the custom for the protection of the Sovereign has been that two gentlemen of noble birth, who must be natives of the city of Espinoza, should watch the whole night through outside the King's room, in Court uniform. The King himself never sees them, or even knows them, for at such an hour he never enters the

Comera, in which these gentlemen have to stay, but the noble families of Espinoza prize this privilege so highly that many resort to that town, simply in order that their sons may come into the world there, and thus acquire the right to exercise this strange office.

Many times, on coming home at night, I purposely went past the King's apartments in order to convince myself of this marvel, and, sure enough, in the dimly lighted room I always found those two *Cáballeros* in gold-embroidered coats, holding three-cornered hats in their hand, who then inclined themselves before me. With the impression of this mediæval performance, I then had to go on through the dim Throne Room and the rest of the Reception Rooms before I could reach my own apartments.

Madrid, December 2, 1883.

As we were driving to the English Chapel, where I attended Divine Service to-day, a young man sprang on to my open carriage, clung to it, and spoke excitedly to General Blanco, who was sitting at my side. It turned out that he was a member of the "*Estudiantina*," a students' association, who had petitioned some days ago

to give a performance of their musical achievements, and who, since no answer had yet been
vouchsafed, hoped in this extraordinary fashion to
obtain the decision.

After service there was a luncheon at Sir
Robert Morier's, at the conclusion of which the
King showed me his stables and carriage-houses,
called *Las Caballerizas* and *La Real Cochera*. Here
a fair proportion of old Spanish pomp is still
displayed, notably in the harness, liveries, and
trappings for the Gala bull-fights.

Both their Majesties are extremely fond of
horses, and the animals, which are partly bred
in the country, partly imported from England,
are splendidly managed ; the stables, too, are in
admirable order. The King, as well as the Queen,
who appeared some time after, showed off their
riding-horses more particularly, after which some
fast trotters were exhibited, till I was called away
by enforced audiences.

I had, of course, to conform to the custom
here, by which distinguished Spaniards can claim
a special reception,—even when they have already
been presented, and when one has met them
before, and perhaps daily.

This time there was a deputation from the
Grandees, consisting of the heads of the first

families of the Kingdom, and further of the Field-Marshals Novaliches, Martinez Campos, Quesada, and of the Minister-President Posada Herero, the President of the Upper Court of Justice, the Marques de la Ribera (formerly Ambassador to Berlin), Don Manuel Silvela, Don Manuel Uriarte, Conde de las Almenas. And lastly appeared a deputation from the *Academia de Jurisprudenzia*, headed by their President, Romero Robledo, to incorporate me as an honorary member, upon which the customary tokens and diplomas were handed over to me.*

From the speeches of to-day and of previous days, I see very well that many far-sighted

---

* On this occasion Romero Robledo addressed the Crown Prince in the following words : " The Academicians beg Your Imperial Highness to accept an Album that we are dedicating to the Crown Princess. This Album, which contains the names of the Academicians who admire in Your Imperial Highness the love of Art and of the Sciences, has been illustrated by one of our finest artists, and requires some time longer for its completion ; we shall rejoice in the moment when we shall be able to forward it to its distinguished destination." The Crown Prince replied, "I am proud of the nomination as member of your Academy, an honour that will be prized in my Fatherland. I have had a predilection for juristic studies from the time I was a student in Bonn. You know that the legislative work of Germany is still being actively pursued. In the first place, at this moment, there is the codification of the Civil Law, a task that is much heavier with us than in Spain. Your Fatherland has been a united country from very early times; the German Empire consists of different States, which have different justice, and different legislations. The equalizing of these differences, the formulating of a legislation, based on scientific principles, is the problem that jurisprudence now has to solve in Germany, and as I hope will solve. The first task of the law-giver, however, in my eyes, is that of obtaining equal rights for all."

Spaniards, some party-leaders at their head, are disposed to study us Germans pretty closely. The martial deeds of our people, crowned by the restoration of Emperor and Empire, excite in them as much admiration as that feeling so innate in Germans, of fidelity in duty, self-sacrifice, and devotion for the good of the Fatherland. These men earnestly desire to awaken the same ideas among the Spaniards.

Last night at half-past ten the city of Madrid gave a *fête* in my honour, the announcement of which ran, "*Recepcion que en honor de S. A. J. y. R. el Principe heredero de Alemania celebra el Ayuntamiento de Madrid en su primera casa consistorial.*"

Since the Court went "in gala," we descended the Grand Staircase of the Palacio, escorted by Halbardiers, and preceded by lackeys bearing wax-tapers, and then remained a long time in the vicinity of the illuminated town hall, with the carriage, until all the gentlemen and ladies of the *suite* had passed us, and had alighted.

The Alcalde (Chief Burgomaster) received us at the foot of the stately staircase at the head of a line of firemen, while on the steps of the Alguazil powdered lackeys stood in picturesque Old-Spanish costume, none of whom might stir a finger to remove our cloaks, since this is never the duty of the servants! During my stay here, I have never found out whose business this really is, since I have always had to accept the kindness of the nearest bystander, or, at the theatre, to help myself.

The *fête* consisted only of a "rout," in which the middle-class inhabitants of the town, the diplomats, and a small number of the upper ranks of society took part. The scene of the festivities was the glazed-in court of the Ayuntamiento building, which was lit with electric light.

After we had made several turns, there was as much conversation as was possible among the many unknown guests; the *fête* closed with a supper at the buffet.

Prince Louis of Bavaria, the eldest son of Prince Luitpold, and husband of the Queen's step-sister, has arrived from Lisbon.

I have received an intimation from Berlin that my visit must not be further extended; the King, on the other hand, begs me in the most cordial manner not to leave before the entire programme arranged for my stay has been carried out, and in addition he insists upon a journey through Andalusia, before I leave Spain—all of which I communicated in reply to the message I had received.

Y

Madrid, December 3, 1883.

A day's shoot, for rabbits and red-legged partridges, under the broom-bushes and cork-trees of the *Casa del Campo*, not far from Madrid, gave us the promised enjoyment of fresh air and fine warm sunshine. Here I slew eighty-six of those fleet little four-footed animals, and sixteen "partridges," as these birds, which are double the size of our partridge, and have red beaks and claws, are called here.

Both Queens appeared at our second breakfast in the open, as also the Infantas, with the Austrian Ambassadress, Countess Dubsky. We all sat down under some very large old oaks, while a band of music entertained us with Spanish National Airs, and the most unconstrained good-humour reigned.

We returned with our bag of 1264 rabbits after sunset, but in the golden illumination of the evening glow that has been daily repeated so long as I have been here.

At the Spanish Theatre Apolo, we attended the performance of the national opera *Marina*, greeted on arriving and leaving with a *fanfare*.

Madrid, Escorial, December 4, 1883.

The King took us to-day by rail to the *Escorial*, which one must have seen in order to appreciate the past glories of Spain.

A Prince whose sole joy was in things ecclesiastical, and who at the same time, as King, was capable of great thoughts, produced with astonishing energy (in both church and monastery), a gigantic work which has for ever immortalized him, and one may say his age, with him. Every labour on that gigantic structure is thought out even to the least detail, and executed in the most polished manner from the best materials. Since, however, no colours, but only stone and metal were employed in it, the spectator feels no impressions that benefit or satisfy, much rather is the only feeling left him one of astonishment at the mighty proportions of this burial-place of the Royal House, built in honour of the Blessed Lawrence in the shape of the gridiron on which he found his martyr's death.

Inasmuch as the Escorial is consecrated to the memory of the dead, the plan of it made upon me an impression as earnest as melancholy, and I then understood why most visitors to it speak of the gloomy horror inspired in them by the work of Philip II. I found myself, however, somewhat compensated by the right royal dignity which is stamped on the magnificent pile, and this helped me to shake off the melancholy of the place.

The church forms the middle point of the monastic buildings, it is built of fine greyish-yellow squares of stone, and reminds one in the interior of the side-aisle of S. Peter's in Rome; it is full of altars, possesses carved choir-stalls, and wrought-iron ornaments of the finest work, with splendid decoration. In contradiction with the bareness of its walls are the gilded bronze groups to the right and left of the High Altar, which represent Charles V., Philip II., and their relatives. Close by lay Philip's dwelling-room, very simple, but decorated with majolica, with the seats and tables he used—which I found in no wise so repulsive as is commonly made out by strangers. Under the High Altar, that King constructed the *Panteon*, the family vault of the monarchs, a tall, octagonal chapel, completely inlaid with marble plates, upon whose walls six stone sarcophagi of precisely similar workmanship are ranged opposite to one another in niches, inscribed only with the names of those who rest there. From Charles V. onwards, all the Kings, with the consorts who had borne them heirs, found their rest in this place. The other Queens, however, with the exception of the first wife of the present King, Mercedes, who rests in a side chapel of the church itself, as well as the members of the Royal Family, collectively, were buried in side-vaults. King Alfonso has prepared a new and more dignified burial-place in the strong adjacent vaults, resembling my plans for the Berlin *Friedhofhalle* in the Cathedral, and intends to translate the bones thither.

The wide Halls of the Convent lead into the magnificently appointed rooms of the Library, which reminds one of the Vatican, and possesses a great wealth of manuscripts and books. The celebrated picture-gallery formerly collected in the Escorial was carried off to Madrid to the Museo: its monks left the cloister in consequence of the secularizing; ecclesiastics, among whom some were able to speak German, took over the superintendence of the Library, and a school for commissioners of taxes took the place of the Fathers of the Convent.

The part occasionally inhabited by the Royal Family is in sharp contrast with that above described; the walls are hung with a profusion of Gobelin tapestry; the Empire arrangement of the rooms is disturbing, though the view on to the plains indeed gives compensation. The little country house in the garden, in Louis XVI. style, is prettier, from it one sees the high mountains that form the background to the Escorial.

We concluded the day at the opera, *Mefistofele.*

Madrid, December 5, 1883.

After the morning hours had been devoted exclusively to the inspection of arrases and tapestries, under the guidance of the Marques Alcanizes (Duque di Sesto) and the Count of Valencia, the King rode with me to the *Ochesa de los Carabancheles*, the great exercising-ground of the garrison, where Brigades of Infantry, Cavalry, and Artillery, respectively exercised before us.

The troops formed up in three divisions, the first of which was made up from the 1st Battalion of the Regiments "Mallorco" and "Garellano," as well as the Jäger-Battalions "Manila" and "Puerto Rico;" these stood in the oddest way in the middle of the Pioneer Exercising-ground, so that, as we rode down the front, a wide scarped trench suddenly opened before us! This, of course, was taken incontinently by the King and myself, but the *suite* had time to select a less unpleasant way.

The second skirmish included the 4th Regiment of Field Artillery as well as the 2nd Regiment of Mountain Artillery. The third was made up from the Hussar Regiments, " Princesa " and " Pavia."

The Infantry stood to their arms in good order, went creditably through their manual exercises, and later, in the sham-fight, showed good " fire-discipline."

Of the manner of fighting, it may be said that they are trying to adapt it to the experiences of modern times.

The subsequent display of Mounted Artillery was dexterous, and the training of these men was the most satisfactory. A target practice, which was to follow, had to be omitted, because there were spectators within range, and also because the Cavalry brought their horses too near the targets during the long period of waiting. The range was only clear after the manœuvres of the Mountain Artillery, but, as the sun set meantime, even the marvellously clear light that prevails here after that would only have permitted the targets to be seen imperfectly. The dexterity of the troops in bringing the guns into action, and un-limbering them, as well as the transport of the latter by mules, was the chief part of the performance.

Queen Christina, who, with the two Infantas,

had appeared a little later than ourselves, and also on horseback, stayed through a great part of the manœuvres, taking her place among the spectators, but had returned to the house earlier than ourselves.

Queen Isabella, however, without our knowing it, was on the Lisbon road, which we only got on to in our return to Madrid, and so it fell out that she was smothered in the thick clouds of dust that accompanied us before we had even recognized her carriage.

In the evening, after dinner, the *Estudiantina*, consisting of simple young people, appeared to perform a little concert in the Royal Saloon. Most of them wore morning coats, or any attire that was convenient, only a few boys, who led the singing with tambourine and castanets, had put on a kind of national costume. Their Majesties and the Court moved about unconstrainedly among the hundreds of people who formed the company. Finally, some individuals of the above Association seated themselves at the piano, and performed their own compositions.

To me there was a great charm in seeing the apartments—at certain hours devoted solely to the old Spanish etiquette—thrown open now to the studious young people of the middle classes, and in watching the King as he conversed and jested with them, with that natural affability that won the hearts of his subjects from the moment when he first came to the throne.

To-day I received His Majesty's permission from Berlin to visit Andalusia on the way home. But as the express to the South only goes three times a week, I must avail myself of the next opportunity, which will be on the 7th, and accordingly I have fixed my departure for the evening of that day.

Madrid, December 6, 1883.

To-day, to my intense surprise, brought me commands from the highest quarters to pay a visit to the Court of the King of Italy in Rome, on my return journey.

After visiting the Assembly Room of *El Senado* (the Senate), and *El Congreso de los Diputados* (the Lower House), which are splendid modern edifices, and in which a goodly number of portraits of celebrated party-leaders and delegates are hung upon the walls, I glanced round the parish church of Madrid, *S. Isidro el Real,* which is lavishly decorated in the *rococo* style, and takes the place of the Cathedral proper, that is still wanting. After we had been shown innumerable models, and also many historical relics and pictures in the Marine Museum, I betook myself to the Museum of Archæology, which has only been built in the last few years, so as yet there is no great number of objects, although it includes some excessively interesting remains of monuments and products of art from different centuries.

I drove through Madrid for the last time, and now looked at its gay, busy traffic with quite other eyes than those of fourteen days ago, when under the charm of its novelty I could not recognize, as I do to-day, that the character of the Spanish Capital is essentially modern. For streets and squares have already assumed the appearance that conforms best with the ideas of our contemporaries. With the exception of the Ministerial Buildings and the *Palacio Real*, there is hardly a house of which the architecture strikes one's eye; in particular those buildings are absent which, *e.g.* in Italy, testify to the splendour and eminence of the families of the nobility.

Monuments, too, of earlier ages are few in number; the best is an equestrian statue of Philip IV., which came from Florence, and stands in front of the East Façade of the Castle. It is surrounded by pleasure-grounds, with colossal figures of ¡sandstone that were formerly on the cornice of the King's residence.

Among other things I drove over the *Plaza Mayor*, which resembles a large court, in the centre of which, where now stands a bronze equestrian statue of Philip III. by Juan di Bologna, the *autos de fe* formerly took place. A monument, *Dos de Mayo* (May 2), in charming surroundings, is dedicated to the memory of the Patriots who struggled against Murat's usurpation, and belongs to the grounds of the Prado, standing not far from a tasteful, triumphal arch, erected in the time of Charles III., which bears the name of *Puerta del Alcala*.

At my return my audiences were awaiting me. Among others appeared the Minister of War, and the Minister of the Interior, to offer me works that had been brought out at the cost of the State.

The last evening was filled with the Italian Opera *Rigoletto*, in which the tenor Masini dis tinguished himself. Castelar, known on the Republican Opposition, had taken his seat immediately *en face*.

Madrid, December 7, 1883.

Snow showers and frost, alternating with sunshine, for my last day in Madrid.

After wandering once more to-day through the splendid Gobelins, a picture of Old-Spanish Court Ceremonial unrolled itself in their midst, the anniversary, namely, of the Founding of the Order of Charles III., with a procession of the Knights in the dress of the Order. Investiture and High office in the chapel of the castle.

The King, with all who bore the chain that distinguishes the Knights of the highest grade, wore an Old-Spanish costume, with a light-blue trained mantle, rich in silver embroidery, over it, and a baretta with feathers on his head; the same cloak was worn by the Patriarch and various ecclesiastics in their capacity as prelates of the order. The stately procession, at which both the Queens, near whom I was standing, looked on from one of the windows to the great corridor, went, preceded by a corps of music, and escorted by Halbardiers, into the beautiful church of the castle, which was draped with rich stuffs, even on the seats of the Knights. The King took his place under a marvellous white satin baldachin, very tastefully ornamented with arms and arabesques, in which the newly-received Duke of Medina Sidonia, after fulfilling certain formalities at the Altar, where he was surrounded by the ecclesiastics, knelt down, and received the

investiture with the chain. After that a musical
High Mass was celebrated, attended by the Queens
and the Infantas from their stalls in the church.
Directly afterwards I had a long and searching
talk with Adjutant-General Count Mirasol over
the military affairs of Spain.

At the close of the service I had expressed a
wish to see the treasures of the chapel, and the
Patriarch suggested that he would wait there
for me, and himself show me the costly treasures
and reliquaries which had escaped the plundering
hands of Napoleon, or had been amassed at a
later time. Stones and precious metals, with
which many coffers are filled, are better represented here than fine types of form. The Library
of the Palace interested me more, in which, among
other costly missals, they preserve that which
formerly belonged to Ferdinand and Isabella.
Among the innumerable manuscripts, I saw
many deeds, to which attached the special interest that they had been signed by both the
" Kings."

On my final visit to take leave, the Royal Pair
showed me their private apartments, which are
comparatively small; the sleeping-chamber takes
up most of the space. Here the present King
was born, and on its wall his wife has hung the

cross which Queen Mary of Scotland carried with her on the scaffold.

After I had taken leave of Queen Isabella II., as well as of the Infantas Isabella and Eulalia, who all treated me with touching cordiality, the King invited me, notwithstanding the driving snowstorm, to go with him to the church of *S. Francisco*, which is undergoing restoration. In this church, which is in connection with the Jerusalem Order of the Holy Sepulchre, some magnificent paintings on the walls and cupolas were being splendidly executed by the best followers of the modern school, and will certainly be heard of again.

Near the Church are the barracks of an Infantry Regiment; when its Commander presented himself to the King, he was informed that he would be amongst those officers who had been selected to go to Berlin for the next Spring-Manœuvres.

Immediately after, the Patriarch and various dignitaries appeared, to take leave of me. The King then accompanied me to the railway station, after I had made my adieus to the Royal Family, from whose circle I parted with regret, since they had all met me with such extraordinary kindness and cordiality. At the Station I found all the

Ministers and Marshals, the Diplomatic Corps, headed by the Nuncio and the French Ambassador,—also deputations, and country people. And here I finally bade the King " Farewell."

And now the beautiful days in Madrid are over! I part from King Alfonso with the feeling of genuine friendship, and the greatest respect for his penetration and strength of character, as also for his courage, and the perseverance with which he has endeavoured to bring his country back to more pacific conditions, and to raise it. Developed in advance of his years, endowed with the true instinct of a King, as well as with the needful self-confidence, he surely will succeed in winning new respect for the Monarchy.

Seville, December 8, 1883.

" Die Schönen von Sevilla
Mit Fächer und Mantilla
Blicken den Strom entlang;
Sie lauschen mit Gefallen,
Wenn meine Lieder schallen
Zum Mandolinenklang,
Und dunkle Rosen fallen
Mir vom Balkon zum Dank." *

These lines from Geibel's *Hidalgo* came into my mind as we neared the walls of Seville; by good luck, however, I entered the city with anticipations other than those of the hero of this ballad, as I was to experience nothing of what these poetical lines describe! For the prevailing and wholly unusual frost kept the fair ones in their houses, and spoiled the last of the flowers, among which the jasmine is notably conspicuous, as well as the oranges, whose boughs hang full of fruit. Ample compensation for the flowers was, however,

* " The Beauties of Sevilla
With fans and mantilla
Spy down the stream;
They listen with delight
When my songs ring bright
To the mandoline,
And roses of the night
Drop thanks from hands unseen."

provided by the guidance of the amiable Duc de Montpensier, who resides here, and also at his country house, *San Lucar di Barameda*, with his wife, the sister of Queen Isabella II., and who, with the officials, and the German inhabitants of the place, received me at the railway-station. The King's mother also has her residence at Seville, in the *Alcazar*.

In this, the first Andalusian city I had entered, I was struck by the comparatively insignificant and often wretched houses, the windows of which have balconies in the upper stories, while the lower floors almost rest upon the ground, but are always barricaded by iron bars, like a prison.

In the older parts of the town, the streets are so incredibly narrow that the foot-passenger could touch the houses on either side with his out-stretched arms; no vehicles, therefore, can pass along them. But when the doors of these buildings are opened, one finds a charming court, planted, according to the custom here, with green things in great abundance, and fountains playing in the middle. I was reminded by this characteristic feature, which dates from earlier times, and still prevails to-day, of the scenes in *Don Juan*, in *Figaro*, and of the gipsy maiden in *Carmen*, to which our stages have indeed given

z

other settings than that which properly befits them.

Seville calls herself with pride the native town of Murillo, and accordingly honours this Master, as does Nuremberg Albrecht Dürer. Next to Madrid there is no such collection of his pictures, some of which adorn the churches; twenty-four, however, have been collected in the Museo (the former cloister of *la Merced*), since the year 1836, from all parts of the country. These pictures, however, are not all masterpieces, but are of very different value. To my taste, the representation of a vision, in which the Saviour comes down from the Cross to embrace S. Francis, is, both in drawing and in the ingenious application of the few colours, the most perfect of Murillo's works in this place.

His *Moses* is highly prized, as also the *Feeding of the Ten Thousand*, in the church of the Hospital *la Caridad*, which is decorated with a fine façade, where the figures of saints in majolica, as well as the pulpit of wrought ironwork, pleased me particularly.

The high development attained by the majolica industry in this place, in the Middle Ages, is shown by the wealth of tiles in the Museo, which afford a regular primer of the *technique*, being even used for picture-frames. Unique in its kind is the church of *Santa Paula*, for the turreted *façade* from the time of Ferdinand and Isabella, whose monograms it bears, the interior halfway up the walls, and even the fastenings of the doors, are of the same material.

The Gothic Cathedral, one of the largest in Spain, is of colossal proportions; unfortunately, its outer walls are disfigured by various buildings which partially conceal them, so that the structure of the church can hardly be made out. The more effectively, however, does the beautiful tower, *La Giralda*, spring out of this mass of buildings, its massive Moorish sub-structure standing in the *Patio de los Naranjos*, the court orange-trees, designed in the time of the Saracens for ablutions. The Renaissance period made an addition, which is crowned by the bronze statue of " Faith," and recalls the famous earthenware vessels (*Steingut Gefässe*) of Henri II. of France.

The enormous stone masses of the Cathedral darken the light inside, obscured as it is already by the magnificent old windows, so that Murillo's *S. Antonio*, stolen in 1874, and found again in America, is as hard to recognize as the gigantic carved reredos behind the altar, called the *Retablo*, which fills the entire height of the dome.

There is more light in the *Capilla Real* and in the Sacristy. In the former rests the sainted Fernando (1252), whose sword, the statue of the Virgin he took to the wars, and a wooden figure presented to him by S. Louis IX. of France, *La Virgen de los Reyes*, are held in the highest honour. This life-size image of the Madonna, both as a sculpture of the thirteenth century, and also because its clothing in the dress of the period has been preserved, is of great archæological interest, and contrasts with the enormous mass of waxen, as also of carved wooden statues of saints, with which the churches and dwelling-houses here are overfilled.

In the same chapel rest also Don Alonso *el Sabio* (the Wise), and his consort Beatrix, and that in a right marvellous fashion, in open niches that are more than a man's height, and painted red, with crowns and sceptre lying on the coffins that are covered with cloth of gold.

The Sacristy should properly be called the Treasure-room, for church vessels and ornaments are heaped up there in the most costly materials, and in incredible profusion; a Gothic cross of silver, and more particularly a huge Renaissance monstrance of the finest work, are reckoned as the best Spanish achievements in the art of this period.

As a proof of the lavish manner in which gifts were formerly heaped on the Church, one may take the silver candlesticks, which must have required twenty men to carry them; further, a bronze candelabra, designed for use during the ceremonies of Holy Week, called *Tenabrario,* which is almost thirty feet high, and on which the Saviour with fourteen saints is represented; this, on account of its enormous weight, can only be brought into the church on wheels.

The most remarkable thing in the Cathedral to me, however, was the dance of the choristers, during the evening-vespers, in honour of the Immaculate Conception.

In accordance with a custom four hundred years old, these boys perform a sort of saraband, in the page's dress of the time of Philip IV., in the space between the High Altar and the Archbishop's Stall, where the latter is seated, surrounded by all the Canons of the Cathedral, and the faithful assemble round the choir. These choristers dance in slow step to the sound of fiddles, contrabass, and flutes, turning on their heels, and now putting on their tall plumed hats, now taking them off, while, during the pauses, they follow the time of the music with castanets. This vestige of the mediæval mysteries is a most singular survival, but does not jar on the spectator as much as might have been expected from a dance in the church, because there is nothing frivolous about it, on the contrary, both the ecclesiastics and lay people attend it respectfully, as if it were a service.

Near the Cathedral is the "Library for India," a noble building, rich in manuscripts from the time of the Discovery of America, among which those deriving from Christopher Columbus and Fernando Cortes attracted me most.

The Royal Residential Palace, the *Alcazar*, still contains wonderfully beautiful Moorish structures and ornaments, which are carefully preserved, and count among the finest achievements of Saracenic art. The large garden belonging to it is laid out in a mixture of Oriental and mediæval taste; palms, lemons, oranges, and bananas, alternate with old-world hedges of box, and the jasmine grows luxuriantly.

Majolica-tiles are employed throughout. The highest perfection of this *technique* is seen, however, in the minute domestic chapel of Isabella the Catholic, the painting of which reminds one of Perugino.

In the Palace of the Duque di Medinaceli, *La Casa di Pilatos*, one learns to appreciate the luxury which the great ones of the land formerly developed in their houses, at the same time preserving Oriental forms.

After I had received a deputation of our countrymen residing here, as also the Señore Merry y Colon, father and brother of Count Benomar, the Spanish Ambassador in Berlin, a dinner in the fine *Palacio San Telmo*, the winter-residence of the Duc de Montpensier, brought this well-filled day to a close, the evening being again illuminated by a most remarkable streaming of zodiacal lights. The above building, which was originally endowed as a Marine School by the son of Christopher Columbus, was given to the Duke on his marriage, and is adorned with the productions of ancient as well as modern art, while the taste of the internal decorations dates from the time of his father, King Louis Philippe.

Two sketches of the equestrian portraits of Philip IV. and the Duke of Olivarez, entirely from the hand of Velasquez, as well as some Zurberans, struck me particularly; not less so an Ary Scheffer, which I had seen during the life of Queen Marie Amélie, in her house at Claremont.

The cold of the nights is the more perceptible, as, in contrast to the comfortable warmth of San Telmo, the heating arrangements of the Hotel are very meagre, and we have to fall back upon *braseros*, which yield a most inadequate response to our demands.

San Luca de Barameda, December 9, 1883.

I made use of the early hours to visit some of the antiquities of Seville, and then took a walk in the garden of San Telmo, which is very remarkable. The Duc de Montpensier has succeeded in acclimatizing all kinds of exotic plants here, and in obtaining stately trees from little cuttings; palms and oranges are here in profusion, so that the owner gets a considerable income from the sale of the fruit. Along with these delights of nature, he permitted himself a jest in honour of the *Don Juan* from Mozart's opera (who is, moreover, the hero of an old Seville legend), by buying up the sepulchral monuments of the Tenorio family, to which Comthur and Donna Anna belonged, at the breaking-up of the monastery in which they stood, and set them up here, calling them after the principal persons. Only the tombstones of Figaro, the Barber, and the friends of Mozart's as of Rossini's music, are wanting, in order that all the euphonious names should be united here in one resting-place.

A five-hour steam-boat journey on the

Guadalquivir, which did not indeed afford any attractions in the way of landscape, until towards evening we espied the pine-woods and the rocks of Gibraltar, brought us in the company of the Duc de Montpensier to the shores of the Atlantic Ocean, where the Duchesse received us in San Lucar de Barameda.

A friendly, spacious country-house with a pretty garden provides the princely pair (who of the eight children born to them, have only two living) with a peaceful home in this salubrious air, amid a people who are devoted to them.

Cordial hospitality, and a welcome fire on the hearth, made the evening in the tastefully furnished rooms a very pleasant one.

Granada, December 10, 1883.

From San Lucar, a ten-hour journey took us through Andalusia's red-brown landscape, which exhibited little variety, and also through parts of the Sierra Nevada, to Granada. Only at Xeres, where the proprietor of the largest of the vine-yards there, and also the German Consul from Cadiz, came to meet me, was there any sign of vegetation. Ossuna, the family seat and burial-ground of the well-known Duke of that name, who is now dead,—and which has ten churches and twenty monasteries, but no school,—makes as desolate an impression upon one as Bobadilla, where we connected with the express from Cartagena to Granada, and met the Knoop family from Wiesbaden.

We reached Granada at nine in the evening; so soon as I had got over the reception formalities, I hastened to the *Alhambra*, situated near the Inn of the Seven Stories (*Fonda de los siete suelos*), and entered it in the radiant moonlight.

This evening visit could indeed only give me a general idea of the outlines, along with the internal plan of this marvellous building; yet so much the more effective was the ghostly appearance lent by the moon to those halls and courts immortalized by history as by poetry! As a background rose the glistening snow-covered heights of the Sierra Nevada, while, far below, the valley of the Xenil, and Granada, lay in a silvery shimmer, broken only here and there by a beam of light from the sea of houses, against which the darkened gipsy quarter stood out eerily.

Only the mild air of Andalusia and the murmur of the springs were wanting to make the enchantment of this evening complete. Unfortunately, however, several degrees of frost, to which the cactuses were victims, and even quite thick ice, contradicted my wishes. The present onset of winter, not known here for twenty years, compels us to wear our warmest clothing, not merely in the open, but even in the rooms of the Inn. For here the heating apparatus is confined to diminutive fireplaces, and beyond that exclusively, as in Seville, to the charcoal basins, called *braseros.*

Granada, December 11, 1883.

The cold of the night and early morning hours was succeeded by warm sunshine; the ice disappeared, the fountains flowed, so that to-day's visit to the Alhambra was accompanied by a pleasant warmth, which even permitted us to sit out in the open.

Before we entered the Moorish castle, our way led between two creations of Charles V., a magnificent fountain, and a palace in the luxurious Renaissance style. While the former still flows, and is made use of, the Imperial Palace has, on the contrary, remained unfinished, and even unroofed, on the spot where the Moorish Winter Residence once stood, which was pulled down by Charles V. The glaring contrast between this and the Moorish building is in itself a chapter of history, but there was no time for such reflections, for the threshold of the Alhambra lay in our immediate neighbourhood.

I had already been long acquainted with this monument of architecture—of its kind unique— first from pictures, and then from the plaster reproductions of its most striking rooms in the Crystal Palace at Sydenham. Now, however, as I entered the place itself, this all disappeared from memory, like the images of a cloud, before the splendid reality; it rose before me here in a manner so enchanting that a shiver of joy and satisfaction ran through me.

All that I had seen in my Eastern Journey of 1868, of the works of Oriental decorative art, now seemed to me like piece-work before the gorgeous exhibition of taste and colour brought to its perfection in the Alhambra. Strange to relate, this lavish splendour and fantastic multiplicity contents itself with comparatively small courts and chambers, none of which can be termed a " saloon " in our sense of the word, and however much the architecture of the interior corresponds with that wealth of treasure, it has done equally little for the outside of the Alhambra, which, indeed, exhibits only heavy irregular walls, piled up against each other, and towers devoid of style.

I must not permit myself any even approximate description of the structure, but will only point out how astonishing it is that material and colour should still resist the weather, so that the *chef d'œuvre* of Saracen architecture has endured from the epoch of Charles V. to the present day.

A structure of the age of the Alhambra of course requires careful watching ; unfortunately in the course of past ages this has been most inadequately attended to, while happily at the present day it is managed by clever and capable hands; and since, in addition to this, the Spanish majolica manufactory has now been revived, this form of art, which is so richly employed in the Alhambra itself, can be applied here conformably with the original style.

For many hours we traversed this wonderful work of men's hands in amazed contemplation, for the splendid natural scenes around lend a peculiar charm to the achievement. Out of each window, in front of each balcony, is unfolded a vast landscape, which could only be guessed at yesterday evening in the moonlight, while to-day Granada and its mountains are sparkling under a deep-blue sky in the clearest sunshine.

The *Generalife*, originally "*Jennatu-l'-arif*," which is, being translated, the "garden of the architect," is a structure lying higher than the Alhambra, in which much fine Moorish ornament is still preserved, although it has given way to a great extent to the later European taste. Here garden grounds from the last century present a charming alternation with all kinds of water-works of Arab origin, while there are some very old trees to which all kinds of tales attach. The proximity of the mountains, the distant views of valley and plain, lend to this spot, in which to-day the winter is forgotten in the sunshine, a character of ideal summer freshness.

The *Generalife* is the property of the Marchesa Durazzo-Palavicini, well known to me in Genoa, who greets me here through her officials, and in whose possession is the splendidly wrought sword of the last Moorish King, Boabdil—*El Rey Chico* —which he gave up on handing over Granada to Ferdinand and Isabella. His memory is linked with the mountain pass of the Sierra Nevada, which he had to traverse on the retreat from his lost residence, and which to this day is known as " the last sigh of the Moor," as Heine sings—

> " ' Berg des letzten Mohren Seufzer's '
> Heisst bis auf den heutigen Tag
> Jene Höhe, wo der König
> Sah zum letzten Mal Granada." *

* " ' Mountain of the latest Moor's sigh,'
So they call it to the present;
Height from which the banished Monarch
For the last time saw Granada."

To the Oriental reminiscences of the forenoon followed those of the epoch in which the Moors were driven out, among which the mighty cathedral, dating from the late Gothic transition-period, along with the burial-place of the Conquerors of Granada, the Catholic " Kings " Ferdinand and Isabella, appealed to me particularly. Huge marble sarcophagi in the Renaissance style do honour to their memory, as also to that of their daughter, Joan the Crazy, and her husband Philip of Burgundy. A simple vault under the High Altar, however, covers the bones—within a coffin of curious shape, entirely encased in iron—of this distinguished princely pair, still held in veneration to-day, and whom I am proud to reckon among my ancestors.

As in the church of Toledo, S. *Juan de los Reyos* possesses shields and ciphers, as well as countless historical objects such as the sword, banner, and missals of these conquerors, of whom there are several pictures.

La Cartuja, a former Carthusian convert, contains some really marvellous work in inlaid cedar and ebony wood, mother - of - pearl and tortoiseshell—the doors of the sacristy-chapel, as well as a great number of gigantic coffers, being made out of these materials. In addition, the view of the Alhambra, the Sierra Nevada, and the valley of the Xenil from the terrace of this monastery is as attractive, as the character of the gipsy quarter, located in rock caves, is the reverse. This singular people have here lost many of their original characteristics, partly because they were established in Granada, partly because a mixed race has sprung up by marriage with the people of the country.

The so-called King of the Gipsies appeared before my dwelling in a dress that resembled the costume of the bandits at the theatre, so that at the outset I felt sceptical of his genuineness ; but when His Majesty approached me to present his august photograph, I became convinced, by the unmistakably Indian type of countenance, as well as by the piercing eyes, of the indubitable relationship of this monarch to his race.

Granada's antiquity-stalls have the charm of large rag-shops, in the rust and dust of which the original character of many Hispano - Moorish objects has been preserved from the perils of modern restoration. Close by there is an industry peculiar to this place, which supplies models of Moorish architecture, with exact reproductions of colour and pattern, and, thanks to the execution by intelligent technicians, it has been brought to a really astonishing degree of perfection.

Cordova, December 12, 1883.

I left Granada at four in the morning, in clear moonlight; the discomfort of this early hour was increased owing to the by-no-means Andalusian climate, and the inadequate heating arrangements of the railway carriages, while the want of variety in the landscape on the long journey to Cordova presented little that was attractive.

In the days when this city was still the residence of the Khalîf, the number of its inhabitants amounted to a million, and the life there must have resembled that of the *Thousand and One Nights*; to-day the streets give one the impression that everything has changed into the direct contrary.

So soon as one reaches the Cathedral, or *Mezquita*, one perceives that the Muslims must have developed their full power here; for this marvellous mosque, begun at the end of the eighth century, and containing 1096 columns, is among the greatest that Islam ever called forth.

After passing through an outer court, filled with cypresses and palms, and notably with a real grove of orange-trees, the porch of the

2 A

Cathedral, called *Puerta del Predon*, which is inlaid with Saracen and Gothic bronze plates, admits one to the sight of a labyrinth of pillars, resembling a petrified forest.

The founder, Abd-el-Rahman, and also his successors, collected pillars of jasper, porphyry, and verd-antique, from Constantinople, Alexandria, and Carthage, and from France and Spain, many of which support the ancient capitals to this day. Each pair is connected with the next by high, rounded Saracen arches, of richly chiselled marble, over-arched, as a rule, by a second set, the extraordinary number of which forms a regular maze of geometrical figures, that assume a different aspect at every step one takes. The most lively imagination can hardly form any idea of the strange architectural complexities of this effect, which almost produces vertigo in the onlooker.

A direct contrast to this is afforded by three chapels surmounted by cupolas — the former *Mihrab*, or sanctuary turned towards Mecca—whose costly mosaics, closely resembling byzantine work, alternate with the most tasteful ornaments of stone and stucco. Not far from this is the former Seat of the Khalîfs, designed for the Fridays' devotional exercises, now known as the *Capilla de Villaviciosa*, which rises as a sort of crypt upon steps, and shows in its fine Saracen-Gothic ornamentation that, long after the expulsion of the Moors, Oriental artificers were still employed to complete the works of their forefathers.

When, after eleven centuries, there is still so much that commands our admiration, and defies destruction, in spite of the demolition in which Christianity and the Roman Church bore the principal part,—from religious zeal no less than from defective taste,—we can conceive what the effect of the Mosque must have been in its original and complete splendour, when the Followers of Islam were supreme here.

In the time of Charles V. the ecclesiastics built a high choir in the Renaissance style in the middle of the Mosque, which is, indeed, a stately church in itself, with wonderfully fine carved choir-stalls, but still has a most detrimental effect upon the Oriental structure, and accordingly deserves the reproach which that Emperor expressed in regard to it.*

The treasures of the Cathedral are kept in the *Capilla del Cardenal*, and contains masterpieces of the goldsmith's art ; among other rarities, there

---

* Charles V. remarked to the Chapter, " *You have built here what you, or any one, might have built elsewhere ; but you have destroyed what was unique in the world.*"—Tr.

is here a huge silver-gilt monstrance, in the Gothic style, with magnificent processional crosses, two in that, and one in Renaissance style, works which brought the master-hands of Cordova into the highest honour in the Middle Ages.

The chief ecclesiastics greeted me in the name of the Bishop, and served as guides, along with some of the canons, whose heads would have made real studies. Two of these had a certain acquaintance with modern languages, and were vastly occupied in answering questions made to them about the localities, now in English, and now in German, with the aid of written vocabularies, which they carried in their hats.

It was with great difficulty that my *suite* persuaded me to leave the contemplation of this wondrous Mosque, for its interior surpasses in magnificence all the Oriental monuments that I had formerly seen in the East, although to a certain point I was reminded of that in Old Cairo. Our stay, indeed, could not be longer, for a wearisome railway journey of a day and a half lay before us, and impelled us to a start, in order that we might get without a break to Tarragona, and thence to Barcelona.

Yet I counted these physical exertions as little, because I owed to them the enjoyment of the Alhambra's spells, and the marvellous structure of the Mezquita of Cordova!

At dark we reached the Sierra Morena, and crossed the ridge about midnight, in the moonlight. On gazing at this wild and barren rocky landscape, I involuntarily began to think how easily an accident to the train, which here happens not infrequently, might occur—and what an untoward end such an adventure would make to my journey! While thinking this I went to sleep. In the middle of the night I was awaked, not by bandits, but on account of Queen Isabella, who was travelling from Madrid to Seville, and had arrived at the junction of Alcazar simultaneously with our train, and who had interrupted my slumbers, to bid me farewell once more. The conversation at this *rendezvous* could have been carried on from window to window, since our carriages were exactly opposite each other; of course, however, I jumped out, in spite of my not very ceremonious attire, and paid my respects, in the dead of night, standing on the rails, to the honourable traveller.

Tarragona, December 13, 1883.

At daybreak the landscape had essentially altered to its great advantage—in fact, we were already on the same railway that had taken us, in the night of November 22–23, to Madrid; to-day, however, we saw the beautiful mountainous country of the east coast by day, and reached the famous plain of the *Huerta de Valencia* in the forenoon.

Here, so far as the eye could reach, we were surrounded by a thick hedge of oranges, in which each single tree was quite laden with great fruits of the most brilliant colour. On the declivities of the mountains were country houses alternating with villages; everywhere one perceived labouring men at work, in fields and gardens, cheerful sights we had long been deprived of. And why this sudden transformation? Because in the *Huerta* the system of canals, introduced by the Moors, is still in force, and thanks to this supply of water these plains are a fertile garden, on the rich produce of which the inhabitants live in a certain prosperity.

Whenever the train stopped, great baskets, or branches with the fruit still hanging on them, of the splendid apples which grow so well on this soil were handed into our carriage; they tasted as sweet as if each fruit had been dipped in honey.

At the station of Valencia was a large

concourse of men, and the same officials whose acquaintance I had made on landing. They all gave me a hearty greeting. From here the railway goes uninterruptedly along the beautiful shores of the sea, which we had seen from our ship three weeks before, to Tarragona, which we reached at nine o'clock, and where our night-quarters were taken in the hotel. The municipal authorities, however, had determined to receive me as a guest in the *Ayuntamiento*, or Town Hall. With this object the Council Room had been turned into a living-room, so that I there found a gorgeous reception.

Among all the courtesies which I had to accept, this hospitality took the very prejudicial form of serving a magnificent supper, much against my wishes; but as the fathers of the city collectively partook of it, I naturally could not refuse to attend. While the kind hosts relished this dainty meal—which perhaps is a rare luxury with them—with evident enjoyment, I was silently longing for my bed, and this the more as my companions at table understood nothing but Spanish, so that we were necessarily debarred from conversation.

Barcelona, on board H.M.S. " Prince Adalbert,"
December 14, 1883.

After visiting the municipal museum of Tarragona, which possesses some quite good antiquities,
I went by the railway to Barcelona, where the
whole population of the town had turned out to
meet me.

It had been reported that the fact that my
first landing on Spanish soil had been in Valencia
instead of here had vexed the inhabitants of this
town. The people evidently laid themselves out
to convince me of the contrary, which they did to
the fullest extent. For as I moved by the side
of the *Capitan General* and the Alcalde in an
hour and a half's drive through the principal
streets and squares, amid the lines formed by the
garrison, I found the houses much decorated
with flags, and every window full of people
making friendly greetings, while the close masses
of the populace were in a really enthusiastic frame
of mind.

During the drive I was struck with the modern
character of this commercial city, which is
obviously in the full tide of its prosperity; it
resembles Marseilles in many respects, but in

spite of its rich manufactures is not, as to-day
is mostly the case, disfigured by forests of
chimneys, because the manufactures are situated
more in the side-valleys and the neighbourhood.
Great wide streets, planted with rows of trees, are
the arteries for the traffic of all this moving
life, and stately four-storied houses are speaking
witnesses to the commercial significance of
this harbour, which also possesses a climatic
importance.

Strangely enough, there is here a much greater
show of Toledo wares than in the city where they
are manufactured, or in Madrid, so that a selection
we had not hitherto been able to secure of the
finest works of this genuinely Spanish industry
were, thanks to the forethought of our Consul
Lindau, sent on board for our acceptance at the
last moment before starting.

German work is much prized in Spain as
in France, so that innumerable wares from
home find a market here—of course only so
long as the Spanish firms conceal their German
origin !

From the balcony at the house of the *Capitan
General*, I inspected the march past of the troops ;
during this the Bishop appeared, seated himself
at my side, and was also my neighbour at table,

where he made himself most agreeable, and later escorted me on foot to the Cathedral.

In Barcelona, as repeatedly during the journey, Prefects and superior officers of justice were presented to me, who had taken office in consequence of the recent change of ministry—that is, within the last few weeks.

To show the city some reciprocal attention, I went to the very respectable *Ayuntamiento,* because there is here the picture by the late talented artist Fortuni, native of Barcelona, which represents the Battle of Tetuan, 1859, of which his countrymen are so inordinately proud. From there I went to the Cathedral, which was surrounded by masses of people; since these all poured into the church, the crush there soon became so unbearable that I declined the close inspection of that great Norman-Gothic edifice, and confined myself to the ecclesiastical treasure and the beautiful cloisters. The evening sun cast its beams through the very striking and well-preserved stained glass of many colours, and warned us to depart, as we were to weigh anchor before nightfall.

At the embarkation I caught more friendly cheers, the last we heard coming from our own countrymen assembled in the harbour. After

going on board the *Loreley*, I dismissed the vessel
from the squadron, and took leave of our Ambassador, Count Solm, who during my whole stay
had been most kind and useful, and so departed
amid the salutes of the guns to Genoa, by sea.

And so my stay in this most interesting
country is at an end! I shall always reckon the
days spent here as among the most cherished
recollections of my life.

As I parted from Spain with the most lively
sympathy for the King, his family and his country,
I entertain the hope that closer relations than
have ever yet subsisted with Germany may be
initiated through my visit. At the same time
I feel myself justified in the anticipation that the
Government, as well as those clear-sighted men
who have their people's welfare at heart, will
henceforward recognize our Empire as a prop of
the monarchical principle, and still more as a
disinterested and well-wishing friend.

The more closely the larger States of Europe
approximate to each other the more certain will
be the maintenance of peace. And herein the
wish is justified, that my mission to Spain may
prove to be another element in the prolongation
of this desired state.

I landed in Genoa on the morning of the 16th,

after as stormy a passage as I had on the outward voyage, took leave after Divine Service on board of the officers and men, and was received on Italian soil with the same demonstrations of respect as at starting.   At night I embarked on the journey to Rome.

ERRATA

Page 216, line 1, and page 235, line 3, *for* "draught" *read* "draft."
Page 350, line 10, *for* "Generaliste" *read* "Generalife."
Page 351, lines 17, 18, *for* "As in the church . . . possesses" *read* "Here, in the church of *S. Juan de los Reyos* at Toledo, there are," etc.

INDEX

THE END

ImTheStory.com

Lightning Source UK Ltd.
Milton Keynes UK
UKHW02f1053130818
327155UK00005B/532/P